LION
EYES

ALSO BY VICTOR VILLASEÑOR

Macho!

Jury

Rain of Gold

Wild Steps of Heaven

Thirteen Senses

Burro Genius

Crazy Loco Love

Beyond Rain of Gold*

Snow Goose Global Thanksgiving

Walking Stars

CHILDREN'S COLLECTION

Mother Fox and Mr. Coyote

The Frog and His Friends Save Humanity

Goodnight, Papito Dios

Little Crow to the Rescue

The Stranger and the Red Rooster

*Available from Hay House

Please visit:
Hay House USA: **www.hayhouse.com**®
Hay House Australia: **www.hayhouse.com.au**
Hay House UK: **www.hayhouse.co.uk**
Hay House South Africa: **www.hayhouse.co.za**
Hay House India: **www.hayhouse.co.in**

LION EYES

VICTOR E. VILLASEÑOR

HAY HOUSE, INC.

Carlsbad, California • New York City
London • Sydney • Johannesburg
Vancouver • Hong Kong • New Delhi

Published and distributed in the United States by: Hay House, Inc.: www.hay house.com • *Published and distributed in Australia by:* Hay House Australia Pty. Ltd.: www.hayhouse.com.au • *Published and distributed in the United Kingdom by:* Hay House UK, Ltd.: www.hayhouse.co.uk • *Published and distributed in the Republic of South Africa by:* Hay House SA (Pty), Ltd.: www.hayhouse.co.za • *Distributed in Canada by:* Raincoast: www.raincoast.com • *Published in India by:* Hay House Publishers India: www.hayhouse.co.in

Cover design: Charles McStravick • *Interior design:* Tricia Breidenthal

Library of Congress Cataloging-in-Publication Data

Villaseñor, Victor.
  Lion eyes / Victor E. Villaseñor.
    p. cm.
    ISBN 978-1-4019-3200-8 (hardcover : alk. paper) 1. Tarahumara Indians --Religion. 2. Tarahumara Indians--Missions. 3. Tarahumara Indians--Land tenure--Mexico--Chihuahua (State) 4. Milburn, Jan. 5. Missionaries--Mexico-- Chihuahua (State)--Biography. 6. Totemism--Mexico--Chihuahua (State) 7. Chihuahua (Mexico : State)--Religious life and customs. I. Title.
  F1221.T25M558 2011
  972.16004'974546--dc23

                          2011018259

Hardcover ISBN: 978-1-4019-3200-8
Digital ISBN: 978-1-4019-3201-5

14 13 12 11   4 3 2 1
1st edition, October 2011

Printed in the United States of America

DEDICATION

*This book is dedicated to you, dear readers, and all
of your friends and <u>familia</u>; and to our ancestors, who at
one time were all indigenous people, and who guide us on a
daily basis with their wisdom from the Heavens, through
our hearts. God bless, from my <u>familia</u> and me,
to all of your family and you, dear readers.*

CONTENTS

"If you know my song, you know Charlie. Everyone has a song. God gives us each a song. That's how we know who we are."

— **Charlie Knight**, Ute medicine man, Four Corners

"I myself have no power. It's the people behind me who have the power. Real power only comes from the Creator. It's in His hands. But if you're asking about strength, not power, then I can say that the greatest strength is gentleness."

— **Leon Shenandoah,**
Six Nations Iroquois Confederacy, New York State

"There was a man, a postman here on the reservation, who heard some of the Elders talking about receiving objects that bring great power. He didn't know about such things, but he thought it would be wonderful if he could receive such a thing—which can only be bestowed by the Creator. He knew he couldn't buy one and he couldn't ask anyone to give him one. Day after day, he went around looking for an eagle feather. It got so he thought of nothing else. Weeks passed, then months, then years. He paid no more attention to his family and friends. He started to grow old, but still no feather. One day he took a break by the side of the road and got out of his Jeep mail-carrier and had a talk with the Creator. 'I'm tired of looking for that eagle feather. Maybe I'm not supposed to get one. I've hardly given thought to my family and friends. I've missed out on a lot of good things. So I'm giving up the search. Maybe I still have time left to make it up to my family and friends. Forgive me for the way I have conducted my life.'

"A great peace came into him. He suddenly felt better inside than he had all these years. And just as he finished his talk with the Creator and was walking back to his Jeep mail-carrier, a great shadow passed over him. Holding his hands over his eyes, he looked up into the sky and saw, high above, a great bird flying overhead, then almost instantly disappear, and he saw something floating down ever so lightly on the breeze—it was his eagle feather! This was when he realized that wisdom comes only when you stop looking for it and you start living the life the Creator intended for you.

"The postman still lives and he's a changed person. People now come to him and he shares everything he knows. Even though he now has the power and prestige that he searched for, he no longer

cares about such things. Now he's concerned about others, not himself. This is how wisdom comes to us, when we start living the life the Creator gave us, and stop thinking just of ourselves."

— **Leila Fisher**, Hoh, Washington State's Olympic Peninsula

"Secrets? Mysteries? I can tell you right now, there are no secrets. There's no mystery. There's only common sense. And the first one is that you've got to keep things pure, especially water. Keeping water pure is one of the first common sense things in life. If you destroy the water, you destroy life."

— **Oren Lyons**, Onondaga Faithkeeper of the Turtle Clan, Upstate New York

"It's not who you are that holds you back, it's who you think you're not."

— on a Dumpster in San Diego

"At a seminary in Bangalore, a nun once said to me, 'Mother Teresa, you are spoiling the poor people by giving them things free. They are losing their human dignity.' When everyone was quiet, I said calmly, 'No one spoils as much as God himself. See the wonderful gifts He has given us freely. All of you here have no glasses, yet you all can see. If God were to take money for your sight, what would happen? Continually we are breathing and living on oxygen that we do not pay for. What would happen if God were to say, "If you work four hours, you will get sunshine for two hours?" How many of us would survive then?' Then I also told them, 'There are many congregations that spoil the rich; it is good to have one congregation in the name of the poor, to spoil the poor.' There was profound silence; nobody said a word after that."

— **Mother Teresa**

". . . our deepest fear is not that we are inadequate. Our deepest fear is that we are powerful beyond measure. It is our light, not our darkness, that most frightens us. . . . We ask ourselves, Who am I to be brilliant, gorgeous, talented, fabulous? Actually, who are you not to be? You are a child of God. Your playing small doesn't serve *the world. There's nothing enlightened about shrinking so that other people won't feel insecure around you. We are all meant to shine, as children do. We were born to make manifest the glory of God that is within us. It's not just in some of us; it's in everyone. And as we let our own light shine, we unconsciously give other people permission to do the same. As we're liberated from our own fear, our presence automatically liberates others."*

— **Marianne Williamson**, *A Return to Love: Reflections on the Principles of <u>A Course in Miracles</u>* (commonly misattributed to Nelson Mandela, 1994 inauguration speech)

"The secret to life is easy to understand. Where the wind blows strongest, through a pass or over a knoll, even the mighty oak cannot live because its limbs will be torn to pieces, but flowers grow on these passes and knolls with no <u>problema.</u> Why? Because they dance with the wind. They don't hold strong and rigid. So the secret in life is to always dance with our <u>problemas,</u> our upsets . . . dance and be happy. Or in technical words in Spanish, '<u>¡El secreto de la vida es saber cómo bailar con los chingasos!</u>'"

— **Doña Margarita**, mother of my father,
Juan Salvador Villaseñor;
"A little sack of Indian bones," my dad always called her

KEYS FOR UNDERSTANDING

About capitalization: Ever since I can remember, our dad, Juan Salvador, would shout at us kids, "YOU GOT TO FEEL IT!" and he'd shake his fist at us, with eyes ALIVE WITH JOY! And so ever since I started writing, I have used capital letters to emphasize the intense emotion that I have found to be true in my family and culture. And I fully realize that in English, understatement is a prominent style, but this isn't what I found to be true of my *familia*'s background. In fact, wild passion and unbridled emotional intensity, I was raised to believe, is what helps us open our hearts and souls so we can impregnate and expand our everyday reality into other realms and possibilities. Also note that I have capitalized certain terms in Spanish such as *Indios* and *Mexicanos* to give them dignity, even though this does not conform with standard Spanish orthography.

Curandero: An Indian healer who works with natural herbs, ancient remedies, and massage to specific points in the body to treat specific ailments.

Indigenous: Born, growing, or produced naturally in a region or country; native, innate, inherent, inborn.

Shaman: A monk, a priest, a medicine man, a tribal worker of magic, a magic healer to whom unseen worlds of gods and demons and ancestral spirits are believed to be responsive.

Tarahumara: One of the three original tribes of the Copper Canyon of northwest Mexico; considered to be some of the greatest long-distance runners in the world.

Totem: One of a class of living or sometimes inanimate objects regarded by ancient people as having a relationship to any animal or plant; sometimes, an individual's animal guardian spirit.

FOR SAFETY AND CONFIDENTIALITY PURPOSES, some names and identifying details in this book have been changed.

PREFACE

This book is a gift to us, dear reader, straight from the stars! How else can I explain how this incredible true story came to be?

You see, what happened was that back in 2006, I was hired by the Durango, Colorado, school district to give a weeklong series of talks to faculty, parents, students, and the community at large.

On the first day I spoke to 980-some faculty, administrators, and groundskeepers—anyone who had contact with the students while they attended school. Also, I understood that a lot of teachers and staff had driven in from Arizona and New Mexico when they heard I was going to be giving a series of talks in Durango.

I was exhausted, but still I gave a pretty good, blunt talk. Most of my audience loved it and gave me a standing ovation, but a few felt threatened and remained seated, which is normal wherever I go. About 10 to 12 percent of my audiences always seem to get pushed out of shape, which is good, of course, for how else can a human be open enough to move into new shape-shifting possibilities?

I was into the third day of the conference and autographing books, when a young Mexican guy sat down beside me to get his book signed. He told me his grandmother had been born and raised in *la Lluvia de Oro,* the Rain of Gold canyon, the exact same one where my mother had been born and raised in Chihuahua, Mexico.

"Impossible!" I said. "That canyon is tiny! It's just one of the little fingers of the great big arms and legs of the Copper Canyon!"

"I know," he said with a big smile. "I hiked in to see my grand-mother's birthplace. She lived right next door to the rock that your mother's house was anchored to."

"No—you've got to be kidding!" I exclaimed. "You mean you saw the iron bolt that my mother's house was tied to so it wouldn't slide down the steep mountainside?"

"Yes." He nodded. "I e-mailed your office and told them you need to talk to my dad. He's a white guy, yet he's put his life on the line to help get over two million acres returned to the Tarahumara Indians, land that was stolen from them by the logging compa-nies. This could be your next *Rain of Gold* book, 100 years later."

"Just wait," I said. "If your dad is a white guy, then how could his mother have been born next to where my mother was born in the Rain of Gold canyon?"

"No, that was my grandmother on my mother's side of our family," he replied. "My dad is from the San Jose area, in Califor-nia."

"You're confusing me," I said, "and besides, I have enough ma-terial to last me three lifetimes. Tell your dad to write his own story."

"I have. We all have. But his story is so big and unbelievable that it would take a great talent like yours to make it even a little bit believable."

"And you're his son?"

"Yes—Aaron Milburn. I'm his son from his first marriage. Now he's married to an Indian woman from *las Barrancas del Cobre.*"

"And he was instrumental in getting over two million acres returned to the Tarahumara Indians?" I asked.

"Yes. His story starts in the '60s in San Francisco. He was a young hippie Christian minister. He knew Joan Baez and Jerry Garcia and all those people. He rode a motorcycle, and with his faith in Jesus Christ, he has helped keep that wild idealistic spirit of the '60s alive. Please," he added, "just come out and have dinner with us."

I was extremely hesitant. Everywhere I went people always told me these incredible stories and asked me to write them down.

"Look," he said, obviously seeing my hesitation, "personally, my degree is in accounting and business administration. I'm not a religious or spiritual person, but I'm telling you, you need to hear my dad's story. We've read all your books. *Rain of Gold* alone I've probably read 15 times. All my family knows your work. We know how you were able to take the magical world of Mexico, which is so full of miracles and God, and make it acceptable to even non-Mexicans. You have a special gift.

"And this story of my dad needs to reach the world. Violence related to drugs is on the rise in Mexico, drugs and terrorism have a stranglehold on the U.S., and wars are going on all over the whole world. People have lost hope. They don't know what to do or what to believe in anymore. My dad's actions were so great and inspiring that they influenced governors and three Mexican presidents. His story can do for today's world what *Rain of Gold* did for your parents' generation, giving people faith and hope and the courage to live good lives. It's no accident that you were brought to Durango. We've been waiting for you for years."

I took in a deep breath. He was quite the salesman. "What are you serving for dinner?" I asked.

He laughed. "Homemade Mexican-Indian food."

Hungry, I was. I'd been autographing books for well over three hours. "Do you live in town?" I asked.

"Just a little ways out, but I brought our big station wagon, so I can take you and all your staff out there for dinner right after you finish signing."

"You got beer and *tequila* and I'm in," I said.

"We bought your favorite, *Herradura,* and my stepmom squeezed fresh limes, so you can have real *margaritas* just the way you like them."

I guess he'd heard my talk. I always mention how I like fresh-squeezed lime juice with quality *tequila* for my *margaritas*. "Okay, I'm in, but we've got to move along right now. We're holding up the line, and I still have a lot of books to sign."

The line was still pretty long, and I had each person sit down beside me so we could make eye contact before I signed a book. Our eyes are the gateway to the soul, and I liked to reach the soul of each individual. Anything else, in my opinion, was shallow. Life is short, so I always like to get to the heart and soul of each person.

That night I met Aaron's father, Jan Milburn, a man in his mid-60s; his beautiful Indian wife, Mireya, who was probably in her late 30s; and their 15-year-old son, Joaquin. We drank and ate and visited, and then after dinner Jan began to tell me his story. It was easy to follow him. He was a natural storyteller.

He told me he had been born in the Midwest; then when he was about nine, his dad died, so he and his mother and sisters moved to California to be with his older brother, who was a brilliant engineer and had been offered a great job at IBM. They bought an estate in the mountains of Los Gatos right outside San Jose. Giant redwoods surrounded their home. Jan found himself alone a lot of the time, as there were no kids his own age to play with. Once, coming home from school, he got lost in a snowstorm and was freezing to death when a huge lion suddenly appeared right beside him.

"A mountain lion?" I asked.

"Yes," he said.

I took in a deep breath. I'd been raised on a ranch and had spent most of my growing-up years in the wild, and no mountain lion had ever come close to me. I'd always seen them at a distance, and usually running away.

"How old were you?" I asked.

"About 11."

"Go on," I said.

"Well, the lion and I looked at each other; then she turned, walking off through the snowstorm, and I followed her."

"You followed the mountain lion?"

"Yes, and I'd lose sight of her sometimes, but I could still make out her huge paw prints in the fresh snow, so I'd follow them until she led me home."

I nodded. This was big. The man wasn't saying it, but his totem had come to him. And it had been a female. This I could write about. This was huge. Because according to Indian belief, we all had our totem, our Spirit Guide, and we never really knew what our purpose in life was until we found it. "So the lioness led you home."

"Yes, through snow-covered brush and under trees, right up to our front door, and . . . and it was after this mountain-lion experience that I began to see the world differently, and, I guess, realize that something very big was missing in my life. You see, I came from a very devout Christian family. We read the Bible every night, and could quote passages with the best of them. But still something was missing, and . . . and I didn't really know what it was until a few years later when I started working in the summertime with the Mexican farmworkers down the hill from our place and I saw how much faith they had, even in the worst of conditions."

"And?" I asked.

"And what?" Jan said.

"What did you find was missing?"

"Happiness," he said with a huge smile. "It was like my family and I had so much and we were devout Christians, as I said, but we were so judgmental and uptight about everything and everyone. On the other hand, these field-workers had nothing, but because they had so much faith, their lives were full of love and laughter," he added, laughing with a big belly laugh. "This is why I agreed to go to Mexico and I ended up taking the cause of the indigenous people of the Copper Canyon. They're illiterate—they don't read.

So their faith in God isn't rooted in the written word, but in life itself."

"Okay." I nodded. "You have a very good, important story, but I think you're looking for a religious writer—and that I am not."

"We know you're not," Jan replied. "We've read all your books. You're a spiritual writer who writes about the indestructible strength of the human heart and soul. This is why we think you're the perfect person to do our story. You don't just understand the Mexican people. You understand the native Indian people of Mexico, and their world of the mystical and miraculous, and I do believe that the time has come when all of us need to return to our natural indigenous faith in God and life itself so we can live a life beyond being uptight and full of judgment."

My eyes got big. "I thought you weren't at my talk today," I said.

"I wasn't," he replied.

"Well, this is exactly what I said today, and I've been saying for years—that at one time we were all indigenous people; and we lived each day not full of thinking, but instead reaching up for the sunlight of God as naturally as a weed, a flower, or a tree."

"Well, then, *amigo*," Jan told me with another big belly laugh, "it looks like we're on exactly the same page, doesn't it? Because I've also been saying for years that humanity needs to reestablish its indigenous roots and live a life of service and miracles."

I was the one who was now grinning and laughing. "So back to the future, eh? To a time when we were all indigenous people the whole world over and we knew how to live with God and daily miracles!"

"Exactly! That's why, over and over again, I was willing to give my life for . . . for . . ." Jan couldn't speak anymore. The words choked in his throat. His young, beautiful wife, Mireya, drew close and lovingly stroked his back.

WOW! I didn't know what to say or think. Jan was right. His story should be written by a spiritual writer. Not a religious writer. And both my parents had been raised by mothers who were indigenous Christian people, so they'd raised my dad and mom in a Catholic Christian world mixed with native Indian Spirituality that was full of joy and daily miracles, no matter what. But for me to write a book took years and . . . it was a huge financial commitment, and most people didn't have the staying power or know-how to let go and allow the writer to do his work as he saw and understood it.

"And so this mountain lion," I said, "she came to you in a snowstorm in San Jose, California, where it never snows, and led you home, eh? And you were an 11-year-old kid and not terrified out of your mind, eh?"

He instantly saw through my resistance and started laughing. "It happened way up in the hills above San Jose, in Los Gatos, where it does snow every now and then. The place is called *Los Gatos,* 'the cats' in Spanish, because of all the mountain lions in the area. Many a night we would hear them scream."

I breathed and breathed again. I really didn't want to get involved with this job. "But why weren't you terrified and ready to run for your life, and instead, were willing to follow this beast through a snowstorm?" I asked, wondering if he'd use the word "totem."

"Those feelings did cross my mind," Jan replied, "but then I closed my eyes, said a little prayer, and when I reopened my eyes, it was like the whole world was different. I was no longer afraid of the lion, or anything else. It was like I'd been touched by Spirit, and I could now see that this wild beast meant me no harm. In fact, somehow I knew she was my friend and would lead me home to safety."

I smiled. He hadn't used the word "totem," but he'd said what a totem does. It touches our Spirit and leads us Home to God. I glanced around at everyone else in the room to see how they were taking in the story. Then Aaron, who was sitting beside me, spoke up.

"Mr. Villaseñor," he said, "this is exactly why we've come to you. Because, you see, after this incident with the mountain lion, my dad's whole life changed. The redwoods began singing to him and he understood their songs, and you have written about this. Indian totems aren't foreign to you."

I had to grip my forehead. He'd said it. He knew. And my own mother's mother had raised me like this, to talk and pray and sing to our fruit trees and the garden we planted. Then years later a great big, old tree in the Yucatán Peninsula of Mexico spoke to me, telling me the entire story of humanity. Yes, I could do this book. I should do this book. But my God, I was up to my ass in debt, and this would be a huge commitment, with no monies coming in for at least three years!

"Aaron," I said, "so you honestly think that this book could be a new *Rain of Gold,* 100 years later, and people would get it?"

"Yes," replied Aaron. "Your original *Rain of Gold* establishes a world of uneducated, ordinary people doing extraordinary things, because of their faith in God. And my dad's life shows us that even well-educated white people can still be moved back into their indigenous roots and live a life full of faith and miracles that are beyond all civilized reason and comprehension." He stopped and drew in closer to me.

"Mr. Villaseñor," he continued, "more than ever before, the world needs to know about this—that no matter how terrible circumstances look for us in modern times here in the U.S. and in Mexico and the world at large, there's still hope for humanity. Because we ordinary people, educated or not educated, aren't helpless once we are connected to our God-Spirit. All your books show this."

I took in another deep breath. Aaron was right once again. This was exactly what I wrote about: hope and miracles and the power and goodness of human beings when we were spirit-connected. But I'd always done this through *mi familia* and their natural accessibility to the Spirit World. And Aaron's dad was a white guy. He looked like an older version of an actor like Brad Pitt or Tom Hanks, so it was really difficult for me to hear these stories coming from someone who wasn't a *curandero,* an Indian healer. I mean, coming from him, these stories sounded false and exaggerated.

Also, who wanted another do-gooder story of the great white man saving the poor indigenous people? I certainly didn't. And I fully realized that I was being a hypocrite and racist in reverse, but oh wow, what could I do? This was when I decided to do something I'd learned to do a long time ago as a writer.

I excused myself, got up, and went to the kitchen, pretending I wanted some water. I approached Mireya, who'd done very little talking all evening and had gotten up and left the table when I began to question her husband.

"Tell me," I said to her, "are all these stories that your husband is telling me really true?"

"Yes, they are," she replied as she continued to rinse the dishes and put them in the dishwasher.

"Okay, let's say they are," I said. "Why do you think your husband's life story is worth telling?"

"Because, well, I'm not educated," Mireya told me, "and I don't know much about books, but I can tell you that with my own two eyes, I saw how this man was willing to risk his life over and over again for people who weren't even of his blood. They tortured him. They broke his back and arms and legs. They left him for dead several times, but never once did he give up. Even on crutches, he continued to do his work for the good of my people."

Suddenly her eyes filled with tears. "DON'T WRITE HIS BOOK!" she yelled at me. "Don't believe the stories he tells you! Ridicule us if you want! But my people and the stars in the Heavens already know what this heroic man has done! I feel privileged to be his wife!"

Saying this, she quickly turned and left the kitchen and went down the hallway to the bathroom. She was really pissed. But I'd gotten what I needed. Not only had Mireya validated Jan's stories, but she, an indigenous person, had done it with a voice of passion. A voice full of heart and soul and such gut-core feelings that a whole book could be anchored to her voice. Not just to her husband's. Suddenly I glimpsed pay dirt.

Jan came over to me. "It's okay," he said. "She'll calm down in a few minutes and come out smiling and happy once again."

"Oh no," I told him, "I hope she never calms down. Without her passion and conviction, there's no chance for a book. We'd just have the account of another do-gooder white guy who's done great things for native people because of his Christian faith, which is a good story for Christians but nothing really special. But with her fire, and her beautiful use of language, bringing in the stars and the Heavens with such passion, oh boy, then we'd have a book that can electrify the world of believers and nonbelievers alike. SHE ADORES YOU! And look at you, Jan—you're nothing but an elderly-looking, fat white guy."

At first he couldn't believe what I'd said, but then he burst out laughing; and in that moment of his open, natural laughter, I knew that he, too, had a good voice, because he didn't take what he'd done and accomplished so seriously that there wasn't room for laughter. And laughter, *carcajadas* from the gut, was what gave the Mexican culture its power and its eyes into the miraculous.

Over and over in interviewing my father and mother for the trilogy *Wild Steps of Heaven, Rain of Gold,* and *Thirteen Senses,* my dad had roared with laughter, especially when he'd told me about the most awful things that had happened to him and his *familia* during the terrible Mexican Revolution. They'd been starving, ready to die, but then their mother would tell a joke or see something so funny in their predicament that it would give them the heart-*corazón* with which to laugh and go one more step into the unknown.

Or, as the *L.A. Times* said of my first book *Macho!* . . . it was as if laughter and tragedy were twins, married together through life—and I didn't invent this. This came to me firsthand from my parents, who in turn had learned it from *their* indigenous mothers, this power to dance and laugh and love life even in the face of terror and starvation and death.

Mireya came out of the bathroom smiling and happy, but her passion was still intact. You could see it in the way she coquettishly slipped her arm around her husband's large midsection, hugging him close.

"Well," Jan said to his wife, "it looks like our great guest is starting to think that maybe he can do a book on us, honey."

"Just wait," I told them. "Hold on. I'm not a fast writer, Jan. And to do a book on you guys will take months of interviewing and going down to Mexico and up to Los Gatos and San Francisco and then years and years of writing and rewriting. I'm going to have to sleep on it before I say yes or no. Ever since I had my vision-dream up in Portland, Oregon, about snow geese and world harmony and peace, I've learned to depend more and more on my dreams for any important decision making."

"Okay," replied Jan. "Well, then, we will pray for Spirit to come to you tonight and lead you into God's love of enlightenment."

"I'll accept that," I said.

So that night we shook hands, agreeing that I'd dream on it, and Aaron drove us back to our hotel in downtown Durango.

And so now, dear reader, I invite you to accept this book as a gift from the Heavens. For truly, Aaron was right. What *Rain of Gold* did in documenting and validating my parents' generation, this book does for modern times, showing us that all the crazy*loco* love and idealism of the '60s wasn't in vain, but is now, in fact, finally coming to fruition, as predicted by the Mayan calendar and so many other indigenous tribes all over the globe—including my other grandmother's people from Oaxaca, Mexico.

So put on your seat belts! Because this book you are about to read is going to take you on a twisting, turning roller-coaster ride that will sometimes "feel" so unbelievable to your modern mind THAT YOU WILL WANT TO SCREAM! But hold on! And just allow your ancestors to come to you in slip-sliding flashes from your Dream World with the highest vibrations of *amor*-love . . . and you will then know that miracles are our daily *tortilla*-bread! Because once upon a time, we were all indigenous people and directly connected to God!

So there you have it! World Harmony and Peace is in the bag as we now Collectively and Individually LEAPFROG INTO OUR FUTURE PAST! Because, you see, there's only ONE RACE, THE HUMAN RACE, when we go slip-sliding with Love and Trust past all borders and boundaries back to a time when we were all free-roaming Indigenous People, Open of Heart and Alive of Soul, and lived our lives directly connected to God and Creation!

And this is where we're going once again! BACK TO THE FUTURE with a Whole New Consciousness of Focused Intent, because down deep inside we're all One *Familia* the whole globe over and we're all good people! Full of magic! Miracles! And the healing laughter *de carcajadas!*

Thank you!
¡Gracias!
Victor E. Villaseñor
September 2011

P.S. As you will see, I chose not to write this book in the third person. Instead, I decided to let each individual tell his or her own story in the first person. There is no way I could ever speak with the beauty and honesty with which Mireya speaks. There's no way I could ever give voice to her world or her son Joaquin's world. These people are the ones who give life and breadth to Jan Milburn's incredible story.

For 50 years I've been awakening to write at about 2 or 3 each morning, and I've always heard my own voice speaking to me. But this wasn't the case with *Lion Eyes*. No, it was as if these three souls had taken over my life and I could only hear their voices telling me their own story—a story of faith and greatness!

INTRODUCTION

SOUL
TALK

JOAQUIN

My name is Joaquin, I'm 16 years old, and the year is 2007. My mother, Mireya, is a Mexican Indian from the town of Creel up high in the mountains of the state of Chihuahua, Mexico. My dad is a white guy, born in Kansas City, Missouri; and raised in Los Gatos, California. Myself, I was born in Creel, Chihuahua; and raised in Durango, Colorado, as well as Creel, so I feel pretty much at home both in the U.S. and Mexico. I speak English without any accent, and I speak Spanish like a native, so I get along very well with my friends and relatives on both sides of the border. In fact, I'd go so far as to say that I've never had any real problems on either side until lately.

Recently my friends and I have all gotten our driver's licenses, and when we're driving around in town or up at the ski resorts above Durango, the cops always seem to stop us and single me out, especially when they learn that my name is Joaquin. And why me? Of all my friends, I'm the one who doesn't drink or do any drugs. I'm pretty straight, so why me? My last name is Milburn, and I'm not as dark skinned as my mother, and I don't speak English with an accent. But my mom always tells me to just keep calm and well behaved and it will all be okay. My dad, he's funny. He says, put a uniform on any monkey and he becomes a gorilla.

Anyway, both of my parents are pretty cool. In fact, when my friends get kicked out of their houses or their dad starts beating on them, they usually come and stay at our place for a few days. We live about ten miles southeast of Durango on a mesa that butts up against the Southern Ute Indian Reservation.

These Indians are way rich. They have gas, oil, and casinos; and they're nothing like the Indians where my mother comes from up in the mountains of Chihuahua. Some of those guys still live in caves, and very few of them even have cars.

Everyone knows my dad, Jan Milburn, in Creel. He's a local hero to the Indians. He got over two million acres of land returned to them after it had been stolen from them by the loggers, the drug lords, and hotel chains. The way my dad tells it, the coastlines of Mexico have been exploited by the tourist resorts, from Acapulco on the Pacific to Cancún on the Atlantic, so the big international-money people of Mexico and the world now want to move their monies inland to exploit and ruin *las Barrancas del Cobre,* one of the last large untouched pieces of land left on Earth. Also, it's the home of the Tarahumara Indians, who are some of the greatest long-distance runners and free spirits on our planet.

My dad is a minister. At 17 years old, back in the early '60s, he became the youngest minister ever licensed in California. He has explained to me that not even the priests were able to get very far into the culture of the Tarahumara Indians. And it's true. I've seen it. I was raised a Christian, and their Catholic church outside of Creel is dirt-poor and has no pews inside, so the Indians have to squat down on their blankets on the big old wooden planks.

And during Holy Week, there are actually more Indians outside the church than inside. The ones outside sit on the cliffs and monstrous orange boulders that surround the church. The women lay out their big colorful blankets on top of the boulders and sit down and nurse their babies, while the bigger kids laugh and play near their mothers. They look like colorful wildflowers out in the bright sunlight. The men, they squat or stand at the foot of the cliffs or boulders looking serious or talking with their friends and laughing so hard that it makes you all happy inside.

My mother, Mireya, laughs like that, too. Her eyes and face light up, and she laughs like there's no tomorrow. The Indians in Mexico, when there are no white people around, are some of the happiest people I've ever seen.

And also . . . something really crazy . . . is that I've never seen a little kid fall off one of those cliffs or huge boulders—and they're jumping around all over the place, having as much fun as newborn goats. But then, on the other hand, my friends and I, we all go snowboarding in the winter up on the slopes above Durango, and then we also longboard all over town in the summer, doing really crazy things, and none of us have ever been killed. So I guess it's not as strange as it seems for little Indian kids to be jumping around the cliffs and tall boulders without getting hurt.

Also, one more thing . . . every year during Holy Week the Tarahumara men get together at sundown, and they escort the priest out of the church, put him in his car, and make sure he leaves. No white people are allowed to witness or participate in the spiritual services that the Tarahumara Indians do for Holy Week once the sun goes down. Only my dad—whom they call their *apolochi,* meaning their sacred grandfather keeper of wisdom—is allowed to stay and join them.

The drumming starts. You can hear it for miles. The women climb down off the cliffs and boulders and help the men make huge bonfires around the church. But not too close to the Catholic structure, because they don't want to burn it down. They simply want to illuminate it. You see, for the Tarahumara, my mother has explained to me, the cliffs and the boulders are the real house of God. Not the old building out in the middle of a meadow. Also, for these Indians, Holy Week isn't just about celebrating the crucifixion of Jesus. It's also about celebrating Judas, the dark side, because they say that without Judas's betrayal, then Jesus Christ could never have done His Holy Work.

My dad, a Christian minister, entirely agrees with what my mother says, and he tells me that this was why even at the young age of 17 he was ready to take the word of Jesus into the streets of San Jose and San Francisco. He drove a Honda 300 motorcycle, and he helped set up coffeehouses so that the hippies and drug addicts of the day could have a clean, safe place to hang out. He didn't just want to stay inside the church that he'd been assigned to in Willow Glen—a couple of miles southwest of downtown San Jose. No, he wanted to take the light of Jesus into the darkness.

Why? Because, he tells me, it's easy to preach to the people who come to church. What the real challenge is, he says, is to also take the example of Jesus out to the lost souls and nonbelievers. Because you don't see the stars during the day. You see the stars in the darkness of the night, and over and over again he witnessed the eyes of hippies and drug addicts light up like stars once they accepted the words of Jesus Christ. Also, he tells me that he didn't carry a Bible, but instead worked with people one-on-one with an open heart; then he'd leave a pamphlet with them with the picture of Our Savior so they could visualize him, and sleep with him close to their hearts.

Drug addicts, I can understand. We still have them today. They want their drugs so they can get high and cancel out. But hippies . . . I just don't get it. My dad tells me that during the '60s they came in droves every day from all across the country to the Haight-Ashbury area of San Francisco. And that most of them had homes, and some even had parents who were way rich, but they rejected all that because of the Vietnam War, and ran away. Young kids. Girls and guys. Fourteen to twenty years old . . . and they played music, smoked grass, and had orgies of sex. Right out in public. And they called it free love and gave each other the peace sign. I don't get it. My friends and I don't especially agree with the war we've got going on in Iraq, but we're not running away and having sex orgies.

I mean, I'm 16 years old, and it sounds kind of good to have sex, but I wouldn't want to do an orgy. I mean, how can that really be called love? And my dad agrees with me. He says that the hippies would laugh at him when he'd tell them that he was a minister and he was saving himself for his marriage. They'd tell him that it was just skin to skin, so to get off his high horse. But he explains to me that he stuck to his belief.

And he saw many deaths. In fact, he witnessed one young boy so high on LSD that he jumped out of a three-story window, saying he could fly. He also saw some real pretty young girls die of overdoses.

And yet my dad tells me that even back then, he didn't see the world as being divided between the good guys and the bad guys. No, he also saw a lot of hippies do some very brave, good things. Like at the park at Central and Haight, which has a huge towering old fern tree, he says that he once saw them stand up to the cops who were harassing them—but not with clubs and violence. They used flowers and smiles and love in their eyes even as the cops beat them with clubs.

My dad tells me that this is when he learned, as a true Christian, not to pass judgment on his fellow human beings, but instead have faith that the light of Jesus can give heart to even the darkest soul when His holy words are given with an open heart. Even back then my dad says he could see that the days of carrying the Bible around like a badge and preaching from a pulpit with a voice full of righteousness was out-of-date.

In Willow Glen, he filled the church that he was assigned to with young people. This was a church that had been running half-empty for years. He'd hardly sleep. Day and night he'd be on the road on his Honda 300 between San Jose and San Francisco. In fact, he says that he did most of his service after midnight when the young kids were really out of it and looking desperate.

He circulated among some of the most lost souls in the world with his guitar and pamphlets, getting them off the streets and into the warm safety of the spacious coffeehouses he'd started. This was when he began to seek the help of the priests and nuns and ministers of other denominations who weren't afraid to leave the safety of their pulpits and take the word of Our Lord Jesus out into the streets at night. Soon every night they were housing over 400 kids between Haight-Ashbury and Willow Glen. The cops would warn him and his priest and nun friends that they were going to get knifed and killed, but they'd just assure their cop friends that God was with them, and so, of course, everything was okay.

But then one night a guy tried to run my dad over with a truck when he was on his motorcycle, because he'd gotten the girl the guy was pimping away from him and to the hospital. But he outrode the wild-eyed pimp with his Honda 300, shooting up the steps of the park off Central and Haight and dodging through the trees, then coming out up on the top side of the park . . . and he was gone. The girl was 15 years old, and the guy had been pimping her to the Army guys from the Presidio for a dollar a go, and sometimes even for 50 cents, so he could get drugs for the girl and himself.

Yeah, my dad tells me that people do some real bad things in every walk of life, but even these people aren't all bad and can change overnight. So the name of the game, my dad says, is not to stand back playing it safe and passing judgment on people from afar, but to jump into the middle of life with both feet and see with your very own eyes that we all have some good and some bad in each of us.

Days later that girl died. She'd gotten released too soon from the hospital, even after my dad argued with the doctors that they had to keep her for at least a week. Then guess who came looking for my dad? . . . That same pimp. But this time not to kill him, but to tell him that he'd loved her, that he really had, and that he would have done anything to get her back so they could marry and quit drugs. Then he asked my dad to go with him and help save another girl three guys were keeping drugged and using as a sex slave.

My dad said it was really hard for him to forgive this guy and trust him, but he did. He withheld his personal judgments, turned the situation over to Our Lord, and went with the ex-pimp; and they almost ended up getting in a big old knife fight to get this other girl away from her three pimps.

But my dad is quick and strong—a champion wrestler—and very good with words, so they managed to get the girl to the hospital and convinced the doctors to keep her for a full week. My dad says that he and this ex-pimp began working together; and the guy ended up accepting Jesus, going straight, and becoming one of my dad's hardest-working people at the coffeehouse in San Francisco.

This really confuses the heck out of me. What did my dad say to this guy to turn him around like that? I don't think that in another year when I'm 17, I'll be able to do what my dad did when *he* was 17.

But on the other hand, I've also seen what my parents do when one of my friends is having trouble at home and wants to stay with us. The first thing my dad and mom tell my friends is: "This is a Christian home, and you are welcome to stay with us. But this isn't about running away. You will need to go back in a few days and face your situation at home. We will not support you in blaming or talking badly about your parents. Life has no easy answers. But for now, you are welcome, get a good night's sleep, and we'll talk some more when you have rested. Also, no drinking or smoking or drugs while you're here with us."

My dad and mom say that life really isn't complicated. That it's really very simple. All you need to do is first be straight with yourself and God, then not be judgmental with others, and state up front where you stand and what you expect. My parents don't let me or my friends get away with very much. But also, they don't rag on us, and they give us our space.

Since I turned 16, I get to live in the garage, which has been converted into this huge bedroom–living room with a 52-inch flat-screen TV and a pool table and my own refrigerator.

My dad also tells me that he knew Jerry Garcia back in his days in San Francisco and that he knew Bob Dylan and Joan Baez, plus a bunch of other musicians before they became famous. He rode his Honda 300 everywhere and carried a guitar. He had two coffeehouses where he did his work: one was in San Francisco in a large basement right off the corner of Haight and Ashbury in the heart of the hippie section of town; and his other coffeehouse was right next to the old theater in Willow Glen, right outside of San Jose, and also in a basement because of the cheap rent. He sang and played his guitar at each place, but mostly he served free coffee and day-old doughnuts and hot soup, giving young people a place to hang out and feel safe. The word quickly spread about a crazy young motorcycle-driving minister who didn't beat you up with the Bible, but instead offered words of kindness, hot soup, and a free place to hang out.

Joan Baez invited my dad down to Carmel, and he told me that he met a tall, skinny actor who'd just lost his job in a Western on TV and was worried about the new job he'd been offered to go to Italy to make Westerns. My dad said that his only bad habit, even back then, was that he smoked cigars, like his dad had done and his grandfather had also done. They were very inexpensive long, slender, square-looking cigars made by the Amish people with tobacco that was grown completely naturally. He offered one of his long, slender cigars to the worried young actor, and they went outside to smoke.

The actor asked my dad what he did, and my dad told him that he was a minister, but he didn't just do his work at a church. He also ran two coffeehouses, one in San Francisco and another in San Jose, so he could take the word of Jesus to the young kids in the street. He explained to the young actor that this was also how he'd personally overcome all of his haunting doubts and fears—by doing service and putting his trust in the hands of something larger than himself.

The tall young actor asked my dad if he believed in destiny. My dad said yes, of course; then he told him the story of how a mountain lion had led him home through a snowstorm in Los Gatos, California, when he was 11 years old. He explained to the actor that even to this day he could still see that lion's eyes inside his mind. They'd been so calm and indifferent that he'd had no fear of the great cat, and so this was how he now chose to live his life, fearlessly, and with a calm indifference to life or death.

My dad tells me the tall young actor was so impressed with the lion story that they visited for hours, and then a year later, just before my dad left the U.S. to go to Mexico on a six-month sabbatical from his church, he saw a movie that all the young people were raving about, calling it a "spaghetti Western." And there was that tall, skinny young actor on the 20-foot screen: his name was Clint Eastwood; and he was smoking a long, slender, square-looking cigar and wearing a poncho, just like he'd seen my dad wear, and his eyes looked just like the eyes of the mountain lion that my dad had seen that day in the snowstorm—fearless, completely calm, and indifferent to life or death.

I'll tell you, it's hard being 16 and having a dad who's lived through so much, met so many people, and always seemed to be so brave and have all the right answers, and then on top of that, finding out he's the man Clint Eastwood learned to portray in his Westerns. What am I going to do? Heck if I know. But well, maybe I'll find my own way. Still, I wish I was older and not going through all this crap—then maybe the cops wouldn't harass me and my friends so much and then single me out because my name is Joaquin and I look Mexican.

MIREYA

I was in love with Jan before I ever saw him. He was kind, they said. He was strong and handsome; but most important, they said he had a noble heart, meaning that just like a mother bird or deer, he was willing to give his life for his family. My grandmother told me that my great-grandfather had been killed protecting our family; and my mother has explained to me that a man is measured by his willingness to work and protect his loved ones.

My name is Mireya, and I was born in 1964 on my grand-parents' *rancho* west of the mountainous town of Creel, which wasn't really a town when I was growing up, but a train-stop station in the state of Chihuahua, Mexico. It took the Mexican government—with the help of the Irish and the Swedes—well over 100 years to complete the rails between Chihuahua City to the east and Los Mochis to the west on the Pacific coast in the state of Sinaloa. In school we were told that it took this long to build the rails because there are nearly 40 bridges and more than 80 tunnels to cross the huge mountainous area of my homeland. And it's not all just huge pine forests and lakes like it is up in the high country. It's also rich tropical jungles with mangos and bananas down in the deep canyons off the main one, which I've been told is more than a mile deep.

I am the oldest of three sisters and one brother, and to look at me, most people in Durango, Colorado—where we now live most of the time—think I am an Indian. But I'm not all Indian. I am also part Spanish and a little bit French. In fact, one of my sisters isn't real dark like me. She's much lighter of skin and hair, but she's not tall like I am. In fact, in my family, I'm called the tall stick with the laughing teeth, because I'm so skinny; and ever since I can remember, I've always been laughing and showing my teeth, which some say are as large as a horse's, but are still, I think, very beautiful.

For the first few years of my life, we were raised on my grandparents' big *rancho* on the large *mesa* west of Creel where the *Divisadero,* the lookout station, is now located for the tourists who get off the train to look out over our beloved great canyon of *las Barrancas del Cobre*—one of the ten wonders of the world, I am told. But when I was little, the train didn't stop at the *mesa,* and my grandparents' *rancho* stretched out all over the great flats of pine and great big meadows.

We had everything a person could possibly want on our *rancho.* We had goats and cows and *burros* and horses. We had chickens and ducks and rabbits. And we had the most beautiful orchards of peaches and apples that would bless us every year with an abundance of fruit. No child could want for more. Also, when we lived on the *rancho,* we didn't have to go to school, so we could run loose and wild, enjoying each day just like the birds in the trees and the deer out in the meadows. And yet, we still had responsibilities like everyone else. We had to remember to close the gates so the goats and the pigs wouldn't get into our vegetable garden, and we had to remember to gather the eggs and watch out for the snakes and *coyotes,* and of course, also be on the lookout for the great mountain lions.

Have you ever heard a mountain lion scream? They don't roar like that big hairy lion from Africa that roars at the beginning of the movies. No, our mountain lions scream like a woman screaming for help, and with such power that you'd think the lion was right outside your house instead of way over there on the cliffs by the rim of our great canyon.

But the *coyotes,* they live in families. Not alone like the mountain lions. So when they start calling, especially during the full moon, they yip-yip-yap as a whole *familia,* and they sound so happy and full of mischief that my sister and I would get on the roof of my grandparents' house and yap right back at them. This was our entertainment. Not TV or the radio, but instead, the happy wild sounds of the night. My other younger sister and brother weren't born yet. They didn't come into the world until we moved into town.

Oh, it was paradise growing up on my grandparents' *rancho,* but then one of our distant cousins came up from the great city of Chihuahua, where he'd been living for nearly ten years, and my grandparents told my sister and me that they could see that our cousin had brought the evil eye with him. I remember I asked my grandmother what the evil eye was, and she told me it was the eye that couldn't see life in the trees, but instead only saw lumber, couldn't see beauty in the mother hen with her baby chicks, but instead only saw eggs and meat. The evil eye was a sickness, my grandmother explained to me, that people commonly caught down in the lowlands where the roads were paved and cars drove fast.

But I had no understanding of what my grandmother said, because back at that time, there were no paved roads in all of Creel, much less up on the tall *mesa* where we lived, so everyone drove real slow over the rocks and holes in our road.

Soon I began to understand what my grandmother was saying, because at first our cousin offered to buy the *rancho* from my grandparents so he and his group of businesspeople could build a hotel and put in a lookout point for tourists to see our great canyon when they got off the train. He explained to my grandparents that even most of Mexico didn't know about the wonders of *las Barrancas del Cobre*—which is called the Copper Canyon in English because of all of its jagged orange-colored great cliffs. He told them that our canyon was one of the great wonders of the world and had to be shared with Mexico and all of humanity. That we'd all been lucky to have been raised on its spectacular rim, but now the time had come to develop it, like the *Americanos* had so wisely done with the Grand Canyon in Arizona.

My grandfather told our distant cousin that he'd talk it over with the *mayori*, the wise old grandfather of the Tarahumara who also lived on the *mesa*. Our cousin said that the Indians were of no concern to him, because they didn't legally own the land they lived on—that the logging companies owned their land. When they heard this, my grandparents both said no, that they didn't want to sell, because the Indians had been family to them for untold generations.

This was when our distant cousin and his men from the city rounded up our cattle and ran them down the railroad tracks into one of the long tunnels. The train killed and maimed half of the herd. It was awful. Even little calves and mother cows suffered. We were told that you could hear the poor *animales* calling long into the night. And when that still didn't get my grandfather to sell the *rancho* to our cousin, then he came in with the backing of the military, and they arrested my two wonderful uncles, who helped work the *rancho* with my grandparents. They stripped my uncle Oscar and his brother Baltazar of their clothes, whipped them with horsewhips, then staked them out on anthills, cutting up their bodies with sharp little razors so the ants would crawl up the rivers of blood running off of their naked bodies.

I, a child, was there, and this was how we found my two beloved uncles, screaming to the high Heavens in the bright hot sunlight as ants ate of their blood all the way up to their eyes. My uncles were never the same after that, and my poor grandmother went crazy*loca* with grief, so my grandfather finally agreed to sell his beloved *rancho* that had been in our *familia* for over 150 years. But now our cousin with the evil eye said that he would not pay my grandparents any money like he'd originally offered, telling them that they'd cost him a great deal of time and money by putting up such resistance. Then we moved into the town of Creel, and my mother got a job cooking at a little restaurant owned by a man named Coco, who wore a flower behind his left ear and sang like a happy bird.

I was ten years old. I began going to school, and it was very difficult for me to sit still and pay attention. But little by little, I began to learn, because I wasn't a child anymore. No, I was now old enough to realize that my beloved grandfather's heart had been destroyed, because he—who'd always been so big and strong—began to get old and weak and smaller and smaller before my very eyes. The human heart, my grandmother explained to me, was the source of all life, because it was the heart that pumped the blood all throughout the body and even to the brain. But the people with the evil eye didn't know this, so their blood ran backward from their brain to the heart—and this was why they had the sickness. No person with an open, noble heart would have ever run cattle into a tunnel to be massacred. No person with an open, noble heart would have turned on his *familia* and staked his own cousins on an anthill.

Our distant cousin with his friends from the city of Chihuahua built a road from Creel to the *mesa* so they could start the construction of their hotel and the lookout point. They decided to keep my grandparents' house intact and use it as a museum for the tourist to see how people used to live in the old days. My two uncles got jobs driving trucks for the logging company that supplied the lumber for the construction of the hotel.

Life had to go on, my grandmother explained to me, but what I couldn't understand or believe was how the talk in town began to say that our distant cousin and his men were wonderful people, and so they couldn't be the ones who'd done all those terrible things to my grandparents—that it had to be the Indians, those savages who still lived in caves and owned no cars. My grandmother also explained to me that people needed jobs, so they chose to believe the story that benefited them and their bosses.

The years passed and the story grew and grew until finally I, too, began to sometimes forget the truth and start to believe the lie. After all, Creel was growing. Even a bank had been put in. Soon I began to think that only the people with the sickness of the evil eye could get ahead in this modern world of trucks and paved roads and needing to sit still and pay attention instead of being able to run wild and free.

But then miraculously, this was also just about the same time when I began to hear all these stories about *el gringo,* whom a priest had brought up into the mountains to live in a tent in the forest by our largest lake. He was kind, they said, and his eyes were as pure as the eagle and his heart as noble as the lion. It was said that he'd fought against the drug lords down in the lowlands, and this was why he was on crutches—because they'd sent men to kill him, but he'd lived even after they'd broken his body into pieces. Now it was said that he and the priest, who was also from the lowlands, were building a camp by our largest lake for kids to come up to the high country in the summer.

I began to think that maybe, just maybe, there was another way for a person to get ahead in this modern world of paved roads and fast cars. Maybe a person didn't need to lie and have the sickness of the evil eye. Maybe kindness and a noble heart still counted for something.

I was 13 the first time I saw him. It was snowing, and he came walking into town with a cane from the forest where he lived. I'd been told that *el gringo* had a big red beard, but this day his beard was all covered with white frost, and he had icicles coming from the nostrils of his nose. He looked so awful that I ran up the street laughing and shouting, "Here comes the crazy*loco gringo!*"

I was almost 15 years old the second time I saw him, and now it was summertime and he was getting off the train at our train stop of Creel. He didn't have a cane anymore, and he looked very handsome even with his big beard, which wasn't really red. It was more of a brown color, and I could also see why he was famous for having such an abundant appetite. His middle wasn't slender like our townspeople of *Mestizos* and Tarahumara Indians. (*Mestizos* are people like me who are part Indian and part European, with maybe a little bit of *negro,* meaning *Africano.*) This time I ran to the restaurant where my mother worked to tell everyone that *el gringo* had come into town without his cane. That's what we all called him, *el gringo,* because he was from the United States.

The owner of the restaurant, Coco, who always wore a flower in his hair, was madly in love with *el gringo* even before I was, and so were the two *señoritas* who'd come up from the lowlands to work at our new bank. In fact, it was these two women, who were in their 20s, who'd told us of how famous *el gringo* had been in the city of Chihuahua. He'd helped set up safe coffeehouses for the drug-addicted people, and he'd also had an evening radio show called *La Hora Romántica,* "The Romantic Hour," where he gave advice about love and played his guitar and sang with a voice of an angel.

We were told that half the young women of the city of Chihuahua were madly in love with him. But I didn't care what they said. I, too, was now in love with him, and he was going to be mine, because he was a good man with a noble heart . . . and I knew how important a man with a noble heart was for the survival of a family. It was just that he didn't know it yet. And it would be a long time before I learned that his name was Jan Milburn and that he was a minister. But what did I care? Even the animals were in love with him, just like they'd been in love with St. Francis, because the dogs would bark and the *burros* would make their huge hee-haw *burro* sounds, and they'd all follow him up the street when he came into town.

It was said that in the middle of the winter when he first came to live in a tent in the forest, the snow was so deep that the priest hadn't been able to bring in food for *el gringo,* who was starving because he was still on crutches and not able to come to town, which was well over 12 miles away. It was said that he spoke to the Mother Moon, as all good Christian people do, and that very night a huge mountain lion screamed in the darkness and once dragged up a deer, placing it right outside his tent. People say that all through the winter, the lion lived outside of *el gringo's* tent, and in the course of that terrible time, he brought him that deer, then a goat, and even one pig.

I was still only 15 years old and so skinny that I had nothing to offer a man compared to the finely dressed *señoritas* who worked at the bank with their nice big *tetas* and well-defined behinds. And yet I wasn't going to let any of this hold me back, because when I'd dream of my *gringo* at night, I'd see us walking hand in hand across the stars, and we'd be so happy and safe and very good together. But also, I was uneducated and had no idea how to say any of this to him, so instead of telling him that we were united together in love in the stars, I'd get so excited when I'd see him getting off the train or driving into town from the camp he was building for the children that I'd run up to him and leap on him, wrapping my skinny legs about his abundant middle and my arms about his neck, kissing him the whole while.

I continued this for months, but then my mother took me aside and told me that I was embarrassing the poor *gringo* and that I should stop leaping on him every time I saw him come into town. Also, she told me I was no longer a little girl, that I was becoming a young woman, and so such behavior wasn't appropriate. But I didn't care about what was appropriate or not appropriate, so I continued screeching with delight every time I saw him coming up the cobblestone street with the dogs barking and wagging their tails and the *burros* squealing as excitedly as if a thunderstorm was about to begin.

But then one day Jan himself finally told me the same thing. He said to me that I wasn't a little girl anymore, so it wasn't proper for me to be jumping up on him. Then he added the strangest thing.

"Look, Mireya," he said, "if you still feel this way about me when you're 18, then come to me and we can talk. But no more of this for now."

His words were like a knife to my heart, but also like gold, because even though the two *señoritas* from the bank were after him as well as Coco, my mother's boss at the restaurant, I now knew deep inside that I'd shown him my love, and true *amor* had the strongest voice of all, especially when it was spoken from the heart as if there was no tomorrow.

By now Creel was becoming a real town. Most of the road coming in from Chihuahua City was paved, and our distant cousin and his business friends had completed their hotel and the *mirador* for the tourists. The tourists weren't just coming in by train anymore. They were also being transported in by buses and taken to the surrounding lakes and waterfalls and Indian villages.

My grandfather didn't live very long after we were forced off the *rancho*. His heart and soul were torn from his body. But I still had hope. For I could see that Jan, who'd also come from the lowlands and knew all about the cities, had no sickness in his eyes. No, his eyes were as pure as the eagle and his heart was as noble as the lion, so I just knew down deep inside of me that fate would bring us together.

Why? Because in Mexico we always say, *"Mañana es otro milagro de Dios."* Tomorrow is another miracle of God. And this isn't just a saying for us, I tell our son, Joaquin, but the very foundation of life itself. Oh, I sometimes worry so much for our son, Joaquin. He was raised with one foot in Mexico and another in the United States, and it troubles him, I can see.

But also, I tell him that he is the future of the world, because the time has come when we humans must all rise up and fly like the eagle, past the ways in which we were born and raised, and reach for the stars, just as my beloved husband and I have had to both do. This is our modern predicament. A chance for all of us to have eyes as pure as the eagle and hearts as noble as the lion, and not fall victim to the sickness of the evil eye.

JAN

I can see it in our son Joaquin's eyes. He feels confused and lost, and my heart goes out to him, but what can I do? So Mireya and I have talked it over, and we've decided to take him out to California to show him where *I* was when I was 16 years old. Maybe seeing San Francisco and San Jose will help him. Maybe seeing the place where I grew up in the giant redwoods will inspire him. I've often told him the story of how my whole life changed the day I was lost in that snowstorm in Los Gatos and I saw those bright yellow lion eyes up so close to me that I could almost reach out and touch them.

My name is Jan Milburn, and I was born in Missouri in 1945. I have an older brother and sister, then another sister who's closer to my own age. We moved to California when I was, I guess, about nine years old; and with the money from the insurance policy after our dad's death and the wages of my older brother, who was a genius engineer and worked for IBM when it was first starting up in San Jose, our mother was able to buy a beautiful wooded 40-acre estate six miles from downtown Los Gatos, just off Highway 17. But back then Highway 17 wasn't a freeway like it is today. Still, it went over the mountains between the San Jose basin and Santa Cruz on the coast. Black Bear Road used to be the name of the dirt road that came off of 17 and wound its way up through the chaparral and redwood trees to our large home, which was built in 1911 as a resort for people to come to on the train from San Francisco.

Truly, I do believe there are no accidents in life and we're all born with a special purpose. Also, I believe it's only after the storms in life that we find clarity and are able to find our purpose, because on our regular days of life, we seem to just take things for granted and don't really open up our eyes. For instance, when I told Mireya that when she turned 18, if she still felt the same way about me, she could come to see me, little did I think that she would actually do it.

It had been snowing for more than two weeks, and all the roads were closed from Creel to the lake where I lived at the boys' camp we'd built. I had a fire going and the wind was howling like the dickens when I heard a knock on the door. I opened the door and Mireya stood before me covered with snow. She could barely move. My God, she'd walked all the way from town, a stretch of well over 12 miles, and she was half frozen to death.

"I'm 18 years old today," she mumbled with great difficulty, "and I still feel the same way about you."

I was so shocked that at first I didn't understand what she was saying, but once I brought her inside and put her by the fire and she repeated her words, I understood. That first night we prayed to God for guidance. She was 18. I was almost 38. There was a difference of 20 years between us. It was one of the longest nights of my whole life. I truly didn't want to take advantage of this beautiful, innocent, young girl.

But then in the morning we heard a lion's scream, and just like magic the storm stopped. We went outside. The lion had brought us another deer, and the entire sky and the whole world was so clear and beautiful around the lake surrounded by pine trees. We looked at each other and knew that Our Lord God was with us. That very day we did an Indian marriage ceremony uniting us. We did it by the water's edge and spent the next week in TOTAL HEAVENLY BLISS! Truly, when two people come together with so much love, it is a RIVER OF HONEY TO THE MOON!

Then we hiked down to the bottom of the canyon where it was warm, even in the middle of winter. In the canyon's bottom grow mangos and bananas and great ferns among the numerous waterfalls. It was paradise for us walking naked all day in the warm, bright sunshine and eating the abundance of fruit and wild roots and fish and mushrooms.

Mireya and I have never been apart since then, and to this day we still feel blessed no matter what circumstances come our way. All this I want to tell our son, Joaquin—that there is a way for people to live life in a blessed way. But I think it might be best to take him to the exact place where it all began for me in the Santa Cruz Mountains, just above Los Gatos, California. This is where I saw the mountain lion who led me home to safety. This is where the Spirit of God first came to me in a tangible way. And now, having lived in Mexico all of these years, I know that the Spirit of God has been coming in the form of totems to people all over the world since the beginning of time. Also, I'd like to tell our son that I was feeling lost and desperate and thought for sure that I was going to die, and yet I somehow felt I wasn't alone, and I turned and saw the lion's eyes.

So I feel I must tell our son that it's natural to feel lost and confused and scared, because that's how I felt when I saw the lion's eyes and I first came to the understanding that we humans really aren't just of body, but of Spirit, too, and we come from the stars. How else can I explain what I saw in the lion's eyes? He, too, was a walking star. This is what so many native people believe—that we all are stars, walking stars, and we were each sent to Earth to do a certain job. So relax, I'll tell my son, have faith, and realize that you, too, will find your own path, just as I found mine, which for me has been to devote my life to helping my fellow human beings in the name of Jesus Christ.

I bought plane tickets; then Mireya and Joaquin and I drove from Durango, Colorado, to Albuquerque, New Mexico, and flew from there to San Francisco, California. We rented a car and drove down to the Silicon Valley in San Jose. We had lunch in Los Gatos and then drove up Freeway 17 to Black Bear Road, which was now paved and simply called Black Road, and I explained to Mireya and Joaquin how that day I'd come walking and running all the way from my school down in Los Gatos, because once again I'd been late getting to the parking lot at school, so I'd missed my mother, who regularly drove me home after school.

I was 11 years old, and it was almost dark and was snowing by the time I got up into the hills, I told them. The whole world had turned white and looked totally different. I was lost and scared and freezing to death and really upset that my mom had left me once again. I had no jacket, and I'd run most of the way so I could keep warm; and now I was tired and out of breath, and the sweat on my body was beginning to freeze. I wanted to cry, I was so frightened, because I just knew that I was going to die. But then as I was walking across the meadow where I figured the dirt road to our house should be, I was feeling so lost that I was ready to give up all hope . . . when suddenly I had the strangest feeling that I wasn't alone, that something was beside me off to my right side.

I turned and just a few feet away from me, at the foot of a gigantic redwood, stood the largest mountain lion I'd ever seen. I mean, it looked to be the size of a horse! My heart leaped into my throat, and I closed my eyes and said a quick prayer, hoping I was only dreaming so I wouldn't be eaten alive. But when I re-opened my eyes, I don't know how to explain it—everything was different.

The lion wasn't that huge anymore, but she was still very large. My heart came down out of my throat, and I could see that some-how even the snow had changed and wasn't falling down so hard anymore. Now each snowflake seemed to be almost gentle as it came gliding down past my eyes to the earth. I was suddenly very happy and I began to smile, and for some strange reason, I also wasn't afraid anymore either. This was when I looked at the huge lion again and I saw it in her eyes that she, too, was happy—that she didn't mean me any harm. In fact, I now felt blessed to be in the great cat's presence.

The cat and I just looked at each other for the longest time, and her large yellow eyes sparkled like golden stars. Then she turned and started walking away from me through the snow and great redwood trees. I don't know why, but I decided to follow her; and I'd sometimes lose sight of her walking ahead of me in the falling snow, but I wasn't frightened, because I could see her huge, deep paw prints in the fresh snow. I was no longer cold. I was warm, in fact, and the great cat led me home, right up to our front door.

It was miraculous. There was no other way to explain it, and I felt blessed and so happy. Of course, I didn't want to tell anyone in my family about this. How could I? My mother wouldn't even wait ten minutes for me if I was late meeting her in the parking lot at school; and my brother, who was ten years older than I was, was an engineer, so everything had to make perfect sense to him or he didn't want to hear about it.

I was the weird kid of our family. At school I was in the drama program—which was after school—and on Sundays, I sang in the church choir. I guess my family thought I was a sissy, but this was before I got into high school and I found out that I was really fast. I guess, because of all the times I'd had to run home up the mountain, I'd developed strong legs, and also because of Miguel, my Mexican friend, whom I ran with all summer. I set our high school record in the 220, and I also grew taller than everyone in my family, including my brother, who was now a whole head shorter than I was.

Anyway, something miraculous happened to me that late afternoon when I got lost in the snowstorm: I was out of breath. I'd been running hard and I was pouring with sweat, and I didn't know which way to go because everything was white with snow. The sweat on my body began turning to ice. But then, I told Joaquin and Mireya, I had the strange feeling that I wasn't alone, that we never are, and I turned to my right and saw the largest mountain lion I'd ever seen. She was huge! I bet almost the size of an African lion, yet I knew that most American mountain lions only reached about 90 pounds, and this giant was 300 or more. But then when I closed my eyes, said a quick little prayer, and reopened my eyes, the whole world was different. The storm had turned gentle, and I wasn't cold and frightened anymore. I was actually warm, and I felt a trust for the whole world that I'd never felt before. And now the lion's bright yellow eyes, which had looked so fierce before, looked—I still didn't quite know how to explain it—golden and not kind, not gentle, but I guess, neutral and calm and indifferent; and I could clearly see that she meant me no harm. So I followed her and she led me home to safety.

This was when I first began to understand that there are no accidents in life, that everything is a blessing and a gift straight from Heaven when we just keep calm and neutral and have complete trust in God. But I didn't know how to put all this into words back then. All I knew was that I'd felt lost and all alone . . . and then suddenly I'd had this little, strange feeling that I wasn't alone, that there was something to the right of me, and I'd turned, and no more than six or seven feet from me stood the largest lion I'd ever seen. I'd been terror stricken, but then I'd closed my eyes; said a little, quick prayer; and reopened my eyes . . . and the whole world had looked totally different.

And so ever since then, I have come to see so clearly that when a person closes his eyes and says a little prayer, what he's doing is accessing the Kingdom of God that Jesus told us is within each of us; and once we activate this place within us, we can be calm and neutral because we are Spirit-connected to God, and then automatically the whole world is full of love and well-being.

Because, I said to our son, Joaquin, in front of his mother, Mireya, this was what happened to me that day in the snowstorm after I closed my eyes and prayed and then reopened them. I was able to see that the lion's bright yellow eyes didn't look fierce anymore, but in fact, it had been my own fear that I'd seen in the lion's eyes before I closed my eyes and prayed.

Also, I explained to our son that back then I didn't understand any of this, and it was only at my present age, 50-some years after the fact, that I was finally able to express what happened to me that day in the snowstorm.

"So relax, Joaquin," I said to our son. "You are young. I am old. Your life is still all out in front of you. My life is basically all behind me. Soon it will be time for me to go, and time for you to move out into the world and plant your own seeds that you brought with you from the stars.

"Believe me, I knew no more than you know when I was your age. So, when people now ask me how I've been able to accomplish all the things I've done and they tell me that I must be very smart and brave, I say no, I'm not that brave or smart or even capable. I'm actually pretty much a coward and confused half the time. But then I explain to them how ever since that day of seeing the lion's eyes in the snowstorm, I always close my eyes and say a little prayer . . . and it is from this quiet, magical place within me that I acquire my confidence, and then miracles seem to happen.

"Then I explain to people that Jesus said it best for me when He simply said that the Kingdom of God is within each of us. Because for me this isn't just another quote from the Bible, but the very foundation of Christianity, because it is only when we allow ourselves to get in touch with this Kingdom of God that's within each of us that we are then no longer alone, and capable of doing extraordinary things.

"That day the mountain lion could have easily made a meal of me, but . . . instead she led me home, and I do believe that she did this, because when I closed my eyes and said my prayer and reopened my eyes, she and I were now both connected to our own Kingdom of God that's within all of God's Creation, which, of course, includes animals and birds and trees and rocks and fish, too.

"This is what I learned that day, Joaquin, when I was 11 years old and lost in a snowstorm: that the indigenous people are right and we all came into this world with a Spirit, a totem, as so many tribes say.

"Also, from your mother I learned that once we are connected to our totem, we have intuitive and psychic powers, because after Mireya and I performed our Indian marriage ceremony and your mother and I hiked down to the bottom of the canyon, she explained to me that she'd been in love with me before she'd ever met me."

At this time, Mireya stepped into our conversation with laughter and told our son that it was true, she'd been in love with me before she'd ever met me, because the stars in the Heavens had spoken to her of me when she was little; then one day she heard that a white man had arrived from the lowlands who didn't have the sickness of the evil eye, like most people who came from the world of paved roads and fast cars. That all of Creel could see my eyes were as pure as the eagle and my heart was as noble as the lion, and this was why even the dogs and *burros* were so happy to see me when I came to town that they began to bark and hee-haw with joy.

And I told my son that I understood what his mother had told me, because I, too, as a boy would listen to the stars, and more than once I was filled with so much love that I just knew that pure courageous love was truly our way of living life. But I explained to him that at home I was called a dreamer because I spent so much time being with nature, and more than once I was taken out behind the barn and whipped and told that if I didn't straighten up, I'd never be able to hold down a job. Still, sometimes I'd be gone for hours and come into the house singing—I always liked to sing—and I'd be told that once more I was late for dinner and I hadn't done my job of cutting wood and attending to the fire to heat the house.

I grew up feeling like a total misfit in my own family until that miraculous day when the lion and I looked into each other's eyes. It was like I'd finally found a friend. A best friend.

"And this, I have come to believe, is what is missing in all of us who live in the modern world of paved roads and fast cars," I told Joaquin. "We just don't take the time to acknowledge the Kingdom of God that's within each of us and allow our hearts to fill up with so much love and song that we then automatically find our best friend. And this best friend can be a rock, a tree, a dog, a cat, a bird, a goldfish . . . any part of God's Creation that we can talk to with our whole heart open and full of so much love and song that this is when the Kingdom of God within us comes alive! And then we automatically walk in beauty, as the Navajos say, because we see beauty in everything and in everyone; and then love and trust become our way of life—and so there'd be no room for doubt or greed or selfishness once we've found our song and know who we are.

"I truly believe this with all my heart and soul, because I understand that what we feel inside is exactly what we see outside ourselves, because reality is a mirror; and God, in His infinite wisdom, didn't send us to Earth to have domain over the fish and birds and animals. No, He sent us with love and trust to find His Holy Kingdom within all of His Holy Creation, without exception, just as Jesus did when He was born in a manger, surrounded by such loving parents and animals that He could do nothing other than grow up giving love even as they drove nails into His flesh."

So all of this I told our son, Joaquin, when his mother, Mireya, and I took him to California and he saw where I had grown up in a grove of gigantic redwoods, and I showed him the place where I saw the lion eyes.

"Life is full of miracles," I told him, "so don't worry, just relax, be happy, and have faith and trust that this world is a wonderful paradise all around us . . . once we open our eyes and see through the doorway of the Kingdom of God that All of Creation is Alive and Singing Our Song with Love!

"The great redwoods aren't just so many feet of lumber, and mountain lions aren't just wild beasts to be feared and killed. No, both are beautiful and our best friends, and they give song to our hearts and souls once we're living in the Kingdom of God that is within each of us."

This was what I told our son. In fact, I explained to him that this is how I see life, especially when the going gets tough. I just relax, say a little prayer, and remember how beautiful and gentle even those snowflakes became . . . gliding, dancing, down to the earth before my very eyes, and I wasn't even cold anymore. Life, I told him, isn't complicated. It's really quite simple once we place our complete trust in the LOVING, GOOD HANDS OF OUR HOLY LORD GOD AND ALL OF CREATION!

BOOK ONE

CHIHUAHUA

CHAPTER 1

Jan*

I was shocked.

At 17 I received my degree from the Divinity School Extension of Harvard University; then I took the state test, passed with ease, and became the youngest minister ever licensed by the State of California. Immediately I began working the streets of San Francisco and San Jose, bringing kids into the two coffeehouses I had set up so they'd have a safe, warm place where they could sleep and hang out. But I was exhausted from constantly going back and forth between both places, sometimes several times a night. Twice I almost crashed my Honda 300 motorcycle because I was so tired. Finally, the superiors of my church decided I needed a six-month sabbatical. And they suggested Mexico, which was fine with me, because ever since I'd worked with the Mexican farmworkers in the fields while I was in high school, I'd wanted to visit that country.

---

*All chapters in Books One and Two are from Jan's perspective.

But what shocked me wasn't that my superiors had decided to send me away. No, what shocked me was that more than 200 young people came from San Francisco and San Jose to see me off at the airport. I thought I'd failed. I thought I hadn't reached any of the street-tough kids. I figured they just considered me a crazy fool for even suggesting they not take drugs or have sex until they got married.

It brought tears to my eyes when I saw that a whole crowd of young people had come to see me off. They had flowers and were tossing them up in the air to me. And I'd truly thought they'd only seen me as a joke, as a stupid idiot who refused to take drugs or have sex before he was married. But hundreds of them came to see me off, waving, crying, and telling me how much they loved me.

I was 23 years old. I'd been doing service for nearly six years.

I'll never forget my first night in San Francisco, when I was cleaning up the dirty basement to make it into our safe house and I heard a SCREAM, like the ear-piercing shriek of a mountain lion, up on the street. I raced up the stairs. Outside, I found three drunks harassing a young girl. I yanked the guys away and took the girl downstairs and shut the door, bolting it.

The girl, Nancy, was covered with puke. I helped her wash and gave her my sleeping bag and jacket so she could lie down. Then I continued cleaning, and filling cans with garbage. By the next morning, there were three young girls sleeping on the floor of the safe house.

Nancy woke up and watched me quietly as I was working. "Who are you?" she asked.

"I'm a Methodist minister," I told her.

"Really?" she asked. "And what's all this . . . this place about?"

"I'm working with Father Gabriel, the local priest, and some nuns," I explained. "We're turning this place into a safe house for people to come in out of the cold and crash at night and sober up."

"And find Jesus, right?" Nancy asked.

"Jesus isn't lost, as far as I know."

Nancy burst out laughing, but then, still grinning, she returned little by little to her hard skepticism and said, "Yeah, sure, whatever." But then, I guess, because she watched me keep working and saw that I didn't have any intention of making sexual advances toward her and the other young girls, she finally asked if she could help.

"Of course," I said to her, and she started working with me. Then my second overnight guest, Brenda, woke up.

Brenda's first words were: "Is there any coffee?"

"No," I told her, "but would you like to go out and bring some back for all of us?"

Brenda agreed, so I reached into my pocket and gave her some money.

Nancy laughed at me. "You know she's not coming back with the coffee, right?"

"No, I don't know that," I told her. "All my life wonders have happened when I've put my trust in people in the name of Jesus."

"There you did it! Selling Jesus!" Nancy yelled at me. "I knew you'd do it! But get real! She's going to use that money for drugs, and you know it!"

But with calmness and love, I asked her, "Tell me, did you have a pet growing up?"

Nancy nodded.

"Did you love your pet, and did your pet love you?"

"Well, yes, of course, but what's the point?"

"The point is, I've found that once we turn our hearts over to Jesus with complete trust, like we did with our pets when we were kids, then miracles happen."

Nancy yelled at me, "BULLSHIT! YOU'RE A FOOL! THAT GIRL WILL NEVER COME BACK IN A MILLION YEARS!"

Just then, like a miracle, Brenda came walking in with coffee and a bag of doughnuts, and said that when she told the manager of the coffee shop who the coffee was for, he said he'd deliver his day-old doughnuts to us at the end of the day.

Nancy broke down crying, and I took her in my arms, giving her comfort. But she resisted, and kept crying, "NO! YOU CAN'T DO THIS TO ME! I never want to believe in anything again!"

Then it was Brenda who broke the ice by saying, "Don't believe. Just drink the coffee. It's pretty good."

Nancy started laughing. "Okay, I . . . I can do that."

So the three of us just sat down on the floor, drinking coffee and eating doughnuts, talking about our pets and our lives. The word spread, and by the second night, the priest, the two nuns, and I had more than two dozen kids in our shelter.

Father Gabriel and over 200 young people came to see me off at the airport, and a couple of these girls, who came from prominent, wealthy families and had been trying hard to "de-virginize" me for years, ran up and began kissing me. One said I'd changed her life and she was no longer going to take drugs or be giving her body to anyone, and that she loved me and would wait for me to return, because she owed her new life to me.

It was difficult, but I was finally able to pull myself away from her, and I immediately corrected her, saying that Jesus was the one she loved and owed her new life to. Not me.

They blew me kisses and gave me a beautiful arrangement of flowers. On the plane people asked me if I was a rock star. "No," I said. "A Christian minister." They were astonished, and so was I.

Chihuahua, Mexico

Jorge, the assistant to the pastor of the church where I'd be working in Mexico, picked me up at the Chihuahua City bus station, which was quite small back then, in 1969. At the church,

I met with the pastor and his family, and I was asked if I spoke Spanish.

"A little bit," I said in English. "Mostly what I learned from the field-workers when I used to work in the summers while going to high school."

Jorge, who spoke English quite well, translated for me, and the pastor, I guess, then told Jorge to ask me to demonstrate what I knew in Spanish.

I said, "Sure, of course," to Jorge and cleared my throat. We were seated together in the rectory of the church. *"Buenos días,"* I said, which of course meant "Good morning." They smiled and nodded their approval.

"Buenas noches," I said, which meant "Good night." They smiled and nodded their approval once again.

"Una Coca-Cola, por favor," I said, which meant "May I please have a Coca-Cola." They smiled and laughed and vigorously nodded their approval again.

"Un taco, por favor," I said, which meant that I'd like to please have a taco.

They were all very happy now, smiling and laughing among themselves, especially the older woman and the beautiful young woman, who I guessed were the pastor's wife and daughter.

Then with great delight I said, *"¡Chinga tu madre!"* which meant "Thank you very much." But all their smiles and laughter stopped, and they stared at me in total shock; then they began speaking rapidly in Spanish among themselves.

They seemed very upset, and I had no idea why; then Jorge turned to me and said, "That last one, our pastor doesn't want you to ever say again."

"Why not? Doesn't it mean 'Thank you very much'?" I said.

Jorge shook his head vigorously, telling me no, and the two women quickly got up and left the room. The pastor then spoke very sternly to Jorge, and I guess we were told to leave the church, because Jorge asked me to follow him out of the house of God. Once we were in the street, he explained to me that *Chinga tu madre* meant "Fuck your own mother."

I was shocked!

The guys I'd worked with in the fields had totally misled me. Now I could see why they'd laughed so hard every time they had me say this after I'd been given a Coke or a taco.

"I'd like permission," I said to Jorge, "to go back inside and apologize to the pastor, and especially to his wife and daughter."

"Not now," said the young assistant, laughing. "I was told to take you out for dinner to a taco stand and start teaching you proper Spanish so other vulgarities don't also accidentally come out of your mouth. My pastor thought you were fluent in Spanish."

"Well, not fluent," I told him. "But I didn't realize I was this far off the mark. Those field-workers, they really had fun with me, didn't they?"

"It sure sounds like it," said Jorge, laughing again.

After that, I quickly learned Spanish. My six-month sabbatical came and went; and six years later, in 1975, I was still in Chihuahua, 30 years old, and was married to my pastor's voluptuous daughter. Her name was Catalina; and she had large, beautiful green eyes and dark, gorgeous skin. It was her mother, who'd been born in the Rain of Gold canyon, who first began telling me about the Tarahumara Indians who lived in the Copper Canyon—a wild, mystical place where there were pine trees and snow up on the high ridges, and waterfalls and tropical fruit trees down in the bottom.

Catalina was the love of my life. I'd never been with a woman before, and she'd never been with a man. We were both so innocent and excited and happy and perfect for each other. We soon had our first son, whom we named Nathan, and then we were quickly pregnant again. No couple had ever been happier. Our only conflict was that Catalina didn't want me to go out at night to take the word of Jesus to the young people in the streets. She wanted me to be a stay-at-home-at-night minister, like her father.

She began to go to her parents' home on the nights I was sched-
uled to go out.

One evening I was on my way to give a presentation to the
parents of drug addicts in the poor, southern part of Chihuahua
City, but I had forgotten my box of charts in our apartment, so I
went back to get it. To my surprise, I saw that there were two bullets on a pillow of our bed. I quickly took the bullets and put them
in the shoe box where I'd put the other bullets, so that Catalina
wouldn't see them. Whoever was doing this had been leaving only
one bullet on our pillow for weeks now. This was the first time
that he—I assumed that it was a male—had left two. I wondered
what this meant. I had no idea, but I was sure that if my wife saw
these bullets, she'd probably never come home again and want to
permanently stay at her parents'. But I wasn't really disturbed by
them. After all, I had faith and I was doing God's work, so what
could possibly go wrong?

Without hesitation, I picked up the large chart box I had come
for and hurried out of our tiny apartment and down the stairs to
my little motorcycle. Chato was waiting for me. He was a tough
street kid from Juárez who'd accepted the word of Jesus about six
months ago, and he was now my right-hand man. Most people in
Mexico and all of the kids I worked with addressed me as Don Jan
even though I had a beard and long hair and still only wore Levi's
and T-shirts.

I gave the wooden box to Chato, and he got on the bike behind
me. This motorcycle was no Honda 300. It was just a little two-
banger 110 Apache put out by Islo in Mexico that could hardly
hit 50 on a flat straightaway. But it was all I could afford. I had no
money. The Christian school I'd been assigned to in Chihuahua
was dirt-poor and only gave me the equivalent of $50 a month to
live on, and I was married and we had one son and another child
on the way.

As I pulled out into traffic, I noticed that two large dark vehicles were also pulling out with me. I thought nothing of this
until one of the big four-door cars came up real close behind me,
acting like it was going to ram me. I gave my little Apache some

gas, but I couldn't get it to go any faster. Chato and I were late as it was, so I continued down the street, then turned onto *División del Norte*, the big main boulevard of Chihuahua City, and got into the flow of the traffic.

This was going to be a very important presentation. The wife of the governor of the state was coming to this meeting in the poor section of the city, along with a few of her rich, powerful women friends. The grand lady had a lot of faith in me, because when I'd first come to Mexico, eight years before, I'd been instrumental in getting some of her grandkids off drugs.

Now I noticed that the two large dark cars were still with me. One was pulling up beside me on my left, and the other one looked like he was going to hit me if I wasn't careful. Instantly, my instinct for survival kicked in and I quickly turned to my right, barely cutting in front of a big smoke-belching city bus. We were coming into the main center circle of *División del Norte* with the huge statue of Pancho Villa on horseback. I was safe now. The two cars couldn't get at me anymore. But then the bus turned right, going out of the circle, and I was a sitting duck once again, because I had to keep going straight to get to the presentation on time.

This was when the car on my left side suddenly sped up real fast, pulling alongside me, and for the first time I could see that there were four big men in the vehicle who were staring at me. The one in the backseat of the car started laughing, but I could see in his eyes that it wasn't a happy laugh. Chato must have seen his face, too, because he tightened his grip around my waist.

I swerved to the right, trying to get away from the big four-door car, but the other car now hit me from behind. But not too hard. Just hard enough so I almost lost control of the little Apache. The four guys in the car beside me all started laughing. Now I knew that Chato and I were in real danger. This wasn't a game of just having a little fun with a long-haired, bearded *gringo*. No, these guys were serious. They were going to kill us. Then I remembered the two bullets that had been left on the pillow.

I began to pray, hoping for a miracle, when the car that had pulled up beside me now suddenly sped up ahead, then cut right in front of me, slamming on its brakes. But I'd been riding motor-cycles for years and I'm very quick, so I jerked to the left, thinking I could miss him, but this was when the car behind Chato and me hit us with such force that they rammed us into the other vehicle.

I caught sight of Chato flying over my head with the wooden chart box still in his hands as the little Apache and I were pushed underneath the big four-door car in front of us. Then I don't know how to explain it, but it was like my soul came out of my body and I was now a few feet above everything, and I could see that Chato had flown entirely over the car in front of us and had landed on the wooden box out in midstreet in heavy traffic. The four-inch-thick chart box that I'd made of fine maple wood shattered, and it must have cushioned Chato's fall, because he looked okay and got right up.

But my body, on the other hand, wasn't okay. I could see that it and the little motorcycle were being crunched into pieces as both were rammed farther and farther under the big four-door vehicle that had cut in front of us. I could hear the bones of my legs and arms breaking. I'd never realized that human bones made so much noise when they were broken. Now my body was half under the car, and the big vehicle went forward, driving over me, then stopped and began backing up over me, too. I guess I was still conscious enough to realize what was going on, because I now saw myself turn my head away as much as I could so the rear passenger tire of the vehicle wouldn't run over it, crushing my skull.

Then both cars stopped, and the eight men in the two cars got out of their vehicles and were asking each other if I was dead or not. Then I guess, for good measure, a couple of them tied ropes to my arms and legs and began yanking me in four directions while the others kicked me in the head and ribs. This was when I saw the people in the ice-cream parlor across the street come outside and start yelling at them to stop.

Two of the men pulled out guns. Instantly, the people from the ice-cream parlor scattered. One of the eight men now came over and spat on me, then kicked me one last time, right in the groin. Then they got in their vehicles and drove off.

Chato now came over to see me. He looked terrified; and I guess he figured I was dead, because he carefully put the remains of the chart box down beside me and stroked my cheek gently, with tears pouring down his face. Then he took off running past all the people who had gathered. As for me, I disappeared after this. I guess my soul went back into my body, because I don't remember much after that, except I could hear the sound of an ambulance.

The next thing I knew, there were bright lights and people in white uniforms all around me. They were saying it was a miracle I was still alive, but also they added that I was sure to die. I tried to talk, to tell them that I wasn't going to die—that we human beings, I now knew, weren't just of our bodies. I now truly understood that we were all also of something else far beyond our physical selves; and this other part of me was never, never, never, NEVER, NEVER GOING TO DIE!

I was put on a stretcher and slid into the ambulance; then it began snowing, and everything all around me turned white. I was freezing cold . . . but then I had the strangest feeling I wasn't alone. Something was beside me off to my right. I turned my head, and just a few feet away from me were those same great big golden lion eyes that I'd seen as a child. But this time the eyes had no head or body. They were just bright yellow eyes that glowed like stars.

I smiled. I was so happy to see them, because I now knew that I'd be led safely home. All of our totems always lead us home. All paths lead home once we are connected to God through our Loving Spirit Guide.

The next thing I knew, more people dressed in white were working on my body, but then they quit, saying I was dead. This was when I heard the EAR-PIERCING SCREAM OF A MOUNTAIN LION, AND I FELT AN EXPLOSION COME BURSTING INTO MY BODY! My heart began beating once again! I HADN'T DIED! I HADN'T DIED! I WAS ALIVE! And I now knew that the mighty lion of my childhood had taken up residence inside my earthly body, so there was no way that this lioness was going to allow me to die. No, she loved me, and she was going to lead us both back home to safety, just as she'd done when I was a child. But this time my home wasn't a big old house in the redwoods. It was a castle up among the stars! This was all of Our True Homes, THE STARS! THE STARS! *LAS ESTRELLAS . . .*

Days passed. Weeks passed. I walked across the Heavens with my golden-eyed lioness among the stars, being shown that I was really doing my earthly work. In fact, this was why the drug lords had hired assassins to kill me—because I had reached so many lost young souls, taking them from the darkness of drugs to the light of God, that the drug lords could see the end of their monopoly over darkness. I was also told that it wasn't any longer enough for us humans to only have one life within our lifetime on Mother Earth. The time had come when it was necessary for us to have two and three and four and five and even six and seven lifetimes within our one life here on our planet, in order to move us all from the darkness to the light.

Reincarnation no longer worked in the old way, because we human beings were no longer just human beings. We were becoming beams of light for the greater good of all of humanity. It was no longer acceptable for us to play small. The time had come for us to accept our great, wondrous burning-light of being human, so all of us could unite together in one vision of greatness!

Over and over again, my good friend the lioness came to me and breathed her powerful breath into my heart and soul. Yes, I had died. I really had . . . and yet I'd been given new life so I could continue to be of service, as we were all doing in our own way whether we knew it or not. Simply, my life was no longer my life, but of God. TOTALLY! COMPLETELY! I FELT WONDERFUL! MAGNIFICENT! Even though my earthly body was in terrible pain.

Then I saw the gorgeous face of my wife, Catalina. She had our beautiful son, Nathan, in her arms, but she didn't look happy. She was crying, and her face looked full of fear and anger. This was when I heard her say, "So they tell me you're going to live. Too bad. I was hoping you'd die so this whole nightmare could finally be over! I just can't stand it anymore," she told me. "I even wish I wasn't pregnant!"

Her words stabbed me like a knife. I couldn't see why she would say such an awful thing. We were happy, I thought. Catalina had learned English, and I had learned Spanish; and she was a fine, beautiful woman, and we'd fallen in love and married . . . but then, I guess, something had obviously gone wrong, and she now hated me and wished me dead.

I couldn't move, but I so much wanted to reach out to Catalina and take her in my arms and tell her about our great friend the mountain lion. But she turned and left, and I was all alone. Once more I slip-slid back into a snowstorm, and now everything was all white again and I couldn't find the road that took me home. But then once again here was my lioness, and we looked at each other eye to eye as we walked side by side from star to star across the Heavens. I began to understand that Catalina and I didn't live together anymore. She had moved out, and I would now be alone in our tiny apartment.

For years, Catalina and I had lived in a huge, deserted, run-down ambassador's mansion that had been given to us by a friend of the governor's to convert into a safe halfway house. The mansion must have been quite the place in its day, because the tall entrance going up the stairs had the most spectacular chandelier I'd ever seen. It was as large as a car and had been given to Mexico by Austria.

The mansion had been in total ruins when it was given to us, except for the chandelier. Twelve of us worked day and night for months to clean the place up and make it into a good, safe, warm halfway house. Everything had been going very well for Catalina and me. We were like the picture-perfect couple. But then one of our kids broke the house rules and brought drugs into the mansion.

I told the boy that he was going to have to leave. He became so enraged that he sneaked into our private quarters and took the oozing puss from his syphilis-infected penis and rubbed it in our sleeping child's eyes. Our boy Nathan slept for days. Then on Sunday, I happened to notice something moving under his eyelids. Opening one, I saw what looked like small white maggots crawling all over his eye. We called an ophthalmologist friend at his home, and he told us to meet him immediately in his office. He scraped and washed the awful crawling worms from both of Nathan's eyes. He told us it was a good thing we'd brought our child in to see him as soon as we had, or he could have lost use of both of his eyes.

Catalina went crazy*loca,* saying we had to quit what we were doing and get ourselves a decent life, that all of my ex-addicts were nothing but monsters. I tried to tell her that this was an isolated case and that most of the kids under our care were good kids and doing quite well. That very day she packed her belongings and left. She wouldn't see me again until I agreed to move out of the mansion and into a tiny apartment just for the two of us.

Now I was beginning to remember why she hated me. Because we'd only been in our apartment a few days, far away from all of our street kids, when we'd found a bullet and a black glove on our pillow. Catalina and I had no idea what this meant, but people told us the bullet and glove were the calling card of *la Mano Negra*—the Black Hand—the most infamous assassin in all of Mexico.

Even government officials hired him, we were told, not just the drug lords. And nobody, absolutely nobody, knew who he was, but everybody knew all about him. He could be anyone. In fact, some people thought he wasn't even a man, but a woman who'd been raped as a young girl, so she had assassinated not only the man who'd raped her, but all the people who'd been witnesses and hadn't defended her. That was one story. Another was that he was a fine, good-looking young man who'd studied to be a priest, but had been abused by an older priest, whom he'd killed and hung upside down by his private parts at the altar of a church at the state capital of Zacatecas for everyone to see.

The stories of *la Mano Negra* were endless, but . . . the reality of his/her existence wasn't questioned. All of Mexico knew about his/her great feats. In fact, I was told that the eight men who'd failed to kill me had all been found dead a few days later just outside Chihuahua City. Their two vehicles had been blown to pieces, and all their eyes had been shot out of their skulls so that they'd be lost and blind when they returned to the Spirit World.

Catalina never came to the hospital to see me again, and it hurt. I truly loved her, and I loved our son, Nathan. Also, she was with child, our other child, and I would never even know if it was a boy or girl.

But I was not going to die! I was going to live! I'd moved my head quickly enough not to have my skull crushed when they'd driven the big car over me, so I still had both my eyes, THE EYES OF A LION! And together my lioness and I were star walkers.

Still, it was several months before I could even sit up. My back alone had been broken in five places, and the muscles of my abdomen had been kicked to pieces. My arms and legs were in casts, and every one of my fingers had been smashed. It was a few more months before they could even get me in a wheelchair. They began to take me down the hallway to the not-very-well-kept gardens outside. My head began to clear, and I was able to think once again. Before this, there had been such a constant echo going on inside my skull that I couldn't even think.

I began to understand why Catalina had never come back to see me. Obviously my situation with *la Mano Negra* wasn't over, and as a mother, she needed to protect herself and our two children. All this I could now comprehend, but what I couldn't understand for the life of me was . . . why God, in His infinite wisdom, had abandoned me and allowed this terrible thing to happen to me when I'd been working so hard doing His Holy Work.

I began to feel so sorry for myself that I could cry. I was never going to get my body back. That wonderful, quick body that I'd had was gone forever. Now all I had was this broken-up mess that was all in casts. But the doctors didn't quit on me. They kept assuring me that it was a miracle I was alive. Yet they just couldn't understand that this was no life for me. I'd been doing God's work, so this should never have happened to me.

Then one afternoon I was taken out to the lousy-looking flower garden behind the hospital, and I was sitting there feeling so upset and lost and lonely, when three large butterflies came flying by. They were beautiful, and I watched them go fluttering all around me in the bright sunlight. I smiled, and my heart filled up with so much happiness that that evening I ate with my old appetite. Dinner was *caldo de res*—beef soup—made old Mexican-style with a lot of bones and vegetables. I finished my whole serving, and that night I slept like a baby.

The next morning I was starving. I ate two servings of *huevos rancheros,* meaning eggs prepared Mexican-style and placed on a corn *tortilla* with *salsa.* After breakfast I asked to be taken out to the flower garden once again. This time the whole place was alive with butterflies. I couldn't stop smiling. I reached out with my broken arms, wanting to be part of their beauty. They landed on my arms. The nurse who was with me laughed with delight and told me that the butterflies were in migration, and they would be coming through all week by the thousands.

Every day became a glorious event for me!

Each day became another MIRACLE OF GOD'S INFINITE BEAUTY filled with so much love and fragrance that the lousy-looking garden behind the hospital began to suddenly transform before my very eyes. Within a week it was a paradise of flowers and butterflies and songbirds. I began to understand that God had never abandoned me. I was the one who had abandoned God when I'd gotten mad because of what had happened to me. The Holy Creator's love had always remained all around me.

Yes, of course! This was the message I'd received as a boy of 11 when the lioness and I had looked at each other eye to eye, and I'd seen that she meant no harm, but was, in fact, full of love and kindness if only I remained open and calm and indifferent even to death itself. It was forever paradise right here, all around us.

A couple of doctors and other nurses began to accompany me when I was wheeled out to the garden. One of the doctors asked if a photographer friend of his who worked for the local newspaper could take a few pictures of me with the flowers and butterflies and songbirds. I said sure, why not, and I just couldn't stop smiling, because once more—not as a child of 11 in a snowstorm this time, but as a grown man in my 30s in the bright sunshine—I was receiving an . . . an understanding and comprehension BEYOND ALL I'D EVER DREAMED POSSIBLE!

Yes, oh yes, just as Our Lord Jesus forgave them as they drove the nails into His flesh, I, too, now forgave those who had driven over my fallen body with their car and then tied ropes to my arms and legs and pulled me in four directions . . . and life, miraculously, had become a paradise all around me. Oh, I could now see it so clearly. I was a boy no longer. I was a man; and as a man I had to understand that all these terrible pains in my broken body were Holy, Sacred Lessons for me to learn from, just like the butterflies that knew how to move from the caterpillar to the cocoon and then into the beautiful, fluttering, dancing wildflowers that all butterflies became.

Tears came to my eyes. God had not abandoned me.

God had never, ever abandoned me. And suddenly I remembered the dream I'd had that nowadays humans had to die several times within their lifetimes so they could do their earthly work. So yes, I had died. I really, really had died. I had not escaped another of my near-death experiences, as I'd done in California with my Honda 300 when I was going back and forth between San Francisco and San Jose. And this death, it had not been inflicted upon me by a drug-crazed kid, but by the most infamous professional assassin in all of Mexico.

Oh yes, I died and had come back to life, just like Our Lord Jesus Christ, because the time had come for us human beings to all start becoming Christlike in Our Living Lives! Oh, this was wonderful! This was fantastic! Because then, this meant that not even the Black Hand of evil could get rid of us when we were in Service with God!

Tears of joy continued streaming down my face. God was with me! He was truly keeping watch over me, and I was suddenly so hungry that I could scream. I wanted meat. Raw meat. I began to laugh. No doubt the mountain lion who'd taken up residence inside my body was starving, and together we were going to not just survive—but be stronger than ever before!

I began doing my therapy exercises with vigor! And sure, it was painful and really hard, but God had given me this lion spirit that was within me, and together we could move mountains! The doctors were amazed by my energy and determination, yet they still kept advising me to slow down and realize that the most I could ever hope for was to get around in a wheelchair. Because, they added, there was no way I was ever going to be able to stand upright. My stomach muscles had been destroyed, and it took strong stomach muscles to hold the back in place so a human could stand erect.

"You must be realistic," my doctor said to me. "Just look at your belly. You're a slender man with a medium build, yet your stomach protrudes like the belly of a seven-months-pregnant woman. This wheelchair is as good as it is ever going to get for you," he added.

I thanked him, but I could also see these men of medicine knew nothing about the lion spirit that lived within me. I stopped taking all of my pain pills and began to look upon all the pain going on inside of my body as a Godsend, as a gift telling me I still had feelings in these parts of my broken body.

I was transferred from the emergency part of the hospital to a health center where every night we were shown movies; and one evening there was that young, skinny actor I'd met in Carmel on the big screen. I was told that it was Clint Eastwood in another of his spaghetti Westerns, which were now the rage among the young people of Mexico.

We watched the movie several times; and how he did it, I don't know, but Clint Eastwood took me right back to that day I'd met him in Carmel and I'd told him of the time when I'd seen the lion's eyes. It was incredible how he did it. I'd only talked to him for a couple of hours, yet he'd taken what I'd said to him and expanded it into something young people all over the world could understand.

I decided that when I got out of the hospital I'd start using his movies at our halfway houses to show kids how they could remain calm and strong and detached even in the face of the temptation of drugs. I could see that Clint Eastwood had become the epitome of the famous Mexican saying that a man had to embody the three F's—*feo, fuerte, y formal,* meaning ugly, strong, and formal—in order to be a good man. But *ugly* in the Mexican culture didn't mean ugly as we understood it. What it meant was that it didn't really matter how you looked on the outside. How you were on the inside WAS EVERYTHING! And *strong* meant not just strong of body, but of character and especially of heart. And *formal* meant that you were formally polite, well mannered, and respectful.

It was right after this that one morning, just as the dawn was beginning to paint the eastern sky outside my window in colors of red and orange and pink, three sets of eyes came to me. Only eyes. And they were bright yellow like the eyes of my lioness. Then the three sets of eyes took on the human form of three elderly Indians who told me they were *Curanderos*—Healers—and that they'd come to see me from the Spirit World. One of them reminded me a great deal of my childhood friend Miguel, who'd taught me to fly like an eagle when I ran, so I listened closely. At the end of our first visit, the one who reminded me of Miguel stepped forward, and with great formality presented me with a long wooden shaft of feathers and claws.

"This will now be your shaft in life, blessed with eagle feathers and lion claws," he said. "Because from now on, you will need the Vision of an eagle in order to do your Holy Work with your lion heart."

I was overwhelmed. I didn't know what to do. This was way too much, even for a dream. But then my pounding heart finally calmed down enough so that I could reach for the shaft, accepting this fate of mine; and this was when the three of them explained to me that yes, I had died and been reborn so that the Vision of the Eagle could now be added to my Heart of the Lion, so I'd have the tools with which to do my Holy Earthly Work.

"Everything up to this point," added the *Curandero* who reminded me of Miguel, "has simply been preparation."

I almost panicked. What did this mean—that all I'd been through wasn't enough? But I didn't panic. Something in their behavior was so calming that I went to take the shaft of eagle feathers and the lion claws in my two hands, and instantly awoke and found my arms reaching out in front of me, with nothing in them. It was the strangest and yet most real-feeling dream I've ever had.

After that, the three Indian *Curanderos* began coming to me every day at dawn when I was in that state halfway between being awake and asleep, and little by little, I began to understand what they were telling me. It was no accident that my body had been broken into pieces. This was a ritual that had been handed down through the ages all over the world since the dawn of time. All Great Souls went through this ritual before they could do their True Service. Jesus and His Crucifixion was part of this long, ongoing tradition. My earthly body was now going to be reassembled in a whole new way, with the deliberate intent and focus of being conscious of my consciousness beyond all I'd ever known.

I began to wake up with little tingling feelings all over the dead, broken parts of my body. The tiny tingles began at my fingertips, then ran across my hands and up my arms. I'd lie perfectly still, and it was as if I could feel the different parts of my body coming back to life. Then my three Indian *Curanderos* started chanting softly as their hands took hold of my body, mending it, soothing it. Oh, it felt so wonderful waking up with all these great feelings going on in the different parts of my physical body.

I began to realize how much I'd taken my body for granted. The wrists, for instance, were a marvel. They moved not just up and down, but sideways, then all around in little twisting circles. Every morning the three Indian Healers would work on my body when I was in that state halfway between awake and asleep, and little by little I began to regain the use of my wrists, then my hands. Each finger reconnected in feeling and movement to the rest of the hand and then to the wrist.

Then my three Indian Healers began to work on my neck and shoulders. Oh, this was pure pain at first, but then I began to understand that my neck had to be strong and was a miracle of movement as it guided my head this way and that way. I began to feel a profound change coming all through my body. This was a body that I'd really never known before. For instance, my neck, I could now clearly feel, was a part of the spine, and my spine went from my tailbone all the way up to my skull.

Tears of joy came to my eyes. I'd never realized what a magnificent creation the human body was. I could spend all day just looking at and feeling how my thumbs worked. I guess it was only now that my body had been destroyed and my three Indian Spirit Guides were helping me put it back together again that I was beginning to truly appreciate what a gift the human body was.

"Thank You, God, for this wonderful body of mine," I said. "Thank You for each part, each bone, each ligament, each muscle. Thank You, thank You, thank You, thank You, thank You, thank You, thank You, thank You, thank You!"

Tears poured down my face. My poor spine alone was a miracle, and it had been broken in five different places.

"I love you, spine," I said to my spine. "I love you with all my heart and soul. You are fantastic, spine. You are WONDERFUL! You are the one who connects life to all of me, up and down my back to my legs and arms, and of course, to my neck and to my head."

And I now knew that the lioness who'd taken up residence in my heart was the one who was pumping blood and life to my whole body. I'd truly become LIONHEARTED! Slowly, carefully, and with great deliberate intent, my lion heart and I began to consciously work love and energy into every part of my broken body, just as the three Indian *Curanderos* instructed us to do.

The doctors had done their job, and they'd done a good job, especially considering what a broken-up mess they'd had to deal with. But the human body wasn't just a physical instrument. It was a Spiritual Being, too, so the knowledge of the *Curanderos* was also necessary. The doctors were amazed that my body was recovering, yet they still kept telling me I'd be in a wheelchair for the rest of my life. They just didn't know what I was made of, and that miracles weren't just possible . . . but were the norm of life once we entrusted our lives completely to God.

Then one afternoon I was looking out the window of my room, taking in the beauty of the flower garden below, when I began to feel a little tingling sensation in my legs. I smiled. This wasn't pain. These were good feelings coming to my legs, feelings I'd missed so much and thought I'd lost forever.

I gripped the arms of my wheelchair and tried to push myself up, but I wasn't able to get very far. And yet this was a beginning. The next day I asked for crutches, and it was disastrous the first few days, especially when I'd fall and my back would scream out in pain. But no, I still refused all pain pills, and little by little, I began to be able to push myself out of my chair and get the crutches under me. Then with focus and great intent and commitment and trust in God, I stood upright, crutches under me, and began to walk. Stomach protruding and back in terrible pain, but still the lion spirit within me could do miracles.

Within a week, I was able to start moving down the hallways and eventually outside to the garden, and it was in the garden surrounded by flowers and butterflies and songbirds that once again I took up my calling, and the words of Jesus Christ began to flow out of me with a whole new understanding of what it was to be a HUMAN BEING!

Above all else, a human being was not of body, but a Spiritual Being and a Miracle Maker, and I now knew firsthand that Peter could have easily walked on water alongside Jesus if he hadn't glanced down and allowed fear to overtake him. I spread the word of God's glorious, miraculous love—not just to the other patients, but to all the nurses and doctors, especially to those whose eyes looked tired and who had the hardest time believing anymore—and that photographer friend of the doctor's came and took photos once again.

This is when I told everyone about the happy, chubby little old priest I'd met when I'd been coming home to California after having spent a summer as a firefighter in Montana. The priest had begun a children's church in New Mexico. Love-*amor,* with a happy, smiling Jesus, was now also my total sense of mission and purpose. Soon I knew I was ready to go back out on the streets again, even though my back and abdomen would never be completely well.

The morning they wheeled me out of the front entrance of the hospital, I couldn't understand what was going on. There were hundreds of people—if not a thousand—outside, and they were cheering. I glanced around, wondering who all this commotion was for, and this was when I realized that all the doctors and nurses had come out of the hospital to see me off, and all these people were cheering for us, for the doctors and nurses and me, because my recovery had been a miracle. And the story of my miraculous recovery had become front-page news for months, and everyone in Chihuahua knew all about me and my doctors and nurses.

Then when I gripped the sides of my wheelchair and began to stand up, ignoring the excruciating pain I felt, the cheering EX-PLODED AND PEOPLE CAME RUSHING FORWARD TO PUT FLOWERS BY MY FEET! This was when I saw that the pretty *Latina* and the big all-American cowboy who'd flown with me when I'd first come from San Jose to Chihuahua almost a decade ago were over to the side with a limousine. They were waving for me to come and get inside their car. Smiling, I got my crutches under me and started toward them. What else could I do? I could see that no one in my family had come to get me.

"I told you so," declared the beautiful woman with excitement. "I told you you'd be a BIG HIT IN MEXICO, TOO!"

The crowd of people parted as we drove off in the limousine. The woman's big husband explained to me that they owned a radio station, and they wanted to create a radio show for me to host about love and miracles. I accepted the offer, and as soon as I could, I began to sing and play my guitar live on the air. And I ended each of my broadcasts by singing a special song-message of love and goodwill to *la Mano Negra,* asking him/her if we could meet face-to-face and bring our powers together for the GOOD OF ALL THE WORLD!

My nickname quickly became *Torero del Diablo,* the Bullfighter of the Devil, and my radio show became one of the most popular— not just in Chihuahua, but across the entire nation. And now with the help of the ex-governor's wife and her powerful lady friends, we were able to open up safe, drug-free houses all over Mexico. Soon we had more than 60.

But then one night I came home to my little apartment . . . and there on the pillow on my bed was a black glove and three bullets.

CHAPTER 2

I guess I'd been riding so high that I hadn't realized how much fear still lived in my gut, because my heart leaped into my throat with such power that I couldn't breathe. I had to sit down. I began to tremble. Just staring at the bullets. Not daring to touch them.

Then I ran to the toilet and threw up. I was sick with fear. The three bullets had done their job. I sank down to the floor next to the toilet, trembling with uncontrollable terror. This assassin, whoever he/she was, was truly a very smart, capable person. I tried to pray, sitting there on the floor by the toilet, but I couldn't get my mind clear enough to do it. Suddenly—I don't know why—it came to me that this assassin had also seen lion eyes at a very young age. Sure, of course, he/she and I were soul mates, just like Judas and Jesus.

I placed my right hand on the toilet bowl, and with my left, I pushed myself up off the floor. No, I wasn't going to panic. I wasn't going to allow evil, no matter how great, to intimidate me. I went to the sink and washed my face with cold water again and again; then I got a towel and dried myself. I was good now. I knelt down facing away from the toilet. I closed my eyes, went within myself, and began to pray for this assassin's soul with all of my heart, just as Our Lord Jesus had done with Judas.

"Dear Lord God," I said, "I am Your servant. Your instrument. And I will walk through the valley of death and have no fear, for I am with You, my Lord Jesus, with all my heart and soul. Please show me the way, for it is in the darkest of night that we see the brightest of the stars, and so into the darkness of this he/she assassin's soul, I will go in Thy Holy Name. I love You, dear God. You are my salvation, my power. Thank You, thank You, thank You, thank You, for once more having such faith in me to do Your Holy Work."

I felt calm once again. I was in my center once more. I decided to go get some fresh air. I went outside and looked up at the stars. I'd never realized there was so much darkness between the stars. No wonder this assassin had chosen the darkness instead of the light. The stars looked so insignificant compared to all the darkness. Maybe this was why so many souls chose the darkness. Wouldn't I myself be better off if I'd chosen the darkness? What did I have to show for all my years of doing God's work—nothing. Not even a family.

Tears came to my eyes. I loved Catalina, I really did, and my son, Nathan, had been the joy of my life. I wiped the tears from my eyes and continued looking up at the stars. Soon I began to feel a closeness to the darkness that I'd never felt before. Strange thoughts entered my head. "Yeah, sure, Jan," I said to myself, "why not choose the darkness? Why not quit all this you're doing and find your wife and Nathan and this other child you don't even know and have a normal life?"

But every time I breathed and my ribs expanded, it hurt so much that I wished I had died. It had been more than a year since they'd run over me with the car and kicked in my ribs and stomach, yet it still hurt when I breathed. I remembered how my Three Indian *Curanderos* told me that I had the heart of a lion and the vision of an eagle, and also I remembered the ear-piercing scream of the mountain lion just before he'd exploded into my body.

I had to get rid of all these sorry-for-myself thoughts. Who was I kidding? I'd seen too much and learned too much to panic. Over and over again I'd see the eyes of lost young souls who came to life after they accepted Jesus Christ. I was not going to panic. No, I was not going to allow evil, no matter how great and overwhelming, to take over my life. I breathed. It hurt. But no, I wasn't going to die. I WAS GOING TO LIVE!

I looked up at the stars once again, and this time the darkness between the stars didn't seem scary anymore, but instead neutral and inviting. A calmness came over me, and I smiled. Yes, of course I could go into this huge, infinite darkness and not lose myself, because I walked hand in hand with my best friend the lioness, who'd led me back to Our Lord Jesus, and together the Three of Us would bring Light to the darkness. I continued smiling and looking up at the stars, and . . . and suddenly I knew that this "he/she" assassin was right here, right now, across the street from me, hiding in the shadows of the night.

A chill went up and down my spine, but I wasn't afraid. No, I felt happy and calm and detached. Why? Because a mountain lion had taken up residence in my heart, and an eagle had come to my eyes to give me vision. Instantly I understood why we knew nothing about Our Lord Jesus after He was 12 until he came forward to do His Holy Sacred Earthly Service. He, too, had a lion and an eagle come into him to help Him know how to be calm, detached, and fearless even as they pounded the nails into His flesh. Love was all that had been in Jesus, and love-*amor* was now all there was in me as I looked across the street.

And further, my eagle eyes saw that there was nothing this assassin could do to me, for we were not just of body. We were all also of Spirit, just like Jesus, so this he/she assassin could never hurt me, could never kill me; and he/she was beginning to see this, too. Why? Because she/he had also seen the lion eyes as a child, so she/he was here within me. We were soul connected. And not just some of us. BUT ALL OF US! Through the Kingdom of God!

I smiled.

I saw it so clearly. This was it.

I was never, ever going to be afraid again. In fact, I could now see that it was my own fear that had been feeding this assassin his/her power. Because it is always our own fears that we reflect out into the world, and which then come back to us a hundredfold. I nodded to him/her across the street from me and decided to go back inside to sleep. I slept like a baby, and in the morning when I awoke, I felt wonderful.

Whistling, I made myself a good breakfast, and I flashed on Jason, the drug-crazed pimp back in San Francisco who had tried to run me over with a Jeep, but then had ended up being one of our best helpers. I flashed on Chato when I had first met him. Everyone had long ago given up on him because he was the meanest, toughest street kid on the block. But after I gained his trust, I had Chato sit in a chair facing me, about three feet apart. I told him to close his eyes and breathe real easy, and I said a prayer for him, then asked him to open his eyes and look into my eyes in the silence of God's eternal love. Not one word. Not one question. No, just look into each other's eyes, and I sent him all my love through Jesus. Without touching. Without judgments. Just clean, pure love. And within minutes, I could see that he was beginning to open up to God's love, and the layers of distrust and frustration began to soften and then dissolve.

This was when I smelled the trapped fear begin to ooze out of his body. It was so awful, so rotten smelling, that I gagged and had to open the windows. Finally, after about a half hour, there was now enough clean, good room inside of Chato for his heart to start to come to his eyes. And he began to cry. Just a little bit at first, then uncontrollably. Big, belly-jerking sobs. Ever since he'd been born and his mother had abandoned him in the street in a cardboard box, he'd been holding back a river of hate and resentment the size of the Mississippi.

Chato fell to the floor like a limp rag and slept for more than 18 hours. When he woke up, he drank gallons of water, and the other kids in our halfway house didn't recognize him. He'd turned into an angel before our very eyes. You could see and feel the warm glow of love coming off of him. He—the toughest, meanest street kid in all of Juárez—had opened his eyes . . . and in one great flash of light, he'd found his life's true purpose: to simply live a loving life like a flower, like a butterfly, like a star in the Heavens.

After this, Chato became one of our most devoted helpers. He'd get right up in people's faces with such love and genuine concern for them that they'd crack open like the fragile shells of human beings that they were, and the gates of love would open and the evil would flow out of them.

Remembering all this, how could I possibly have any fear of the three bullets on the pillow of my bed? He/she could leave a thousand bullets on my pillow and I'd still love him/her with all my heart and soul!

In fact, this time I didn't remove the three bullets.

No, instead I put three flowers alongside the bullets, and I drew up two chairs facing each other and asked for the Soul Spirit of this great assassin to come to me, and I sent love to her/him with every fiber of my being. Three, four, six, eight times a day, I sent him/her my *amor* in the name of Jesus, Our Savior; and our contact became so strong that I'd sometimes actually feel his/her Spirit start to take on human form before my very eyes.

I prayed and asked God Almighty to please help us, because I knew at the bottom of my heart that if this great, famous *Mano Negra* and I could come together, then all the forces of evil across the whole world would begin to heal and unite in *amor*. There was no doubt in me whatsoever. And so 100 times, 500 times a day, I visualized us sitting together and facing each other IN THE LIGHT OF JESUS CHRIST!

My radio show took on a new energy and flourished!

My guitar playing and singing became far better than my limited human talents. I WAS FLYING!

Heart to Heart, I'd passed through the needle's eye and into the Spirit World of Our Almighty God, Who guided All of Us!

CHAPTER 3

A few weeks later, a wealthy banker named Jorge Ramos came to see me. He said he and his wife, Silveria, were great fans of my radio show, and they had talked it over and wanted to open up a restaurant with me as a partner.

"We'll put up the money," he said, "and you put up your name and fame, and we'll be equal partners."

I'd never had an offer like this before, so I told him I'd have to think about it. But then he said the most astonishing thing.

"Look," he said, "it's time for you to do something for the rich of Mexico, too. We're not all bad, greedy SOBs. Good people can also have money. That needle's eye of the Bible is much larger now. In fact, you can fly a whole damn jet through it," he added, laughing happily.

I liked Ramos. He was very charming. And I'd never thought of this before, but I could see that he was right. All of my life I'd been judgmental toward the rich and their money, blaming them for the problems of the world. So maybe it was time for me to start viewing them with as much compassion and understanding as I had for the street people.

Jorge was probably in his early 40s, and he was extremely handsome and well dressed. I was intrigued. He didn't seem to have any hidden agenda. He invited me to his home for a little get-together that weekend. I'd never been to this part of Chihuahua City. His place was like a castle, with gardens and patios and an Olympic-size swimming pool. The little party he'd invited me to included well over 200 of the most powerful people in all of Chihuahua. And surprisingly, most of them were in their 30s and 40s. This wasn't an old crowd of movers and shakers like the couple I'd met on the plane coming from California to Chihuahua. And while I was at the party, I met a beautiful young woman named Emma who was very friendly.

Getting home that night, I asked the Lord for guidance, because I'd had a wonderful time. If I went forward with the deal, it would mean that for the first time in my life I'd be able to afford better shoes and clothes and even . . . a better motorcycle. Ever since I'd left home to become a minister at the age of 17, I'd been dressing in Salvation Army clothes. I wasn't a kid anymore, and if I'd had money, I would have purchased another Honda 300, and then the guys in those two cars would have never caught me that night as we'd come into the circle of the statue of Pancho Villa. I would have leaped the bike through traffic and gotten away in a flash.

The next day I met with Jorge and his drop-dead gorgeous wife, Silveria.

"So how did you like our little party?" he asked.

"I liked it," I said. "I met a lot of wonderful people."

"So you saw that we're not all a bunch of SOBs, eh?"

I blushed.

"So will you accept our offer?" asked Silveria. "We need a nightclub restaurant in Chihuahua that people can go to that feels, you know, modern and open to new ideas."

"I've thought about it very carefully," I said, "and yes, I'm interested, but I also have a couple of . . . well, conditions."

"Go on," he said.

"One is that we pay our employees very well, and the other is that we give a significant part of our earnings to help run the halfway houses that we have established across the country."

Silveria laughed. "I told you," she said, turning to her husband, "that these would be his two requests."

Jorge grinned. "Yes, you did. Jan, my wife and I have already spoken of these points, and we agree. We, too, want to pay our employees very well and give a part of our profits to your halfway houses."

"You do?" I said, feeling happily surprised.

"Yes, of course," Silveria replied. "This is part of the new type of thinking that we'd like to have as an example for all of Mexico."

"What percentage of our profits is this 'significant part' that you'd like for us to give to the halfway houses?" Jorge asked.

"Ninety percent," I said.

He burst out laughing. "Surely you don't mean 90 percent. You mean 10 percent."

"No, I mean nine-O, 90 percent."

He glanced at his wife. He was still smiling, but speechless.

"Well, I must say," Silveria spoke up, "you really meant a *significant* part when you said that you wanted to give away a significant part of our earnings, didn't you?"

"Yes, I guess I did."

I could see that they both thought I was crazy, yet they hadn't completely written me off yet.

"What would you consider a significant part?" I asked.

"Well, being a man who handles money deals in business every day," Jorge said, "I'd say that if we gave 20 percent, that would be seen as extremely significant and generous of us."

"I understand," I said, "that Paul Newman, the actor, and his wife, Joanne Woodward, give 100 percent of all the profits of their salad dressings and other health-food products to different charities."

"Yes, I've heard of that," replied Jorge. "But that's in the United States, and we're in Mexico."

"Yes, and we breathe the same air and we drink the same water that comes to us from the Heavens. You want a modern nightclub restaurant with new ideas . . . well, then let's go for it ALL THE WAY! LET'S THROW OURSELVES TO FATE AND SEE WHAT HAPPENS!"

Silveria began to laugh. "I like this Bullfighter of the Devil," she said. "I totally agree with him and with you, *mi amor.* Twenty percent would be seen as very significant and generous, but . . . it wouldn't be seen as crazy!" she added with delicious laughter. "And I think we need to get into this restaurant-nightclub business with a certain *loco* craziness!"

I laughed. "I find it very interesting that you've used the word 'craziness,' because, you see, all of my life has been *loco*crazy," I said. "It was crazy when I went to San Francisco and tried to talk the hippies out of taking drugs and having sex before marriage. It was crazy when I came down to Mexico and tried to set up that first halfway house. And yet miracles have followed me everywhere I go.

"In San Francisco, I thought I'd failed, and yet over 200 young people came to the airport to see me off when I left the U.S. to come to Mexico. And here in Chihuahua, it was the governor's wife, after I'd helped get her grandchildren off drugs, who introduced me to a friend of hers who gave us the ambassador's deserted mansion to convert into our first halfway house. Crazy*loco* has always worked for me—and craziness is fun and exciting," I added with delicious laughter, too.

Now I told them the story of the mountain lion I'd seen when I was 11 and how her eyes had looked so calm and detached and neutral and fearless, and that this had become my model ever since. I added that I was sure most people would think 20 percent was significant and very generous, especially businesspeople, but I'd also learned that jumping in with both feet, with no rhyme or reason, was the way miracles happened.

"Look," I said, "do you know who Clint Eastwood is? Are you familiar with his spaghetti Westerns?"

"Oh yes, of course!" said Jorge. "His Westerns are the rage here!"

"He is *muy simpático*," added Silveria with a coquettish flair.

"Good," I said, "because I met Clint Eastwood in Carmel when he was an out-of-work young, skinny actor with an offer to go to Italy to do Westerns."

I explained to them how Clint had been nervous and very unsure of himself, yet after I told him the story of the mountain lion and how the great cat had looked at me and led me home to safety, something happened within that young actor. Clint asked me a few key questions, and I answered him as truthfully as I knew how at the time; and with just that little bit of information, he took to the screen—along with the type of cigars we shared— a way of personifying a human being that had never been seen before in movies.

"Oh yes!" exclaimed Silveria with excitement. "We women of Mexico love *Señor* Eastwood. He has the taste of our culture. Surely he is destined to marry one of our *Mexicanas!*"

"So, then, you know Clint Eastwood very well, eh?" asked Jorge.

"Oh no," I told him. "I only met him that one time at Joan Baez's party in Carmel. Jerry Garcia was there, too. But I don't really know any of them that well. I was just there because Joan invited me. I was riding my Honda and wearing my Mexican poncho and headband. I fit right in."

"Just as you now fit right in here in Mexico, and are considered the man who has more lives than a cat," said Silveria.

"Ninety percent?" repeated Jorge.

"Well, I do believe," I said, "that the time has come for Mexico to not be outdone by what is done in the United States, but for Mexico to jump in and help lead the way into doing crazy*loco* unheard-of things that benefit the whole world and all of humanity!"

Jorge grinned. He knew what I had just done with the words "to not be outdone" and making reference to the United States. I'd cut into the heart and manhood of every Mexican male. Silveria began laughing her head off, also fully realizing what I'd done.

"Of course this is with the understanding," I added, "that the national saying of Mexico is *Mañana es otro milagro de Dios* [Tomorrow is another miracle of God], and in modern times this isn't just a saying for the poor and downtrodden, but a call for the new rich of the nation to step up to the plate, especially since you yourself have said they aren't all SOBs."

Now Jorge started laughing, too, and his wife Silveria shouted, "I love it! This is crazy! And it is exactly why our friends will love it, too, Jorge. It is fun and exciting to be crazy*locos!*"

Jorge stopped laughing, and calmly looked from his wife to me and then back to his wife. "How about 50 percent?" he said to her. "That would also be looked upon as crazy, too."

"*Mi amor,* are we to be outdone by Paul Newman and Joanne Woodward?"

He looked at me and burst out laughing again. "What a mouth you have on you! Too bad you're a *gringo* or we could run you for governor or maybe even president! All right, 90 percent it is. And I can tell you two that our friends are going to think I really went off the deep end."

"Yes, exactly!" agreed Silveria. "And this is why they will come just to meet this man who can talk the birds out of the trees, and sings like an angel in the name of humanity and God!"

Tears came to my eyes. Where had these people been all my life? I guess they'd been out there lost in the mist of my own fear and distrust of the rich. I felt so close to this man and his gorgeous wife. She reached out and patted my hand affectionately.

"So you see, Jan," said Silveria, "miracles can also happen among the rich. Eh, where was your faith?"

I blushed. They both laughed.

"Silveria is right," Jorge added. "It is fun and exciting to do business with the man who bullfights the devil on his radio show, and then sings songs of hope and love and miracles for all of humanity."

Tears of joy ran down my face, and it was now my turn to let the smell of evil come oozing out of me, as I had seen happen to Chato. I hadn't realized how skeptical I'd been and how many ill feelings I'd been holding against the rich. This part of me had truly been living in darkness, refusing to accept the fact that God lived in all of us equally. These people—I couldn't believe it—were extremely rich, maybe even billionaires; and they, too, had the glow of God's light all about them.

I asked for some water, and they gave me a glass and I quickly drank it down. Then I went to the bathroom and washed my face with cold water and drank two more glasses of water. I remembered how Chato drank gallons of water after he'd released all the trapped hate and fear he'd been holding in his body.

Feeling a lot better, I returned to the spacious, elegant outdoor living room with cages of parrots and great tropical gardens. We shook hands on the deal, agreeing to sign papers the following week. It took six months for us to remodel an old run-down hacienda outside of town and put in a large parking lot.

Opening night was FANTASTIC! Within two weeks we had the hottest, most successful restaurant nightclub in all of Chihuahua! Even our 10 percent of the profits was enormous, and I bought shoes and clothes and began to play my guitar and sing to all the rich people who flocked to our place, wanting to meet the Bullfighter of the Devil. My partners and I had more money pouring in than I'd ever seen. And we paid our employees very well and kept our word about 90 percent of our profits going to the halfway houses.

This was when Emma, the woman I'd met at the original "little" party, came to see me at my office at the mansion late one evening. The year before, I'd moved back into the great old ambassador's mansion. I was busy doing paperwork when Emma entered. I'd gotten to know her a little bit over the past few months. She was a very attractive woman who worked at the offices of the new governor. I had spoken to her a few times when I'd gone to see the governor, but that was all. We'd just talked. Nothing more.

So what she did next completely took me by surprise. She closed my office door, locked it, and then with a great big smile, came across the room walking with the most suggestive gait I'd ever seen, all the while unbuttoning her blouse.

Emma had the most beautiful breasts I'd ever seen. I didn't know what to do. Part of me felt like jumping up and running away. But another part of me was exploding inside. I hadn't been with a woman since Catalina had left me well over a year and a half ago.

She saw my fear and confusion, but she only laughed and came around my desk. She was standing so close to me, I could smell her. She smelled delicious. And she now spread apart her long, strong, young brown legs and squatted down on my lap, facing me.

And of course, I'm a man of God, but also I'm a human being, so my reaction was instant. She felt the rise in my Levi's, smiled, laughed, and stood up. She unzipped her short skirt and began pulling it off, inch by inch. This was when I saw that she wasn't wearing any underwear, and her bush had been shaved into a thick dark heart.

We never said a word, and she got back on my lap and just kept smiling and moving back and forth on my Levi's as she reached for my belt. I never knew a man's pants could come off so quickly. Then we were skin to skin and kissing and my hardened member found her juicy hot treasure, and she took me inside of her, laughing so loud and having so much fun!

I'd forgotten how wonderful it felt to be inside a woman! And she now began moving to me with a rhythm that I'd never known, a twisting, turning action. Real fast! Then real, real slow! And I suddenly realized that I'd been pretty inhibited all my life, because for the rest of the night, she taught me things I'd never known.

We never slept, and daybreak found us still at it. Oh, I'd never had an experience like this in all of my life. I was in love! No doubt about it! And with the powerful people she knew at the state capital, Emma was able to get me a divorce within weeks, and we married the following month. Why did we marry? Because I was a man of the cloth, so I couldn't continue to have such a passionate relationship with a woman outside of marriage.

Also, the bullets had stopped, so I thought that maybe, just maybe, I'd somehow miraculously made peace with the assassin on the night we'd stood across the street from each other, and now my life was going to go smoothly.

But then came word that Chato and two of the kids who'd helped us set up our safe halfway house in Juárez, just across the border from El Paso, had been beaten and shot in a parking lot while they'd been handing out pamphlets. Learning this, I ran to the toilet and threw up. This felt way worse than when I'd been rammed by a car underneath another car.

Emma decided she should leave the mansion, and I bolted my bedroom door and gave orders that no one was allowed to enter my room. But still the bullets came, and this time there were six.

I WENT INTO A RAGE! How had the bullets gotten on the pillow of my bed? I asked the only people who had access to my room if they'd seen anyone. They all said no. I showed them the bullets, demanding that they be completely truthful with me, but they all swore they didn't know anything and they hadn't seen anyone.

"BUT YOU HAD TO HAVE SEEN SOMEONE! These bullets didn't just get on my pillow by themselves!" I screamed.

I FELT HELPLESS! Either they really hadn't seen anyone, or if they had, they were so terrified that they weren't going to tell me.

The following week we got word that six of our helpers had been arrested in Zacatecas, and they'd hung themselves in their cells. I couldn't believe this. These were tough street kids who would never think of suicide. Killing yes, but not suicide. Also, where had the cops been? My God, the kids had been in jail when they'd supposedly hung themselves.

I drove down to Zacatecas, and at first they wouldn't let me see the boys' bodies. When they finally did, I saw that their bodies told the whole story. They'd been beaten and tortured, and hot irons had been placed to the soles of their feet. Our wonderful boys had endured unbelievable pain; and all the while their hands had been tied behind their backs, because their wrists had deep, awful rope burns. They'd never hung themselves. But here, nobody had seen anything either.

Going back across town to our halfway house in Zacatecas, the mother of one of the boys came running up to me. "YOU ARE THE MONSTER!" she yelled at me, with tears of agony pouring down her face. "If you had left my boy alone, he would still be alive! It's all your fault because of all those fancy ideas that you put in my boy's head that got him off drugs. YOU KILLED HIM!" she screamed. "YOU DID IT!"

I didn't know what to say. She was right. If her son hadn't gotten off drugs and hadn't been handing out pamphlets in the name of Our Lord Jesus Christ, he would never have been killed.

Back in Chihuahua, the ex-governor's wife and three of her lady friends were waiting for me. They told me I had to get out of town immediately. That this was the only way the killings would stop. I felt totally helpless. Now it wasn't me who this assassin was going after. No, it was my family of kids. Three bullets had meant three kids. Six bullets had meant six kids.

Suddenly a large part of me knew exactly what my ex-wife, Catalina, had been feeling when she'd wished that I had died so this whole nightmare could be over. Because that mother in Zacatecas was right: if I had died, then none of these killings would have ever happened.

For the first time in all of my adult life, I lost all hope.

It was over for me!

How could I, with a clear conscience, ever again ask anyone to accept Jesus? Oh, what a fool I'd been! The forces of evil were just too great for anyone to overcome them!

Sure, we now had 83 safe houses set up throughout Mexico, but they weren't safe as long as I was involved. The ex-governor's wife told me that she'd met with the wife and the mother of the current president of Mexico, and they assured me that the drug-free safe houses would continue to be maintained by the government, but that I was now so famous a personality that I had to get out of town. I was bringing too much attention to the situation, and it would only get worse if I stayed.

Silveria and Jorge agreed with the ex-governor's wife, whom they knew very well. I had to take a sabbatical, they said. This reminded me of when my superiors had told me that I had to leave California. I didn't know what to do. I often thought I should have never left the coffeehouses I'd established in San Francisco and San Jose. They'd both closed down shortly afterward.

This was when Carlos Rochín, the priest who'd been helping me set up the halfway houses over the last two years, came forward and we talked. He told me that he agreed with the ex-governor's wife and that he knew just the place for me to hole up until things cooled down. It was in the highlands of *las Barrancas del Cobre* in western Chihuahua, just outside Creel. He and his family liked to go camping and fishing up there at a lake during the summer.

I finally gave in. They were right. And also there was just nothing left inside of me to give to anyone anymore. The tears poured down my face. Once more I'd failed. I'd failed! I'd failed! Chato had been like a son to me, and so had all those other boys who'd been gunned down. It was almost as if whoever had killed them had known exactly which boys were closest to me, and these were the ones they'd gunned down or hung.

Then to cause me further confusion and doubt, a few days before I was to leave town with Carlos Rochín, a car came screeching up on the sidewalk straight at me, and I leaped down a flight of stairs into a basement, trying to escape. A man and a woman immediately jumped out of their vehicle and came to help me. The man told me that his wife had been driving, and she'd turned around to the backseat to give him instructions on changing diapers when she'd lost control of the car.

"But you were almost half a block away," she told me, "so why did you scream and leap down a flight of stairs? We would never have hit you."

I could see she was right and I'd completely overreacted. But the damage was done. I'd reinjured my back, and I was back on crutches the day Rochín and I drove out of town. I'd been down in Mexico for nearly ten years, and I'd originally only come down for a six-month sabbatical. I had no idea what was going to happen to me next, and . . . and I really didn't care.

I was DONE!

I was FINISHED!

I was 33 years old, and I had nothing more to give. I'd hit bottom! The Kingdom of God within me was totally empty!

Book Two

BARRANCAS DEL COBRE

CHAPTER 4

I was feeling very quiet, deep inside myself, as Father Rochín drove us west out of Chihuahua City. We drove over dry hills and white-hot high-desert valleys in his old blue Renault. I felt like I was in a faraway trance. I couldn't even comprehend the things that Rochín was saying. We traveled for hours, mostly on dirt roads, over a terrain of nothingness. Then we came over another small dry hill, and there ahead of us lay a luscious green valley as far as the eye could see on both sides of the road.

I sat up. It felt like we'd entered Heaven. Seeing my reaction, Rochín burst out laughing and told me that this was one of the largest Mennonite settlements in the world. As we drove by, I saw buckboards full of blond kids with large, well-fed European-looking fathers and even larger, better-fed European-looking mothers. The horses that pulled their buckboards were also huge, magnificent, well-groomed, well-fed animals.

Rochín was talking, telling me the history of the settlement, but it was very difficult for me to pay any attention. Up ahead was the town of Cuauhtémoc, with small, dark, slender-looking Indians, and behind the town stood tall towering cliffs and mountains in the distance. I'd been in Mexico for years, and this was one of the first times I'd traveled outside the cities.

After Cuauhtémoc, we began to climb, following the rail-road tracks, and now there were scrub oaks and a lot of bone-dry riverbeds that I was sure became torrents of water during the rainy season. We were going very slowly on the mostly dirt roads, but then strangely enough, here and there we'd hit a section of poorly made paved road.

Rochín was still talking and laughing, having a grand time. This story I was able to hear. He was telling me that a few years back, when Luis Echeverría had been president of Mexico, he'd given a large chunk of money to the state of Chihuahua to finish blacktopping the road from Chihuahua City all the way to Cuauh-témoc, and beyond to La Junta.

Father Rochín was laughing so hard that it was difficult for him to speak. "But what did our ingenious people of Chihuahua do? They decided to out-corrupt Echeverría himself. They lay down a solid rock-and-gravel foundation, building a good road for the first two hours out of Chihuahua City; then after that, they pocketed all the rest of the money Echeverría had given them and just sprayed black oil on the rest of the dirt road.

"I tell you, it was nothing short of genius," he said, laughing, "because after that, when Echeverría flew over the entirety of the road he had commissioned them to build, he saw a fine black-topped road all the way to Cuauhtémoc and even beyond to La Junta. His term was coming to an end, and he wanted to go out of office feeling that he'd done a lot of good for his country, and he was so proud of his fellow patriotic millionaires for doing such a great job that he even gave them some more money before he stepped down.

"I tell you, Don Jan, my fellow Chihuahuans are brilliant people! If only they stopped wanting everything for themselves and began to want for the good of the state and the people of the nation, they could move mountains! My very own cousins were involved in this great scheme. And why did they do this? Because they all knew that Echeverría was by far the biggest thief Mexico had ever had. Corruption begins at the top, Don Jan. This is what a president does for a nation. He gives a vision of honesty or corruption; and we here in Mexico win the lottery for having some of the most abusive, lying, thieving presidents in the world!

"Your presidents in the United States are Boy Scouts compared to our presidents! Ours would have done well even in Rome, or when Spain ruled the world. I die laughing every time I drive this piece of road. There was Echeverría flying overhead in his plane, looking down and thinking that his *compadres de Chihuahua* had done a great, honest job. Does this mean that Echeverría thought he was surrounded by honest men and he was the only thief? I doubt it. Mexico has a long-standing tradition of getting robbed by its leaders, even before the Spanish came. The Aztecs were a warring tribe, and they came down from what is now your United States and conquered and raped and enslaved everyone in their path.

"So what can we do, Don Jan? What can we do? Or are men like you and me always going to be on the losing side of good versus evil? I hope not. I pray that someday we will have a string of presidents who love this land and the beautiful people of Mexico and will want to give, instead of take, like my rich cousins do.

"And now the big question is, why do people feel free to rape and take from Mexico without any remorse whatsoever? I'll tell you why, Jan. Because they see Mexico as a land of Indians, of stupid *Indios,* and so they steal and take all they can. The Spaniards, the French, the Chinese who escaped from your country, and now the Arabs and Jews or whoever else comes to our land have no respect for the native people. Even in my own family, the darker ones like me are looked down upon as being less than the whiter ones.

"Look at you, Don Jan, and see how far you've come in your short time in Mexico. If you were black or dark brown, these doors would have never opened for you. You're white and tall and handsome. If you were short and dark like me, do you really think you would have gotten that radio show? If you were *Mestizo* or even worse, pure Indian, do you think those rich people would have opened up that nightclub restaurant with you?

"You're white, Don Jan, but I'll give you credit, you are a giver and not a taker . . . and yet, I ask you in all sincerity, my friend, are you racist? And please don't get offended, but understand that where I'm taking you, you will not see any white persons. You will be living among full-blooded Indians. Will you be able to handle this? Even my own family, when they come here to camp and fish, have a very difficult time, particularly when they see that many of the *Indios* still live in caves, and most of them have never even been inside an automobile."

I stopped listening. He'd asked me if I was racist. How could Rochín ask me such a question? He'd been working with me for more than two years. He saw how hard I worked day and night with the lowest of the low. I wasn't racist. I was . . . but I'd just said inside of my own brain "the lowest of the low," so then he was right. I was . . . well, not really racist, but elitist.

He continued talking, but I quit listening. Yes, I could now see that I enjoyed telling people that I'd left a home of money and prestige and lowered myself to work with the street people of the world. And yeah, I also had to admit that doors had opened for me in Mexico because I was a white American. But also, hadn't some of these doors opened for me because long ago I'd chosen the light, and people could see this in me?

I quit. I didn't want to think anymore. I was feeling so low that I wasn't sure I even had the strength to go on. Chato and those boys . . . how could God have allowed that to happen? I would have gladly died in their place. They were just kids. And I was the one who had convinced them to trust the light. I was such a damn elitist hypocrite, coming down to Mexico, thinking I could make a difference. Tears were pouring down my face when we came into the tiny cobblestone plaza of the town of La Junta.

"This is where we will spend our first night," said Father Rochín. "From here on, the going gets tough. It will take us over 18 hours just to go about 80 miles. It's nothing but logging roads after this. Believe me, *amigo,* I'm taking you so far away from all civilization that no one will be able to find you, except for God Himself."

I nodded. Maybe this was good, to be so completely alone that only God could find me. I figured it was my last chance.

CHAPTER 5

I awoke to the sounds of goats, and cocks crowing in the distance. Then I began to hear a profusion of birds and *burros,* and kids and adults talking and laughing. Then I heard the sound of the church bells and galloping horses on the cobblestones of the plaza outside my window. I guess I'd slept way better than I thought I would. A knock sounded on my door.

"Yes!"

"Get up, Don Jan! Breakfast is ready! We've got to make an early start. It's going to be a much longer day today than yesterday. And tougher, too. Up on the *mesa,* we'll have to cross a thousand streams!"

"Okay, okay, I'm getting up," I said.

I was groggy. I'd had a lot of confusing dreams. Chato had been in most of them, and so had Emma, but I had no idea what the dreams were telling me. Long ago, I'd stopped trying to figure out what dreams meant, and instead I simply began to realize that dreams, for me, were more like signs that would somehow seem to appear later on down the road in the course of my living. And the more I did this, the more it gave me peace, because when I always used to try to figure out what my dreams meant, it had just kept me in my head and caused me to worry and have expectations. Now, I just took note of my dreams and lived my life with a relaxed calmness and my dreams gave me joy and not worry, because *que será, será*—what will be, will be.

At daybreak Rochín and I were back on the road. We now began to climb very fast, zigzagging back and forth as we followed the rails of the train. Up on the *mesa*, the scrub oaks turned into great oak trees, and there weren't a thousand streambeds to cross, but I'm sure there were at least 200. After about the 20th, I began to drive so that Rochín could get out and move the rocks so we could get across the rocky streambeds without tearing out the Renault's underbody. Every few hours we stopped, and Rochín gathered wood and built a small fire so we could cook up strips of beef into *carne asada* and heat up some corn *tortillas*. I'd never seen him so full of energy. He was really very happy being out in this wild terrain.

"Isn't this the way to live?" he said, eating his tenth *taco* of the day. He ate two every time we stopped. "Lifting rocks and sweating and bending and breathing this wonderful pure mountain air. You're going to love Creel. It was nothing but a tiny train-stop station until a few years back when a man who'd been living in Chihuahua City returned home to his grandparents' ranch and helped them build a hotel and a lookout point for the tourists to see the great canyon. Now I'm told that next year a Hollywood movie is going to be filmed in Creel, and a bank has come to town, too. The place is exploding. I think they have 400 people living in town now—but I also think that probably includes the pigs, goats, horses, and *burros*," he added with great laughter.

It was midafternoon when I saw the three Indians. We'd come to another dry riverbed. I was driving and Rochín got out to move a couple of big rocks so we could drive across, and this was when I saw them. The Indians were squatting in the rock and brush just above us.

"Rochín," I said, "there are some Indians up on that embankment."

He laughed. "So you finally noticed them, eh? They've been with us for the last ten miles or more."

"With us?"

"Yes, they've been running along with us watching what we do, so they can go home and have a great laugh tonight, talking about us. Two crazy *loco chavochi*—non-Indians—who worship their car so much that they work all day in the hot sun to bring it along with them."

"Do they live around here?"

"Probably not. They probably live all the way on the other side of Creel."

"Then what are they doing down here?"

"Taking a run. You see, the Tarahumara are some of the greatest runners in the world, and sometimes they take a little day run of over 100 miles."

"A hundred miles in a day?" I said. "This reminds me of my friend Miguel, who I used to run with back in Los Gatos when I was going to high school. He said that he grew up running races of over 60 and 80 miles."

"He must've been Tarahumara, or at least part Tarahumara. Did he tell you what town he was from?"

"He told me, but I forgot. He was a schoolteacher, but I guess they paid him nothing, so he'd go to work up in the States every year so he could buy school supplies."

"That definitely sounds like a Tarahumara. Good-hearted people, and their teachers get paid nothing, even less than the rest of the teachers of Mexico!"

For the next several hours we watched the three Indians run alongside us, dodging through the brush and leaping over rocks. A couple of times I gave the old blue Renault some gas, when the road allowed it, and their faces would light up with joy and they'd go into a sprint, easily keeping up with us. Then just before sunset, four more Indians suddenly appeared out of nowhere, and now all seven of them took off in earnest, running like deer through the brush and boulders with such speed and ease that I now knew why Miguel had told me to forget my legs and fly with my arms like an eagle. Because these guys were, indeed, now flying, and within moments, they were up over the ridge and gone!

"They got their fill of us and want to get home before dark," said Rochín. "They'll really move now, and cover the next 15 to 20 miles in close to world-class time."

"But they've been running all day," I pointed out.

"Did you also notice how they kept laughing?"

"Yes, I did."

"They can catch deer like that, too, running and laughing. That's how they hunt, laughing with *carcajadas* as they run the deer down. At the 1968 Olympics in Mexico, the government took a dozen of them to Mexico City to show the world that the Tarahumara are some of the greatest runners on the planet, but they all got sick from the food they were given and none of them were able to compete. But what our government doesn't understand is that the Tarahumara would have never competed effectively because, you see, for them it's not about any individual winning a race. It's about all of them laughing and having fun and giving each other encouragement. In fact, they are famous for closing down and not running well when white people come and try to push them into individual performance."

"Why is that?"

"Because like all tribal people I know, they have no individual egos. They see themselves as belonging to the tribe. Think about it, Don Jan. Can there be any room for individualistic ego in a society in which each one depends on the other for survival?"

This one I had to think about.

Rochín started laughing. "Mexico's greatest asset, I tell you," he said, "is its indigenous people, who know how to live happy and in harmony with each other and with nature. There are two other less numerous tribes that also live up here with the Tarahumara: the Tepehuane and the Xixime. One tribe is well known for being cannibals and the other for being fierce fighters."

He laughed again. "And what do the Tarahumara do, who are peaceful and mostly vegetarians and outnumber both tribes and could easily crush them? They let them be. They let the Tepehuane keep the cannibalistic Xixime at bay, and they enjoy the reputation of both tribes, allowing the outside world think that they, the Tarahumara, are also cannibals and fierce fighters. This way they've managed to keep all outsiders away from this whole region. They're brilliant, I tell you, and they are going to continue to be brilliant and live very well in their huts and caves even after all this that we call modern civilization falls apart and is gone with the wind. I love my indigenous *gente de México!* They are the salt of the earth!"

I'd paid attention and heard everything Rochín had just told me, but being an ex-runner, I was still stuck in my head, wondering how he actually thought they'd make it home before dark.

"Excuse me," I said, "I'm not dismissing what you said, Rochín, but knowing what I know about running, it's very difficult for me to believe they can make it home by dark. You said they have 15 or 20 miles to go, right?"

"Yes."

"And they probably only have about an hour more light."

"No, up there they'll maybe have about half an hour of extra light."

"Okay, so then they'll have about an hour and a half in which to cover 15 to 20 miles through rock and brush and mostly uphill, so my question is, how can—"

"Don Jan, please stop a moment," interrupted Rochín, "and ask yourself why you are having so much trouble believing in what you've just seen. Why are you so full of resistance? Tell me this, could an Olympic champion cover a distance of 15 or 20 miles in this amount of time?"

"Well, yeah, sure, of course," I said.

Father Rochín burst out laughing so hard that I thought he'd choke. "See," he said, "you are racist, Don Jan! You really are!"

I turned all red. "No, I'm not!" I objected. "It's just that Olympic champions are trained, and . . . and they've been selected out of tens of thousands of other top athletes. And—"

"And are these men less trained by needing to catch deer so they can eat? And are they less selected by having 30,000 years of only the fittest of the fit surviving? You are racist, my dear friend. How can you not be? You're white and a *gringo* on top of that and—oh, I could go on for three days," he said, laughing and laughing. "Racist you are, and it's okay, my dear confused friend!"

I said nothing more. I knew I wasn't racist, and he wasn't going to convince me I was. Ever since I'd been a kid, I hadn't been racist. I was the only one in our family who'd take my plate of food when no one else was home and I'd go eat in the kitchen with our black maid. I loved Gladys. I actually sometimes felt closer to her than I did to my own family, who were always looking down their noses at everyone, even at white people who didn't have as much money or education as we did.

I'll never forget the day my grandfather and grandmother came home early and found me eating my dinner with Gladys in the kitchen. They quickly put me in the dining room to finish my dinner, and my grandmother closed the kitchen door, but I could still hear her yelling at Gladys. I was four years old, and I was never allowed to eat with Gladys in the kitchen again, no matter how lonely I was and how much I wanted to be with her.

"Don Jan," said Carlos Rochín, "don't be too hard on yourself. Just realize, *amigo,* that you were raised in a very narrow-minded country, so even though your heart is in the right place, your brain still sees everything in racist ways. For instance, here in Mexico we call a fat person *gordo,* meaning 'fat,' and we mean this as a term of endearment, and the people who are fat take it as a term of endearment. We call a short person *chaparrito*—shorty—and there's no offense meant or taken.

"But in your country, oh boy, call a person fatso or shorty and it's all heavy-duty stuff, except maybe among some of your blacks, especially in their world of jazz. I've lived in your country. I've seen the uptightness and how everybody is so scared of offending each other, and why? Because down deep inside, all of you *gringos* know you're totally, totally, completely racist!"

I took a deep breath. I could see what he meant. Calling a person fatso wasn't taken as a term of endearment in the U.S. "Look, maybe it's true that we're uptight and take offense, but it's not because we're racist," I said, "but because we're highly aware of the health issues of being overweight, and we're—"

Rochín burst out laughing with *carcajadas!* "That's so beautiful, Don Jan! Go on, and explain away everything I just said by showing me how great and idealistic you *gringos* really are! Go on, do it, *amigo,* and never question why you call Mexicans lazy, while at the same time they do all of the hardest work in your agriculture and in your slaughterhouses. Call your blacks shiftless and not as smart as whites, yet they are some of your most gifted and creative people. And you say that Asians are hardworking but can only produce inferior products, yet Japan is already producing trucks and automobiles that are equal or better than your American cars. Go on, *amigo,* stick your head in the sand and let all these facts stare you in the face, but you hold on to your old beliefs and prejudices."

He continued laughing like there was no tomorrow, but I certainly wasn't laughing. I didn't think he was funny one little bit!

"Oh, Jan, you should see your face! You look so upset! Jan, we're all racists and full of prejudice all over the world! Not just you Americans. Here in Mexico we still call our Indians *Indios sin razón*—Indians without reason—because they don't meet our standards. Here, I'll give you a perfect example. If I was traveling with my cousins and their kids, by now they'd be angry and cussing out these Indians because they never came down off the ridges to help us get our vehicle across the streambeds. They'd be calling them stupid, *sin razón,* no-good Indians who are just too lazy to be of any help. But that's not the way I see it. I've lived up here with these Tarahumara. This is why I'm explaining all this to you, Don Jan, because, you see, you are going to be living among some of the most untouched people in the world.

"Of course, they didn't offer to help us when they saw us struggling so much to get our car across the dry riverbeds, like decent, good, civilized people would do. And why not—because would a deer offer to help us? Ah, Jan, would a rabbit or a fox or a coyote? And would you take offense if they didn't? No, you'd realize that the deer, the rabbit, the fox, and the coyote have no comprehension of what we are doing. And if they did, what do you think that they would do?"

"I don't know."

"Come on, think—try to imagine yourself as a deer, a rabbit, a fox, or a coyote."

"They'd probably laugh at us," I said.

"Exactly, they'd probably laugh their heads off because they can see we have two good pairs of legs and feet, so why not just walk or run. Why struggle with a piece of iron all day long? Also, they wouldn't want to interrupt us, because they'd see how much we enjoyed our struggle and figure they'd have a great story to tell when they got home. A story that would keep their families laughing for weeks. Jan, we are their entertainment! Our whole way of life is pure ridiculous entertainment that has no rhyme or reason for them."

It was really very difficult for me to grasp what Carlos Rochín was telling me. "But Rochín," I said, "they've had a train coming through their country for nearly a hundred years, you say, and they've seen logging trucks coming and going for years, so how can they see all this and still not understand, or at least be affected?"

"Who do you think lives a longer, happier life, Jan?" he asked me. "Those large Mennonites or these slender, small Indians who can run like the wind?"

"Well, at first I'd say the Mennonites, of course, because of their endless food supply, but now in the way you ask the question, I'm beginning to think that maybe the Indians live longer, happier lives. Because, well, when I was running, I felt such joy and health and power all through my body that at times, I'd just start laughing—I'd felt so good!"

"EXACTLY! And this is why the powerful overfed bodies of the Mennonites start breaking down at 50, and they're old people by 70 and dead by 80, whereas—and no one believes this—some of the Tarahumara live in perfect health to 100 and 110, still walking upright without any back problems.

"Jan, we've lost our faith in God! We've replaced our faith in God with material things. Tell me, do civilized Christians really believe that Moses parted the sea? Do we, even the men of the cloth, really see God's grace in everything all around us anymore? Or did we lose sight of the miraculous with the Fall, as it says in the Bible?"

"Wait. You're not trying to tell me that—"

"Yes, exactly, that's what I'm telling you. Not all of us lost sight of the Garden, Jan. These people still see and live in the Spirit World of God's Daily Miracles."

I breathed deeply, and blew out. Maybe he was right. After all, personally I'd lost faith and fallen out of the Kingdom of God when Chato and my other boys were killed.

We drove on in silence. The sun was going down. I just didn't know what to think anymore. Because Rochín was right: I, a man of the cloth, had become a totally, totally Doubting Thomas.

"Jan," Rochín finally said, "we all know what a huge loss it was to you that those boys were killed. But they were our kids, too, and even in a situation like this, there is much to be seen and learned."

This broke the camel's back.

"LEARN WHAT?!" I yelled, snapping at him. "That the more and more I try to convince people that there really is a God and we should turn our lives over to His Son Jesus, the more painful and horrible the journey gets?!"

Rochín looked at me and kept quiet for many miles. Then he spoke. "I heard you, *amigo*," he said. "I really did. But now I'm going to ask you something that might sound quite silly and un-important to you, but please be patient. Okay?"

"Okay," I agreed. "And I'm sorry I snapped at you."

"That's quite all right. Now, Jan, do you think that we really landed on the moon, or do you think—as a lot of people are beginning to say—that it was all a hoax?"

"What does that have to do with anything?"

"Please, just go along with me. Do you believe that it really happened?"

"Yes, I believe that we really did it."

"Why?"

"Well, because I saw it on TV, and I read enough articles and newspapers accounts to . . . well, make it seem real to me beyond any doubt."

"Exactly. You saw it on TV, and you read enough background information so you have a basic trust and acceptance that it really occurred."

"Where is this leading?" I asked.

"Jan, these people you're going to be living with up here don't read and don't watch TV, and they have no reason to trust or accept our system. So all this movement of trucks and trains is seen as nothing but an unanchored dream."

"An unanchored dream?"

"Yes, a dream that you don't bother remembering or putting energy into. Because for a dream to be anchored in their belief system of reality, the Tarahumara must first and foremost see miracles."

"What are you saying?" I asked.

"I'm saying that for the Tarahumara, even this that happened to us with our boys would be seen from a spiritual point of view, and be miraculous."

Tears came to my eyes. I'd had enough! I didn't want to hear anymore! This was just a bunch of crap as far as I was concerned!

"Jan, I also recently read an article," continued Rochín, "that says the indigenous people of the Caribbean couldn't see the three ships of Columbus because they had nothing to anchor them to what they knew."

I shook my head. I had no idea what he was talking about, and I really didn't care.

"The article went on to say that we can only see that which we've been trained to see. That it's now been proven scientifically that children can see spirits when they first come into the world, but they lose that ability as they begin to learn how to speak. So, Jan, where this is all going is that I'm preparing you for the world you are about to enter, so you won't think that you're losing your mind when you begin to see miraculous things happen, or at least visualize realities that you've never seen before."

Suddenly I flashed on the three Indians we'd seen squatting in the brush and rocks. They'd looked very familiar. A chill went up and down my spine. Could these be the same three Indian Healers who'd come to me in the hospital just before dawn? Then I remembered the night I'd gone outside my apartment to look up at the stars and I'd felt the presence of *la Mano Negra* so strongly that I'd known . . . without a shadow of a doubt . . . that he/she was across the street.

"Or more precisely," Rochín was now saying, "maybe you've seen all these miracles your whole life, but you didn't give them importance or energy because you didn't have the background with which to let them register except in your dreams. This is why the Tarahumara have no problem accepting the miracle of Jesus and the Bible, but they will not allow a priest or a minister to preach to them."

I was now really listening.

"Jan, I've seen with my own two eyes a *mayori*, meaning their wise elder, take his bullwhip and crack it in front of the priest's face when he closed the Bible and began to give a sermon. They ran the priest out of the church and quickly escorted him off their land, and this is why even to this day, no priest can rule them. In fact, during Holy Week all priests and white people are prohibited from remaining for their night services. These people don't have much respect for white people, because they only have respect for realities that are anchored in the miraculous, and they don't see us as being a very miraculous people. Things like trucks and trains aren't miracles for them. They're just things. Unimportant things that aren't worthy of their attention or energy."

93

I inhaled deeply and then blew out. "Rochín," I said, "truly, I do believe that a few months ago everything that you are telling me would've been so totally foreign to me that I couldn't have heard you. But, you see, when I was in the hospital, I had this recurring dream of three Indian Healers coming to me just before dawn, when I was half-asleep. They are the ones who guided me and healed me and got me strong enough to get out of my wheelchair after the doctors had told me that I'd be in it for the rest of my life."

"I knew it! I just knew it!" shouted Rochín. "This is why I brought you up here, Jan! I knew you were ready to step into the Spirit World of what Mexico is really all about! You see, those three healers are the same Three Wisemen who came to Jesus."

"What? What are you saying?"

"I'm saying that for most of the indigenous people of Mexico, the Bible is still alive."

"Alive?"

"Yes, it is still happening. It never ceased happening."

"But how can this be possible?"

"Easy. Because for us, the miraculous must be anchored in what we call reality or it's not believable. But for the Tarahumara, reality must be anchored in the *miraculous* or it's not believable. So now can you begin to see why our world, our whole way of life, is so unreal for them, but the World of Spirit, as you saw in the hospital when you were half-asleep, is *totally* real for them?"

I again inhaled deeply and blew out. This was a big one. My God, if what Rochín was saying was true, I was really in for the largest experience of my life since I saw the lion eyes when I was a child. So, then, maybe those three Indian Healers had been right and my life service was about to begin, and everything up to this point had just been preparation.

"Understand, Jan," my friend was now saying, "that even if those runners who were taken to Mexico City hadn't become poisoned by the food they ate and they had participated in the Olympics, I'm quite sure they wouldn't have been able to compete, because they would have stopped before the finish line and just looked out on all people watching them, and they would have rolled on the ground with laughter. We're a joke to them, because our dream is so ridiculous. We have no love for the rocks and trees. We don't recognize each day as a gift from God. We don't stand in awe of the sunrise as the right eye of God and the moon as the left eye. We're blind and lost, even to the miraculous beauty of a butterfly or a flower."

I nodded. What Rochín was saying was now beginning to make a lot of sense to me. It had been three butterflies in the garden behind the hospital that had opened me up, and after that was when those three healers had come to me; and they'd seemed so real, especially when they'd taken hold of my body with their warm, strong hands and had begun mending it and soothing it. Maybe what Rochín was saying wasn't that far-fetched. In fact, maybe those three butterflies had actually been the healers. Sure, why not? They'd first come to me as butterflies so I could open up.

"Look, Don Jan," Rochín now said, "from the Tarahumara point of view, life isn't about winning, and it certainly isn't about competing. It's about having joy and giving heart to each other in the Living Grace of the Holy Creator. And I'm not saying all this so that you'll now go into your head and start idolizing these people. No, they're full of faults and ignorance. I'm saying this so you will understand how extremely practical the Tarahumara are. You tell me, how else can a people possibly chase down a deer if they don't help each other? Do you see what I mean? Wouldn't it be very practical if we all started helping each other all over the planet instead of competing? Couldn't we then accomplish great feats with joy and untapped energy, cooperating even as we competed?

"Could it be that our self-centered ego is what drains us all of our spiritual powers? Could it be that pure, unconscious joy was the type of energy that Adam and Eve had in the Garden and was the same kind of energy that enabled Moses and his people to part the seas, and the same kind of energy that allowed Jesus and Judas to do their Holy Work together? You see, for the Tarahumara, Jesus was joyful in His Crucifixion. Not sad. And they greatly admire Judas, too.

"I envy you, Don Jan. This winter you will live with some of the most pure and untouched people left on the globe. By spring you will not be the person you now are. You will experience situations that will just not be explainable to your educated mind. This is why I'm willing to make this long drive every month to bring you supplies. I want to witness the transformation you will be going through.

"And remember that the key to this transformation, my friend, is laughter. *Carcajadas,* as we say in Mexican Spanish—big, strong belly laughs—because you will learn that according to these people, no matter what life brings you on this planet, life, *la vida,* is meant to be joyful, for the Spirit World is real and surrounds us with God's infinite love and well-being. You are going to love it, Jan, but you will need to drop all expectations. That's what I was forced to do. That's why I can now finally love and laugh at my rich, corrupt relatives."

I rubbed my forehead. I was now at last finally beginning to think that I maybe understood a little bit of what Father Rochín was telling me, but how could I ever really drop all expectations? I was an ordained Christian minister, after all, and those boys had been brutally killed and—OH, HOW IT HURT!

"And Jan, we're going to build your camp at the exact place on the lake where it came to me in a vision to leave my family's wealth and become the richest human on Earth—a priest, a servant of God. You and I, *compadre,* we have a lot in common. This is why I chose to bring you up to this untouched Heaven on Earth."

On this point, I couldn't disagree. We really did have a lot in common.

CHAPTER 6

We didn't make it to Creel that day and ended up sleeping on the side of the logging road on the bedding we'd brought with us. I'd never seen so many stars since I'd been a firefighter in Montana. The Milky Way was a thick, wide, bright river of dazzling stars across the sky. We heard owls, and coyotes; and once we even heard the mighty scream of a mountain lion! Once more I slept like a baby, and in the morning we hit the road at daybreak.

"Don't be too surprised if today we have 20 or 30 Indians watching us getting our car across the riverbeds."

"You're joking, right?"

"Wouldn't you want everyone in your family to come and see your latest large-screen TV show?"

"Well, yes, probably so, but—"

He burst out laughing. "But on the other hand, there's a good chance they won't be back," he said. "They've already had such a good laugh from us."

The streams were no longer running dry up here. There was a little water in each one, even though this wasn't the rainy season. All morning I half expected to see a group of Indians watching us when we approached each streambed, but it wasn't until we came to the flat mesa of the town of Creel that I spotted a large group of Indians watching us from the tops of huge loaf-of-bread-shaped boulders. This time there were also women and children with the men, and they looked like wildflowers, wearing colorful clothes and sitting on their even more colorful blankets on top of the wind-smoothed boulders, as we drove past.

Rochín burst out laughing with *carcajadas.* "They even dressed in their Sunday best to see us, the latest TV show of *los chavochi*—the non-Indians," he said, still laughing.

I started laughing, too. I guess we were a great comedy show from their point of view. We drove past them into Creel. Beyond the sunbaked little town there were towering rocky cliffs and pine forests. Entering the tiny settlement, I could see that Father Rochín was right. Four hundred people couldn't possibly be living in this town. It had to be closer to a hundred, unless of course you counted the *burros* and pigs and goats and cows and horses, which were happily running across the road every which way.

We had lunch in a little patio restaurant that was owned by a man named Coco who wore a beautiful flower in his hair, and I bet every person in the whole region came by to say hello to Father Rochín. He'd changed clothes before we'd come into town. He now wore a white *guayabera*—a Mexican wedding shirt—and clean slacks, and he looked very proper and priestly. I was still wearing my regular T-shirt, Levi's, and sandals, and hobbling about on my crutches.

We bought some local tropical fruit and fresh vegetables, which we were told were grown at the bottom of *las Barrancas del Cobre,* and some deer meat that we were told had been hunted on the top rim of the great canyon. Then we drove out of town to the sawmill, where we bought the lumber to build the foundation for my tent. The men working in the mill loaded the lumber on a broken-down old truck, and they were ready to follow us out to the lake where I was going to stay, when a very good-looking, new-ish pickup came driving up.

"Don't say a word," Carlos Rochín said to me under his breath. "I was hoping that we wouldn't see him. I'm embarrassed to say, but he's a fellow Jesuit. His name is Luis Van Housen. He's a German. We send up free clothes for him to give to the Indians, and he sells them the clothes. We send up free food, and if they don't have the money to buy or the means to trade something for it, he holds the food in storage until it rots. I've reported all this to our diocese, but they tell me he's the only one willing to stay up here, and he does have more Indians coming to our services than ever before. I've gladly offered to come up here, but they don't want anyone but Luis. I wonder," added Rochín half to himself, "what could this man possibly have on them?"

"On whom?" I said.

"On our superiors in Chihuahua."

Pulling up in a cloud of dust, the German priest got out of his Chevy with a grand smile. He was taller than I was, maybe 6'2", very lean, and in his late 50s; and he wore a plaid Pendleton shirt buttoned up all the way to his neck even though it was hot. He had on dark sunglasses and a Safari-type helmet, and what hair we could see was dyed a blue-black. And he wore red lipstick on his lips, which I would come to understand wasn't that uncommon as we moved farther out of Chihuahua City, because, I guess, Chap-Stick was difficult to find out here.

"Father Rochín!" he said in a large, booming voice. "How good to see you! It's all over town that you brought a stranger on crutch-es with you!"

"Yes, his name is Jan Milburn," said Carlos Rochín. "He's a Christian minister, but don't worry. He hasn't come to preach. He just needs to get some rest and do a little fishing."

"Oh, I see," said the other man, stretching out his hand.

This was when I noticed that he wore white gloves. He did not remove his glove to shake my hand.

"Glad to meet you, Jan Milburn! Luis Van Housen at your ser-vice."

"Jan Milburn. Very glad to make your acquaintance."

"I'm sure my little friend has already told you what a tyrant I am. I don't give the clothes free to the Indians, and I don't give them the food free, either. I ask them for a little something in trade. Anything. Just a little milk or a few eggs, whatever they can afford, because I don't believe, like our little friend, that we should give anything free to these people. For 500 years we have been trying to educate them, to get them to understand the benefits of hard work, but do they learn? No, of course not, because people like Father Rochín and his backward-thinking acquaintances keep giving them things free. So they continue to be spoiled, lazy, unproductive children.

"Yesterday you drove through the Mennonites' valley. You saw what good, hardworking European people can make out of even a desolate land. We show these *Indios* what can be done, but do they listen? Do they learn? Oh no, they continue in their backward ways as they've been for the last 20,000 years, and they refuse to learn even the most rudimentary civilized knowledge.

"Do not listen to this little man," he went on. "I do not even know how they allowed him to become a Jesuit. We have standards, and they must be upheld or we, too, will become lost souls."

He continued smiling and talking, but I'd quit listening. Never had I heard a man of the cloth be so insensitive and harsh to another man in the service of God.

Father Luis now turned to Father Rochín, and they talked but never shook hands. Then it was time for us to go so we could get to the lake before dark.

It was slow going with the lumber truck following us out of the flat, long valley of Creel.

"Did you notice that he never offered to shake hands with me?" asked Rochín.

"Yes, I noticed."

"For years I was quite offended by that," he said, "and I tried to befriend him, but I finally realized that he would never accept me. I thought that because you are light of skin, he would take his glove off to shake hands with you, as he does for white people, but he didn't, because, I guess, you're with me. I just don't know how he's managed to be up here all these years and yet not be able see the spiritual beauty in these people. But I guess, just as it is said that the native people couldn't see Columbus's ships . . . European people, even to this day, still can't see the beauty in Tarahumara, because you see, these tribes of the Copper Canyon are so pure that they are still in the first stage of civilization."

"First stage? So what is the first stage?" I asked.

"In stage one," explained Rochín, "native people make pots and utensils only for their own use. In stage two, native people begin to paint and beautify their pots and wares so they can use them for trade. In stage three, pots and baskets and other wares become elaborate so they can be taken to market. In stage four, commerce is now done, not just trade, and the use of money begins. That is when the whole world gets turned on its head and people begin to think in terms of profit, not just trade.

"You see, in the first two stages, profit and personal wealth is inconceivable, just as private ownership is inconceivable. This is why I love to come up here. Of course, most people prefer indigenous people who are at stages three and four because in Oaxaca, for example, these people are great weavers and potters; and in Taxco, great silversmiths; and in Puebla, great tile makers. But for me the native people of stages one and two are the most rewarding to come to know because they are as close as we can get to what it must have been like to live in the innocence of the Garden of Eden.

"Oh, I so wish that my diocese would allow me to replace Father Luis. They must know how much he dislikes the Tarahumara. So what is it that he has on them, and why is it that he insists on staying up here? I wish I knew."

I had listened carefully to Rochín. He was truly giving me an education. Up ahead I saw some smoke coming from a cave-like crack in a rock cliff. There were thin, tall upright fence posts tied together at the huge entrance of the cave-like crack.

"Do people live there?" I asked. "Or is that where they keep their livestock for the night?"

"No, that's a home and a very good one, which has probably been handed down for 20 or 30 generations. You'll see, they're large and spacious and cool and clean inside. Three generations of 20 or more people can live in one of those structures, and live very well."

I'd never seen anything like this. I saw a dozen more places like it as we drove southeast of town. The lake, I was told, was about eight miles from town, but where I would be staying was around the lake past a spot called Elephant Rock. It was more like 12 miles from Creel.

The going got tougher and slower. It wasn't even a logging road anymore. Out here, we were following goat paths. Up ahead, I spotted a huge formation of rocks that did, in fact, look like an elephant, and I could see the lake beyond the outcropping of stone.

"To the left around Elephant Rock is where they will film the Rod Steiger movie in the spring," said Rochín. He hadn't spoken a word for the last few miles. I guess that the tall Jesuit priest had really shaken him up. "That's the largest part of the lake. It looks a lot like Canada, they tell me. But we'll go straight, toward the right side of the lake where it is smaller and better protected from the winds. This is where I used to bring my nephews, nieces, and cousins to camp. We always had such a good time."

"How did you ever find this place?" I asked. "It's even more remote than some of the places where we parachuted in to fight forest fires in Montana."

"We came by train," Rochín told me, "which we would have done this time, too, only two bridges are out and it will be months before they will be repaired."

It was almost dark by the time we got the lumber unloaded. The lake was beautiful, surrounded by outcroppings of rocks and tall pines. It felt a great deal like some of the high country above Yosemite, California, where I used to camp when I was a teenager.

"Even though the movie is supposed to take place in Canada, I was told that they want to film it here because the snows aren't as severe as they are up north," said Rochín. "So you should have an easy winter. The little bit of snow we get melts off by the end of the day. We haven't had a big snowstorm in more than 20 years, and even that one wasn't very severe."

"That's the way it is for us in Los Gatos, California. It hardly ever snows, and when it does, it only holds for a day or two before it melts off."

We continued making small talk. I could feel that something very big had gone out of Carlos Rochín ever since we'd met with Luis Van Housen. We set up the smaller tent, built a fire, and settled in for the night. I just couldn't believe I was still in Mexico. This truly felt so much like the Sierras above Yosemite and the Rockies of Montana. I loved it. The fresh air was invigorating.

"You're very lucky, Jan," said Rochín. "Very lucky. But be careful and stay close to God. Then everything will be okay."

"Yes, of course, I'll do that. And thank you for bringing me up here, Rochín. I feel like I've returned home. I've always loved the outdoors."

He laughed, but there wasn't much energy in his laughter anymore. "Sleep well, my friend. I'm going to call it a night now, and if you have disturbing dreams, just relax and go easy. The Indians here don't believe in dream catchers, as their native cousins do in the States. Here, they say that all dreams are equally good. So it's just up to us not to get frightened, my friend, and then even our bad dreams will be enlightening. Good night."

"Good night," I replied. I really didn't think that he was giving me advice. I thought that he was giving *himself* advice. It was almost as if a huge evil spell had consumed Rochín when the big German had come wheeling up in his pickup in a cloud of dust. But I decided not to say anything and just snuggled into my sleeping bag, looking up at the stars. I could hear the tiny waves of the lake slapping up on the shore. As for me, I hadn't felt such peace in a long time.

But then I'd no more than closed my eyes when here came Chato and the others who'd been tortured and hung, and I could hear my boys screaming in unison as they refused to give up the LIGHT of Our Lord God Jesus!

And when they broke Chato's bones with clubs in the parking lot with people watching, he didn't spit in their faces, as the old Chato would have done. No, a calmness came over him even as they beat him, and he began to pray. The other two boys who were with him saw their leader's actions, and they, too, began to pray even as their earthly bodies were being beaten. The people watching made the sign of the cross over themselves and began to pray, too. A golden-white light came over the bodies of my three boys.

I awoke in a sweat. Tears were pouring down my face. I got up and went to the lake's edge to urinate and look up at the stars. My heart was pounding. Gazing upward, I began to pray, asking God to please help me understand. Why had He allowed this to happen? I would have gladly gone in their place.

"Beautiful, eh?" said Rochín, coming up by my side.

"What?"

"The stars."

"Oh, yeah, sure," I said, taking a huge breath. "I had such a realistic dream that I don't really know if I'm here by the lake or . . . if I'm still in my sleeping bag dreaming."

He laughed. "Maybe both."

"Both?"

"Sure, why not. Was it about our boys?"

"Yes," I answered. "Yes!" And the tears poured down my face.

"Did you know," said the priest, "that people are now calling them the three saints of Juárez and the six saints of Zacatecas? Too bad you Protestants don't believe in saints like us Catholics," he added, laughing. "Oh, just look at those stars! That's where our boys now are! Up there giving us hope and light. Ever since I was a kid, I've felt so close to the stars."

"Me, too!" I said. "Like they're my best friends."

"They are, Jan, they are."

"And our boys are up there now?"

"Definitely! From the stars we come, and to the stars we do return."

"Good," I said, wiping the tears from my eyes. "Good."

The breeze picked up, singing in the tree branches, and the coyotes began yapping; then an owl called in a nearby tree, and the little waves of the lake made a quick, tiny slapping sound. I took in a large, deep breath and blew out.

CHAPTER 7

In the morning, I awoke tired and feeling very strange and confused. It was like the realities of the night were so much larger than the realities of the day that they made no sense once we awoke. My boys, my boys, THEY HAD TRUSTED ME! That mother in Zacatecas was right. If I hadn't filled her son's head and heart with all of my ideas of God and Jesus, he'd still be alive. And . . . last night I'd been forced to see how much they'd been tortured before they were killed.

"What is it, Jan?" asked Rochín.

"Remember last night when we peed together by the lake's edge?"

"No," he said, shaking his head.

"You don't remember?"

"No, I don't remember."

"But you came up beside me and—" He started laughing and laughing. "YOU *CABRÓN!*" I yelled. "You really had me going!"

"Good," said Rochín, still laughing. "It's good to have you start doubting your sanity, or believe me, you will never be able to get into the world of the Tarahumara, who make no distinction between dream and nondream. So tell me, my ignorant *gringo amigo,* why are you here? Why did you even come to Mexico in the first place? What even caused you to want to be a minister? All those questions are going to haunt you until, to the depths of your bones, you realize that it was all written in the stars before you were born."

"Then you believe that we are all predestined?"

"No, I believe that we each have an ongoing story."

"A story, eh?"

"Yes . . . and so what is yours?"

I took a deep breath and another deep breath and then told Father Rochín about the lion experience I'd had at the age of 11. He listened very intently, and then he told me that he'd had a very similar experience. We built a fire and drank coffee as we continued talking. It was another beautiful day.

"I, too, was about 11 years old," Rochín began, "and I didn't know how to swim. We were at my grandparents' *hacienda,* and we were having a huge family event with hundreds of people. I wasn't into horses and roping poor animals and knocking them down, so I went to the pond behind the corrals. It was full of water lilies, and I only went in to my waist, so I thought I was fine, until I slipped on some green algae and went underwater.

"I was drowning and yelling, but no one could hear me with the *rodeo* going on. I finally gave up and went sinking down to the bottom of the pond, which had little mosquito fish and tiny frogs. A peace came over me, and I knew that I'd died . . . and this is when I came face-to-face with the huge bubbling eyes of a bullfrog, no more than inches away from my eyes.

"We looked at each other, and he smiled at me, and then— BOOM! A light came bursting into me, and I don't know how, but I was out of the pond and people were yelling, and I was on the grass alongside the pool and gasping and throwing up water. And yet I'd died. I know I had. And after that, the big golden eyes of that frog would come to me in my dreams, and we'd travel together across the stars."

"Golden . . . you said 'golden,' right?"

"Yes, I said golden, and frogs became my obsession. I read every book I could on them. I found out that there are hundreds, if not thousands, of different frogs all over the world. And I loved the way they transformed from a pollywog to a tiny frog, and then burst into a huge, monstrous bullfrog with bulging eyes. Why did you ask if the frog's eyes were golden?"

"Because my lion's eyes were also golden."

"Very interesting," Rochín said. "Because . . . according to legend, back at one time a race of golden-eyed creatures came to Earth from another planet."

"Were there people, as we know people, among these creatures?" I asked.

"Who knows?"

I nodded. "So, then, did you accept the frog as your totem?"

"Absolutely! And I feel privileged to have such a fine creature as my guide from Our Holy Spirit World! Totems, you realize, are nothing more than what we Catholics call our Guardian Angels."

"Yeah, I guess you're right," I said.

And so Rochín and I talked and worked together for the next week, and I can truly say that I've never felt closer and more connected to another human being. He helped me build the platform for my tent; and little by little he got over our encounter with the German priest, and I seemed to get over my screaming nightmares about my boys. This was when Rochín began to tell me that it had always been his dream to one day build a summer camp for kids up here by the lake, like the summer camps he'd seen in the United States.

I told him that I happened to have a lot of experience with kids' camps, that I'd helped build and run a Christian camp at Lake Tahoe in the Sierras and another one in the Santa Cruz Mountains along the coast. By the end of the week, both Rochín's and my energies were totally back, and we shook hands on a deal. He would buy the material, and I would help him build a camp for kids in the spring when I was well enough to get off my crutches.

The day Carlos Rochín left, he was once more laughing with big *carcajadas* like he had when we'd made our way across all those streambeds, with me driving and him moving the big boulders out of the way. He was now saying that no matter how much he detested some of the greedy, bad ways of his rich family, he still knew that they were good people, and they would help us, financially, build a summer camp.

"We will make it big enough to handle 400 kids at a time," he said, full of energy. "We will bring kids in by the trainloads from Los Mochis to the west and from Chihuahua City from the east. And we want our camp to have a bare minimum of facilities so our kids can get into the feel of nature, just like when I used to bring my nephews and nieces up here. We're a team, Jan! And no matter how much greed and evil there is in the world, we will help the Light of Our Lord Jesus Christ come through to all. Just keep the faith, *amigo!*"

"Amen," I said to him. "That's what it's all about—keeping faith!"

It was a sad day for me the morning Father Carlos Rochín was ready to leave. I'd grown to feel very close to the priest. We were both men of the cloth, yet neither one of us put on airs or carried our Bibles around with us. We didn't want that separation from the people. We both liked to meet people as people, and only if the subject of the Bible came up would we refer to the Holy Book.

"Are you sure that you're going to be all right, Jan? I can stay a few more days if you'd like," he said.

"No, I'm fine," I told him. "And you need to get to your niece's baptism."

"Okay, I'll go, but remember, I'll be coming in every month to bring you supplies and the news."

"Thank you. I'll be okay. In Montana we'd parachute in to places that were so remote that once we fought the forest fire, it would sometimes take us ten days or more to walk out to our rendezvous place. We'd always try to do it in groups of two or three, but a few times I found myself alone and had to catch mice and snakes to eat so I could keep my strength up."

Rochín laughed. "You're pulling my leg, as you *gringos* say, right?"

110

"Just a little," I replied. "But not much. Go on. I'll be all right."

"Okay, I'll go, but one more thing: Do not say anything to anyone about our idea for this children's camp at this time. I don't want Luis Van Housen to get wind of it, until I have the backing of my family. He and a man named Ortega pretty much run things up here, and they want to keep it that way."

"Rochín, may I ask you something?"

"But of course. Anything."

"Why do you let this German Jesuit take away your power? You are a very powerful person yourself. You don't really accept his premise about not giving out free clothes and food, do you?"

"No, not really."

"Because if you do, then let me tell you that giving freely is the foundation of what we do. It was the giving of food and safe shelter that enabled me to reach kids back in California, in San Francisco and Willow Glen . . . the giving, along with having the rules of no drugs and everyone needing to pitch in and work.

"I've told you, I thought I was a failure, yet over 200 kids came to see me off at the airport when I left to come down to Mexico. And you know what I've done here in Mexico. All the halfway houses are set up with the premise of giving free food and safe shelter. People need to know that someone cares. One of my old mentors used to say, 'Kids don't care how much you know until they know how much you care.' And this isn't just true for kids, but for adults, too."

"I agree entirely," said Rochín. "But something else is going on, Jan. It is no accident that Van Housen has never shaken hands with me."

"Go on."

"Well, it's not just me he doesn't shake hands with. It's all dark, short people. You'll never see him take the hand of an Indian. You're tall and white, Jan. That's why he took your hand. He considers you his equal. But not me, even though I'm a fellow Jesuit.

"Once, in Chihuahua City, before I knew him, our archdiocese had organized a gathering of priests. I was talking to some of my colleagues when Van Housen cut in front of me, giving me his back, and took over my conversation with that big smile and grand voice of his. I was shocked. I didn't know what to do. I couldn't very well move around in front of him and confront him. That would have been rude, so I just moved away, feeling very small. Which I am—I'm only 5'4", and his back completely blocked me out like a wall.

"And . . . and I had no idea that he'd done it on purpose until it happened two more times, and by then it was too late. If I saw him coming, I'd automatically stop speaking, and move aside. What else could I do? Get angry and cause a scene? You saw how charming he is, with that grand smile of his. Everyone loves him. He's very impressive. And also, no one would have believed me. In fact, it's still hard for *me* to believe it. Be careful, Jan. Be very careful, my friend—the man has haunting powers."

We hugged and he left. That night I was alone, and it felt wonderful, until I closed my eyes and went to sleep. Chato and all the boys who'd been beaten and hung in their cells came screaming to me in a cold black storm, and then there was Van Housen's large laughing face.

I awoke in a sweat. It was just past midnight. I got up and went to the lake's edge, relieved myself, and began to pray. I guess Father Rochín had been right. I, too, had to be very careful of this big, tall, handsome German Jesuit, because somehow he'd gotten under my skin as well.

The weeks passed, and every day I took a little walk, forcing myself to go a little farther around the lake. I began to get stronger once again, and I was able to sleep better, too. And a few times I saw Indians come walking by, but they never acknowledged my presence, even when I'd wave hello to them. I guess I really didn't exist in their reality.

The first month passed so quickly that I was surprised when Carlos Rochín came driving up in his beat-up old blue Renault one day. He had one of his nephews with him.

"So you're alive, Jan!" he said.

"Sitting pretty," I said.

"This is my nephew Pablo. Pablo, this is Jan Milburn, the famous *gringo* of the radio show *The Romantic Hour.*"

"Glad to meet you, *señor,*" said the boy.

He was about 15 and already taller than his uncle. "Glad to meet you, Pablo," I said, taking his hand.

"Pablo wants to help us build the camp for the kids," Rochín explained. "He says that some of his fondest memories are when we used to come up here to camp and fish when he was a boy."

"I loved it up here," added Pablo. "We were allowed to run free as deer, and it was so much fun."

"I know what you mean," I said. "I grew up among the giant redwoods in California; and I would go hiking all through the Santa Cruz Mountains, and then eventually, up into the Sierras and the Rockies."

"My uncle says that you used to parachute in to the wilds of Montana to fight forest fires," said Pablo.

"Yes, that's true."

"And you rode a Honda 300 when you were a minister in California."

"That's also true," I said. "I rode my bike between San Jose and—"

"Okay," said Rochín, cutting me off. "We can tell our stories around the campfire tonight. Right now help me unload things. I'm starving. And Jan, I brought you your guitar, as you asked me to."

I got a lump in my throat at the sight of my guitar. Ever since I'd joined the church choir in grade school, music had been such an important part of my life. Carefully, I took the instrument in my hands.

"Thank you, Rochín," I said. "Thank you very much. I was hoping that you'd remember."

"I didn't," he said, laughing, "I forgot all about it. It was Pablo who asked me if you had your guitar with you, because he looked forward to listening to you play and sing with your terrible accent, like you did on the radio."

Pablo turned all red. "Your accent isn't really that terrible. The girls all thought you sang like an angel, but, well, we guys . . ."

"Go on, tell him," said Rochín, still laughing. "It's good for a person to know how the world really sees him so he can have humility."

"Well, we guys would listen to you, too, and we'd laugh our heads off."

I looked from Pablo to Rochín and back to Pablo again. "And you want to hear me sing?" I asked.

He nodded. "Yes, it was kind of great for us kids to be able to laugh at an adult minister who wasn't afraid to make a complete fool of himself!"

Rochín was laughing so hard that he was fit to be tied. "Go on, tell him the rest. How you kids thought he was ridiculous and yet warmhearted."

Now I started laughing. "Okay, I'll sing tonight. I guess ridiculous and warmhearted is really closer to what I've been doing all my life."

We put things away, built a fire, cooked dinner, and ate; and I played my guitar and sang. Pablo was fast asleep by my second song. Rochín told me that it had been a long day for them.

Rochín and I stayed up half the night, talking the whole while. He caught me up on the outside world, telling me that our halfway houses were doing very well, but at some locations they were beginning to look more like reform schools than warm, heart-giving safe havens. He also told me that Emma was now involved with running the restaurant, but that business had fallen off tremendously since I'd left, and she was very upset.

"Also, Jan . . . she's pregnant with your child," he said, "and she has sent you this letter."

I wasn't surprised that she was pregnant. We'd been going at it like rabbits ever since we got together. I took the letter but didn't open it. It was strange, but once Emma had left me, she was gone, even from my mind. Also, I could feel that there was a lot Rochín wasn't telling me. The fire had died down. It was past midnight, and I'd been going to sleep every night shortly after dark.

"So tell me," said Carlos Rochín, "have you experienced any . . . well, unusual circumstances?"

"You mean miracles?"

"Yes, I mean miracles."

"No," I said, "it's all been pretty quiet and ordinary."

"Are you sure?"

"Yes."

"How about in your dreams? Has anything happened in that twilight time of reality just before you go to sleep and just before you awake?"

"Well, yes, now that you mention it. It's during this time when I'm at peace that I sometimes feel as if the trees are singing to me, like the giant redwoods sang to me back home when I was a kid in Los Gatos."

"Go on," he urged.

"Well, for instance, the night you left I had a terrible dream about Chato and our boys being shot or hung in their cells; and then Van Housen's face appeared, and he was laughing and making fun of the whole situation. I awoke in a sweat."

"And what did you do?"

"I got up and went down to the lake's edge and prayed."

"Perfect," said Father Rochín. "Luis Van Housen has a very powerful spirit. After that initial get-together at the archdiocese, he haunted me in my sleep for months. Like I told you, you need to be careful, Jan, and stay close to God."

"I hear you," I said, "because another thing that has begun to haunt me is, how did *la Mano Negra* manage to put the glove and those bullets on my pillow without anyone ever seeing anything? I'm beginning to think that *la Mano* must be a cleaning woman, and this is why no one notices her."

"Or he could be a plumber or some kind of maintenance man," offered Rochín. "There are countless theories about *la Mano Negra*. So how did you find peace with this?"

"I also went to the water's edge to pray," I said.

"And this helped you?"

"Not at first, and this might sound odd," I told him, "but as I prayed, I kept thinking that I could see three men walking on the water out in front of me."

Rochín smiled. "Go on."

"And as I prayed," I said, "these three men seemed to come walking closer and closer toward me in the mist across the water, and this was when the world began to come alive and I could hear the trees sing to me, just like I'd heard the great redwoods sing to me when I was a boy."

Carlos Rochín was now laughing. "And all this, you don't see as miraculous?" he asked.

"Well, no, not at all. I see it as . . . well, I guess, kind of like a dream."

"Don Jan, you were awake, weren't you, when you were praying at the water's edge and these three men came toward you on the water?"

"Yes, I was awake."

"See, you weren't asleep, as you were in the hospital when the Three Holy Wisemen first came to you."

"That's true, but you see, Rochín, I was also in kind of a dreamlike state as I was praying by the water's edge. There's so much peace and silence here that sometimes it almost feels like I can be dreaming even while I'm awake."

"THERE! YOU DID! YOU JUST SAID IT!" cried Rochín excitedly. "This is exactly what happened to me when I first came up here alone! All that Eastern religious talk about meditation and yoga and how we can experience God. Not just believe in God, but experience the Holy Creator. And I tell you that it was up here with all this peace and silence that I, too, began to feel like I was no longer in my head and thinking all the time, but in my heart in a dreamlike state, and I was finally able to . . . to start experiencing

God and understanding how these Indians up here live and think. You see, Jan, we civilized people automatically marginalize any reality that starts to take us into the miraculous. We live in such a structured, busy world that we can never really stop thinking."

I nodded. "I can see what you mean, Rochín, but—"

"Jan," he cut me off, laughing, "there can be no 'buts' or safety nets to go into the world of miracles. Only 'ands' . . . so a person can then bridge these different realities that are within all of us, instead of eliminating these different possibilities before they can even take hold.

"Relax, my friend, relax; and I promise you that soon these Three Wisemen will be here at your fireside in full form, instructing you in earnest, just like they did with Our Lord Jesus," he said, making the sign of the cross over himself. "And only then will the passing Indians see you. Because at this point, you are as unreal to them . . . as these Three Wisemen are unreal to you."

I inhaled deeply. I was certainly beginning to feel overwhelmed with what Carlos Rochín was telling me. He was a Catholic priest, after all, and if I understood him correctly, he was telling me that walking on water like Jesus had done was common practice up here in this mountainous area of Mexico. This was extremely difficult for me to accept. I was a Christian minister.

I guess Rochín saw my perplexed expression, because he now burst out laughing.

"Jan," he said, "laugh! Remember it's laughter, big *carcajadas* from the gut, that allows us to enter into these other realities. Isn't it well documented that the Spanish explorer Francisco Vásquez de Coronado followed his Indian guides in search of the legendary Seven Cities of Gold, but he never found them? Well, I ask you, could it be that Francisco's Indian guides showed him the cities over and over again, but it was he who couldn't see them because he didn't have the training or background with which to see them? How come, over and over again, they'd be out in the middle of the desert in what is now your Southwestern United States and they wouldn't have any food or water, yet his guides would just go over the hill and come back with an abundance of food and water—and even enough for the Spanish explorer's horses. Laugh, my friend, laugh and see what joy will bring you!"

I breathed.

I shook my head, and I tried to get my body to loosen up so I could laugh, but I just couldn't do it. I was thinking too much. I was in my head and still needing to understand.

But then I flashed on the children's church that I'd seen in New Mexico when I'd been driving back from Montana on the old Harley-Davidson I'd bought in South Dakota, and all the energy in my body changed. On the wall at the entrance of the colorful little church there'd been a big mural of a laughing Jesus talking with a group of happy, smiling, laughing children.

I smiled, then began to laugh. Along with Jesus, I could now join in with Rochín's great booming laughter *de carcajadas!*

Oh, I loved this man! My God, if just one-tenth of what Carlos Rochín was telling me was true, it would change everything we knew, everything about reality and history and the future and . . . and . . . and especially me!

Carlos Rochín and his young nephew stayed with me for five days. We did a little fishing, and I played my guitar for them in the evenings. Then they left. Once they were gone, I immediately opened the letter from Emma. I read it several times. I couldn't believe it. Emma was mad at me and blamed me for our having lost our gold mine of a restaurant, and she added that she'd never meant for us to get pregnant and that she was angry with me for having misled her and taken advantage of her. Me, take advantage of her? My God!

That night it was Emma who came to me in my dreams. Not Van Housen. And once more I awoke in a sweat, seeing Chato and those boys. Now they were all hanging together—not in their cells, but on a hill, just like the hilltop on which Our Lord Jesus Christ had hung from a cross.

I got up and went down to the lake's edge and began to pray. The huge dark vastness of sky was full of magnificent stars. I felt frightened and confused, yet as I continued praying, little by little I began to hear the quiet sound of the tiny waves of the lake slapping up on the shore and the tall pine trees singing in the breeze, and I started feeling better. I went and got my guitar, and I began to play along with the music I was hearing from the water and the pines—and suddenly, without a shadow of a doubt, this was when I saw them.

Three men were walking toward me on the water. I stopped playing and they disappeared. I began to tremble. I just couldn't understand . . . or accept . . . what I was seeing. I started laughing. Really laughing from the gut in big *carcajadas*, and here they were once again. I began to play my guitar again, and once more the three Indians appeared and came walking toward me in the mist over the water. I was finally beginning to let go—not understand— and just accept.

I was finally beginning to see, to see, to accept that life really was meant to be happy and joyful and full of song and music! This was what had been going on back in Haight-Ashbury in San Francisco during the '60s, and this was what was happening with me now in the late '70s . . . crazy *loco* music and unbridled happiness.

And I could now see so clearly that you didn't have to be on drugs to experience a happy God, and you didn't need to relinquish your Christian beliefs and go into yoga and Eastern religions, either. No, all you had to do was be out in nature long enough and be quiet enough to let the whole world all about you come alive and begin to sing to you, AND AWAKEN YOUR VERY SOUL!

Life really, really was meant to be happy and joyful, and Our Lord Savior Jesus Christ hadn't died in sadness on the cross. No, He'd gone to the Father joyfully, and so had my boys, all of them, including Chato. YES, THIS WAS IT! I just hadn't been able to completely, totally, see it before! My beautiful boys hadn't died in vain or in sadness. No, they'd gone in joy, in ecstasy, following the Holy Light to the Father, to Our Lord God Holy Creator!

The tears streamed down my face, but I wasn't crying with sadness. My tears flowed with joy . . . with the deep understanding, for the first time in all my life, that living was a joy! I began to sing an old Joan Baez song, and I'd always had a pretty good voice, but even I could now hear that I was, indeed, singing like an angel. I remembered when Joan had taken me down to Carmel and I'd met Clint Eastwood, and I continued to sing and play, thanking God for all the people I'd ever met. We were all Angels. All of us. It was just that some of us didn't quite realize it yet.

I played my guitar and sang, and the breeze came up and joined me and we became a beautiful sweet symphony of sound. Then here came the Wisemen, closer and closer to the shore, and yet . . . they never reached the shore where I stood playing and singing. I was finally really beginning to comprehend. Of course, we could all walk on water, just as Our Lord Jesus Christ had done. All we had to do was accept Our Spirit of the Kingdom of God that was within each of us and realize that we were all Angels, and not look down. Not lose faith. And instead remain totally in union with the Spirit of Creation, which was Our Natural State of Being.

I continued playing, and the Three Indian Wisemen came closer and closer. Now I could see that they were the exact same men who'd come to me at the hospital, and this time I wasn't asleep and dreaming. I was wide-awake, and they were coming to me. I must have sung and played my guitar all night long, because the next thing I knew, sunlight was beginning to color the landscape across the lake. This was when I saw that there was a large gathering of Indians on an outcropping of rocks by the water's edge, and they were looking at me.

I smiled and continued playing, and they smiled, too, and continued listening. This was wonderful! The locals were finally acknowledging my existence. Several of the children came up close to me, and one little girl put flowers by my feet. It was one of the happiest moments of my entire life!

I'D ARRIVED!

I'D COME HOME!

AND THIS WAS PARADISE!

CHAPTER 8

Several days later the weather changed. It got freezing cold. Large, dark clouds rolled in, and it began to snow. At first it was wonderful. Every snowflake seemed like a gift from Heaven, and it was beautiful how everything became pure white overnight.

But then the snow didn't melt off, as I'd been told it would, and more snow came. And now the Indians began to pass by my tent in large numbers. I guessed they were going to their winter homes at the bottom of the canyon. Rochín had told me that the Tarahumara had summer homes up on the rim of the great canyon and winter homes down in the bottom, where it was tropical year-round.

I continued playing my guitar and singing along with the falling snow, and some of the Indian children would run up close to me. One boy actually came up and touched me, then screamed with joy. I laughed. This was wonderful. Then one day the last of the Indians passed by, and I was alone. But no, I was not going to panic. I had experienced a miracle! I had seen in my Dream World that my boys, my fantastic boys, had not died in vain, any more than Jesus Christ had died in vain.

The tears poured down my face. I'd been so mad at God, the Holy Creator, for having allowed this terrible thing to happen to my beautiful, young, innocent boys that I hadn't been able to see the miracle that was staring me right in the face until I'd come up here and seen in my dreams a whole brave new world, going from nightmares to beautiful dreams of Light and Love and Happiness!

Yes, oh yes, Chato and those boys hadn't died in vain! No, they'd died as brave, joyful souls, seeing the Light! They hadn't been lost, desperate souls anymore. They'd been Angels, who'd known that they'd completed their service on Earth, and it was time for them to return to the Father in all their glory, just as Jesus had done!

I continued to sing and play my guitar, and the snowflakes were so gentle and beautiful! The whole land was Alive with Music!

Rochín wasn't able to bring in my supplies that month. The snow was now three feet deep, and there was no way for anyone to come to the lake to see me. I began to eat less, trying to stretch out what little supplies I had left. And also I began to fish, but it was almost impossible for me to get around in the deep snow on my crutches.

Out of desperation I took a couple of boards off the platform of my tent, and I built myself a sleigh so I could lie down on it and pull myself through the snow. But it didn't work. I began to get frightened. I could see that I was beginning to lose the strength I'd developed in my first few months at the lake. The human body just couldn't function when it didn't have enough food to fuel it.

But still, I didn't panic. I'd experienced a full-fledged miracle, and MY BOYS HADN'T DIED IN VAIN! No, they'd endured the tortures of their tormenters with love and dignity, and they'd gone from this life straight into the Eternal Light of Our Lord Jesus Christ. And I could now clearly see that Jesus had not come to Earth to die for our sins. No, He'd come to show us how to live with such love and confidence and joy that we could even forgive those who crucify us!

I couldn't stop crying.

I could now see that all my life I'd been a blind Doubting Thomas. A lost soul. And I still was when the going got tough. Couldn't I now see the miraculous world all around me? Eh, couldn't I see that I wasn't going to die? Not unless I gave up. And no, I wouldn't give up and die.

No, I had to live so I could go back to Zacatecas and find the mother of the boy who'd felt so devastated and say to her, "*Señora*, I want you to know that your son didn't die in vain. He wasn't a lost soul on drugs anymore. No, *señora*, he'd accepted the word of Jesus. And so just as Our Lord Jesus died a glorious death, so did your son, *señora*, following the Holy Light of Our Lord Jesus straight up in the Heavens of Our Almighty Creator, where your son now lives at the side of God as another true son!"

All this I would tell her with complete confidence, for I no longer lived in fear and doubt and confusion with the Spirit World. And so I could once more, in full conscience, bring people to Jesus Christ and not feel like a hypocrite.

I laughed.

I laughed with CRAZYLOCO CARCAJADAS!

It was as if every day as I grew stronger and stronger of Spirit, I was getting weaker and weaker of body.

I laughed some more. This made no sense. Now that I could finally do God's Holy Work at full capacity, I was to die. This was so funny! So hilarious! Was this a joke, or a lesson for me to learn that we do not live just of our body? We also live of Spirit. I continued laughing the laughter of a CRAZYLOCO INSANE PERSON! And this was when I found myself sitting at the biggest and the most delicious-looking feast of food imaginable. Jesus was at the head of the table, and all my boys were seated at his side.

"THANK YOU, LORD GOD!" I yelled, still laughing as I saw and smelled the giant ham and turkey and mountain of yams, potatoes, and steaming hot vegetables and a platter of *enchiladas* and *tamales* and four huge pumpkin pies, my favorite! "Thank You!

123

Thank You! Thank You! Thank You! THANK YOU! THANK YOU!" I sang as I began to lose consciousness and disappear. My body was going. It was dying, but I still didn't feel scared or lost. No, I felt happy! VERY, VERY, VERY HAPPY!

This was when I suddenly heard the mighty scream of a mountain lion, just as I passed out. The next thing I knew there were two enormous bright yellow eyes directly in front of me. No more than a few inches away. I could smell and feel the beast's hot breath. The lioness smelled of wildflowers.

"Hello," I said to the lioness. I didn't know if I was dead or alive, but I didn't care. I was happy. "Long time no see, *amiga.*"

The lioness turned, opened up her mouth, and reached down, grabbing hold of what looked like a freshly killed deer and dragging it up on the platform of my tent.

"Is . . . is this for me?" I asked.

She didn't answer me. She just pulled the deer up closer to me; then I . . . I understood. This was probably all a dream, so I was most likely not dead and was still alive and dreaming that this huge, magnificent mountain lion had brought me a deer, just as a house cat brings a mouse to the person it loves.

A love for this lioness came bursting up inside me with so much power that I was suddenly full of energy. I thanked and thanked the mountain lion; and she made a low, friendly, growling sound and began to purr. Then she walked over to my smaller tent where I kept my tools and went inside just as if she were a human being.

"Welcome, *mi amor,*" I said to her, "and stay as long as you like."

I built a fire and warmed my freezing hands. I was half-delirious, but still I had the presence of mind to pull myself together long enough to skin out the animal and cook up some long, thin strips of venison. They smelled delicious. I wanted to eat them all, but I quickly found out I could only eat one little strip. My stomach had shrunk that much.

The days passed and the dream continued . . . and the lioness hung out with me all day and we'd talk together, and then she'd go off in the late evenings to hunt.

The dream continued . . . and I cut young tree branches, and with the skin of the deer, I was able to make snowshoes for myself. I didn't weigh very much anymore. I was probably well below even my lean, muscular high-school weight of about 165. I no longer used my crutches by putting them under my armpits. Instead, I began to use them as walking sticks . . . and the dream continued.

At first I could only go about 50 feet with the snowshoes before I collapsed. But soon I was able to go about half a mile, and then a full mile in the deep snow.

Then one evening I was coming in from a long walk around the lake, and I could smell a fire burning at my camp and something being cooked with a lot of spices. It smelled wonderful. Instantly, I was very happy. I assumed it was Rochín and that somehow he and his nephew had made it through the snow. Then I don't know why, but I suddenly knew without a shadow of a doubt that it was my mountain lioness that lived with me in the smaller tent, and she had started the fire and was cooking dinner for the two of us.

I started laughing. Even in a continuous dream this was ridiculous! Lions ate their meat raw, so why would my lioness go to the trouble of building a fire and cooking her latest kill for us?

Then coming around the last group of pines and rocks, I saw that two men were sitting at my campfire, and they weren't Carlos Rochín and his nephew Pablo.

I approached with caution, but then I suddenly realized that these were two of the Three Wisemen *Curanderos* whom I'd seen walking on the water and who had come to me at the hospital. I smiled. Hadn't Rochín told me this would happen, that one day they'd come in full form to my campfire? I laughed again. But where was the Third Wiseman?

"Hello," I said to the Two Wisemen in Spanish as I came walking in. But they didn't answer me in Spanish. They spoke to me in their Indian dialect . . . yet I was able to understand what they said.

They gestured for me to sit down with them; and the tall, slender one handed me a bowl of the venison stew they'd made. It smelled fantastic, and I began to eat. It was at this point that my lioness came out of her tent, and as she approached us, she took on a human form. It was Miguel. Sure, of course, this made perfect sense, because then it had also been Miguel who'd been the lioness who'd led me through the snowstorm back in Los Gatos.

I nodded greetings to Miguel, and he nodded greetings to me; and he took a bowl of stew and began to eat, too. Not one word was spoken as we ate.

"Miguel," I said, after we'd eaten, "I only have one question. Since you are a male human, why do you become a female lioness, not a male lion?"

He grinned. "You tell me," he replied. "This is your dream, *amigo.*"

"My dream?"

"Sure, it has always been your dream."

I nodded. What else could I do, go crazy*loco?* Because even for a dream, this was really so far-out that I had no idea what to ask or say anymore.

Witnessing my silence, all three of the Holy Wisemen *Curanderos* burst out laughing like there was no tomorrow! They laughed so hard and with such joy that the trees and rocks began laughing, too. I joined them, LAUGHING WITH WILD, CRAZY*LOCO* CARCAJADAS, and it felt so good! And I could now see that it was definitely a good thing that Carlos Rochín had taken the time to instruct me on the Spirit World or surely I would have gone insane with what was happening.

The days passed and my dream consciousness continued . . . and every night the Three Holy Wisemen Healers would come and cook dinner and give me counsel. I guess it was now safe to say that I was, at last, living in the actual Dream Reality of the Miraculous. And many times, we'd just sit in silence by the campfire and watch the flames leaping and dancing and little sparkles flying off into the darkness of the night. Little by little, I began to understand that I was receiving my most important information when we were silent.

The weeks passed, becoming months, and the dream continued . . . and I began to understand that we human beings had been building campfires and sitting around these fires and watching the flames leap and dance and little sparks fly off into the darkness for untold hundreds of thousands of years—and not just on this planet, but on all of our other sister planets, too. And all this knowledge—all these conversations of ancient wisdom that people had been sharing around campfires since Mother Earth was young and the Stars spoke and People knew how to listen—was here, right now, in these dancing, leaping little flames and the tiny sparks that flew off our fire into the darkness.

Sure, of course, for untold Timeless Time, human beings had been sitting around campfires watching the dancing, leaping flames and sending their Ancient Sacred Knowledge across the ages with the tiny sparks that flew off their campfires. And this level of communication, I now understood, was what I'd felt as a little kid when my brother Leon and I would build a fire together up at our open meadow above our home and we'd sit around the fire, saying nothing.

And now that I'd had enough life experiences to realize this, I could see that my brother had loved me. He really had, and he and I had been communicating with all of our ancestry, past and future, in a most profound and natural way . . . yet neither one of us had the knowledge at the time to put into words any of what we were feeling as we watched the burning fire in an almost hypnotic trance, until finally it burned down to nothing but glowing coals. Hard coals. Having come from hardwood that had taken a long time in growing, I could now see and feel that my brother, Leon, and I had actually begun to breathe in unison as we'd look down at those glowing coals; and they'd been our window into the universe, but we just hadn't known how to say it.

Tears came to my eyes. Truly, this was when my brother and I had been at our closest. Heart to heart in silence. Because the moment we started speaking was when everything always seemed to get lost.

Then it hit me between the eyes! It was *words,* I could now see, that didn't allow us "civilized people" to be anchored in the miraculous! Yes, yes, yes! I could now see so clearly that words were limiting! That they actually destroyed the magic, the possibility of something being miraculous!

I wiped the tears from my eyes, and from the depths of my heart and soul, I could now see that when we human beings quit all words and just sat around a campfire in silence, we were then still open to communicating across the ages of Timeless Time with all of our ancestry, past and future. Yes, in Our Collective Dreaming, we humans were INFINITE! ETERNAL! AND WONDERFUL! For we were part of Creation! Part of God's personal campfire, and just like moths, we, too, were drawn to light, because we were of the Light! All of us! No exception!

So Rochín had been right when he'd said it wasn't that we were predestined. It was that we each had a story. And realizing this, I now also began to remember what my fellow Indian firefighter up in Montana had told me—that from the Creator's point of view all of Creation was . . . People. That there was a Nation of People Rocks, a Nation of People Trees, a Nation of People Water, a Nation of People Air . . . and People Clouds . . . and People Snow. Everything was a Nation of People, once we people began to see through the Holy Eyes of the Almighty.

I now understood that the Three Large Butterflies who had come to me that day in the garden outside the hospital had, indeed, been People. They'd been my Three Healers, because there was also a Nation of People Butterflies. And the giant redwoods who'd sung to me when I'd been a child had been a Nation of People Redwoods. I began to see my whole life so differently. Everyone and Everything was a Nation of People People and were all Holy, Holy, Holy, Holy, Holy, Holy, Holy, Holy, Holy, Holy, Holy, Holy, Holy, and Sacred and Equal in the Eyes of God.

"Thank You, God," I said. "Thank You, thank You, thank You, thank You, thank You, thank You, thank You, thank You, thank You, thank You, thank You, thank You, thank You!"

The dream continued . . . and then one evening after weeks of counsel, the Three Wisemen asked me to stand up, and they came around the campfire and presented me with the shaft of lion claws and eagle feathers—the same shaft they had first offered me in a dream at the hospital.

I was speechless. And . . . this time when I reached out to take the shaft, I didn't wake up and find myself with outstretched empty hands. No, this time my two hands took a firm grip on a shaft of solid hardwood, which was beautifully decorated with beads and feathers and claws.

Then they told me that they were now officially inviting me to become a *mayori*. But Rochín had told me that no white person had ever been invited to learn the Sacred Teaching of a *mayori*.

"Are you sure?" I asked. All three nodded. "Okay, then I accept," I said, and moved to bring the shaft to my heart, but it disappeared.

The Three Wisemen burst out laughing with *carcajadas,* and the shortest one explained to me that this didn't just happen overnight, that it would take 12 years of instruction, just as it had taken Our Lord Jesus. So yes, I could sleep with the shaft for three nights to begin my apprenticeship, but then I wouldn't get to keep the shaft until I completed my learning.

I couldn't believe it. Suddenly the shaft was in my hands once again, so I, too, began laughing with *carcajadas*. What else could I do? Start thinking and analyzing and destroy this wonderful Dream World in which I now lived? The four of us laughed until the trees all around us were laughing, too; then the rocks joined us. I'd never laughed so hard in all my life!

That night I slept with the shaft of lion claws and eagle feathers under the covers with me. It was all still so new for me, to be living in this Dream Reality of the Miraculous, that I had to keep touching and stroking the shaft to make sure my dreaming was real.

The dream continued . . . and the weeks passed, and every day I could walk a little farther and a little farther in the snow with my snowshoes around the lake. The Dream Reality of the Spirit World became stronger and stronger and more real to me. It was shortly after this that I decided I was well enough to hike into town to get some salt, peppers, and a few other supplies.

Coming into Creel, I must have looked quite a sight, because seeing me, a beautiful slender young Indian girl screeched with laughter and raced up the street shouting, "¡EL GRINGO! ¡EL GRIN-GO!"

People came out of their homes and stared at me. My beard was huge, and I was covered with snow. I was no longer on crutches. I was walking with a stout tree branch. The snow wasn't as deep in Creel, so I had my snowshoes tied on my back. I must have looked like a mountain man coming out of the wilds of Alaska.

Coco met me at the door of his restaurant. He had a letter for me from Father Rochín. He invited me to please come into his private quarters and bathe, and added that he would personally trim my hair and beard. People gathered just to have a look at me. Coco wanted to know if it was true that I lived with a mountain lion and the lion had killed a deer and brought it to me when I was almost dying of starvation.

"But how do you know all this?" I asked.

"Everyone knows," he said. "*Los* Three *Espiritos* who have been visiting with you have told everyone in the region."

"You, too, know about the Three Spirit Wisemen?"

"Of course, how else do you think we manage to survive and prosper in such an isolated, desolate place? *Los* Three *Espiritos* advise us in our sleep every night, and they have told us that you won their hearts when you began to serenade the Holy Night.

They say you have the voice of an Angel, and that you sing to the rocks and the trees and the lake and the stars. That even the very Earth Herself loves you and purrs along with you when you sing. And it is said that they have invited you to become a *mayori*. What an honor!

"Come, it is with great respect that I invite you to bathe, and then I will personally trim your hair and beard. We can't have our visiting *gringo* Holy Man looking wild. Father Rochín was right. He told us all about you before he left, and about the children's camp that you two are going to build. But don't worry. No one has told anything to the mean old German who has the evil eye and whose blood runs backward from his heart."

Coco's private quarters were behind his restaurant, and they were all pink and turquoise. He was very, very happy to help me undress and get me into the tub of hot water. Oh, it was Heaven! I'd forgotten about the luxuries of civilization! Hot water, oh my God, hot water! What a Miracle!

CHAPTER 9

It was another month before Carlos Rochín was finally able to make it out to the lake and bring me my supplies.

"Well, well," he said with a great big smile, "so this time I don't even have to ask you if you've had any unusual or miraculous experiences, eh?"

"No, you don't," I said right back at him, with an equally big smile.

"So in town they tell me that a mountain lion brought you a deer to eat when you were starving and that the Three Wisemen of the Bible came to you and gave you instruction when you were losing your mind."

"That's not all," I told him. "The best thing is that the Indians now see me, and little kids run up to me and give me flowers and touch me, then shout with joy."

"That's beautiful!" Father Rochín said. "I knew you had it in you! I knew you weren't just another do-gooder *gringo* all wrapped up in your head, thinking you were going to save the world. You did it, *amigo!* You really did it! Now you can begin to see that it is your own life that you must save."

"My life?"

"Sure, can't you now begin to see that you could not have ever really made a difference in the world until you saw that *you* were the problem, *you* were the one out of whack, not just the world?"

I nodded. "Yes, I think I'm beginning to finally see that, Rochín."

"Good, because the life you've known up to now has been . . . well, how can I best say it? Shallow. Empty. Limited and full of blaming—even blaming God," he added with laughter. "Am I right, or am I right? Eh, *amigo?*"

"You're absolutely right, Rochín. And now all that blaming is gone. Those boys who were killed in Juárez and the others who were hung in their cells in Zacatecas no longer come to me in fear and pain," I said, wiping the tears that sprang to my eyes. "Now they come to me in joy. In the full Glory of God, and I can now also see so clearly that we all, all, all live in the glory of God once we open up the eyes of our hearts completely."

"YES!" shouted Rochín, bursting with *carcajadas.* "YOU ARE NOW THE RICHEST HUMAN BEING ON EARTH! This is why I left my family's wealth! I saw it all in a vision right here, at this exact same place on the lake. This is a Holy Place! Oh, give me an *ABRAZO, AMIGO MÍO!* We're a team! We are glorious in the Holy Light of Jesus Christ, Our Savior!"

"I totally agree," I said, "but you know, Rochín, I now can also see that Jesus didn't come down to Earth to save us from sin. He came to inspire us to reach for the stars, no matter what type of adversity we encounter. So he's not our Savior, but our Inspirer."

"But wasn't it our sin that we lost sight of the Holy Light?"

Now I was the one who BURST OUT LAUGHING WITH *CARCAJADAS!* "Oh, you Catholics!" I exclaimed. "You just can't get beyond your sins and guilt trips! Come on, loosen up, Rochín, and just laugh from here in the gut. Remember, it's laughter that's the key! Not sins and guilt and all that head stuff!"

He laughed and I laughed, and it was beautiful. Laughing together with big belly laughs of *carcajadas,* from the gut OF CREATION! Even the waters of the lake began making laughing happy sounds, too.

Rochín and I stayed up most of that first night, we were so happy to see each other and had so much catching up to do. He told me that the halfway houses were still going, but having a hard time because the restaurant had folded and the houses had become accustomed to the extra monies they received from it. Jorge and Silveria sent their best and looked forward to seeing me again, but Emma was now a very angry woman, even though she'd given birth to a beautiful child whom I felt for sure was a girl.

"Is it a boy or a girl?" I asked.

"I'm sorry, but I don't know," Rochín told me.

"That's okay, don't be sorry," I said, with my whole heart filling up with longing for Emma and my child. "We need to have faith that this, too, will come to pass, and Emma will start feeling happy again."

But I saw the expression on the priest's face. There was something that he wasn't telling me. "What is it, Rochín?" I asked.

"I don't quite know how to say it, Jan, but Emma is no longer the woman you married. She seems—I hate to say it—almost possessed, and she blames you for everything that has gone wrong in her life. You two were doing so well. You were the toast of Chihuahua. Even the president of Mexico knew of the two of you. You two were rubbing elbows with the rich and famous of Mexico, and then—boom—it all disappeared, and she blames you."

I nodded. "Yes, I've been there, too, and I was blaming God."

"That's kind of it," replied Rochín. "She thought, I guess, that you had been touched by the Almighty, so nothing could go wrong."

I laughed. "That's what I'd thought, too. Now I can understand why she came on to me so strong even from the start. I guess we really do see only what we want to see or are able to see."

"Like the natives of the Caribbean not being able to see Columbus's three ships, and then later seeing Cortés and his men as gods when they saw them mounted on their horses."

"You know, I'm glad you brought this up, because in the middle of my delirium when I didn't know if I was dead or alive, I had all these crazy thoughts. I mean, well . . ."

"Go on."

"Well, I think that maybe those natives of the Caribbean really did see those ships, and it was only that they didn't know what they were. I mean, the deer and the birds I'm sure saw those ships, so why wouldn't the natives?"

"Jan, do deer and birds and other animals ever really see ships?"

"Sure, of course. Birds even land on their masts and live on them when they're anchored in a bay or a harbor."

"Okay, I agree with this, but are they ships that they land on, or just floating piles of wood?"

"Oh, I see what you mean," I said. "I guess just piles of wood."

"So maybe that's the difference. You told me that the Indians didn't even acknowledge your presence when you first came up here and you'd wave to them. So maybe they saw something, but they didn't see you, and certainly not as a human being. Maybe what they saw was just another rock, or a bush waving in the breeze."

I took in several deep breaths. Once more Rochín was presenting me with something that I'd have to think very hard about. Or more precisely, dream about and see what came to me, because truly, I was beginning to feel that when we were awake was when we were dreaming. And when we were asleep and dreaming was when we were awake and finally truly Living in the Center of Reality.

We called it a night and went to bed, and the next day Rochín and I began to physically lay out the plans for the kids' camp. Rochín had gotten the backing of his *familia* in Chihuahua City, and he was ready to start ordering lumber from the mill and sending up the rest of our supplies by train with his nephew Pablo. The two bridges that had been out for months were now almost ready for use again.

Then as we were driving to the mill, he once more warned me that we had to be very careful of Van Housen, because the priest had strong connections at the mill.

"So, Jan," my friend said, "we'll have to inspect every piece of lumber to be sure they don't give us inferior material. I've heard that Van Housen wishes that he'd come up with this idea of a children's camp, so knowing him as I do, I'm sure that he wishes us to fail so he can then take over."

I didn't know if Rochín was being paranoid or not. But it turned out he was right, because we had inspected the lumber thoroughly at the mill, but then the board feet that they delivered was not of the same quality. And when we went back to the mill for the second time, the Jesuit priest was waiting for us outside with his newish black pickup.

"So," he said, cutting in front of Rochín and coming face-to-face with me, "what have we here, another catastrophe that this little man brought upon himself, and then he tries to blame the mill?"

"Excuse me," I said, "but what business is this of yours? Is this your mill? And about Father Rochín, he's my friend and my boss, so speak to *him,* and do so with respect, or I suggest you get out of our way!"

He was shocked and stared at me in utter surprise, then turned on his heel and left in a big rush.

"Thank you," Rochín said to me, "but . . . I really think this will not be the end of it, *amigo.*"

A few days later the first of the Tarahumara began returning to their summer homes up on the rim of the canyon. They brought me fruit and vegetables and sacks of corn. Then one evening I saw a caravan of trucks. It was the work crew for the Rod Steiger movie.

This meant that the bridges had been repaired, so I decided to go down to Chihuahua City to see Emma and my newborn child.

I was gone for a week, and things went well between Emma and me for the first night. Then I have no idea what happened, but things turned awful. She was so full of hate that I had no idea what to say. Just like Catalina, she blamed me for everything. I suggested that we pray together. We had a beautiful boy, I pointed out, and they could both come and live with me in the mountains so we could be a family. She went berserk, yelling at me to get out of her life, saying that she'd die before she would live like a backward, stupid Indian *sin razón* up in the desolate mountains.

I came back to Creel feeling pretty well beaten up and disillusioned about my ability to ever get along with any woman. My God, for me, women were even harder to figure out than the Spirit World.

Then the dream continued, with another miracle just as I was getting off the train at Creel. In front of me stood the same beautiful young Indian girl who'd seen me come into town all covered with snow. Once more she shouted with joy to the Heavens!

"¡EL GRINGO! ¡EL GRINGO!"

And she turned, racing up the street as agile as a deer, and people came out of their homes to look at me. I went to Coco's restaurant and saw that the young girl was in the kitchen, helping the woman who was cooking. I guessed the lady was her mother, but she didn't look all Indian, like her daughter. Coco was so happy to see me that he gave me a big hug and a kiss right on the lips. It was disgusting, and I wiped the kiss off my lips. He laughed and asked me if I'd like to bathe in his private quarters once again.

I said, "No, thanks," and saw that the girl and her mother were laughing with *carcajadas,* truly enjoying my predicament.

"But you loved the hot tub that I prepared for you last time," insisted Coco, stroking my long hair. "And I can also trim your beautiful hair and your beard once again."

"No, thank you!" I said once more. The last time he'd gotten just a little too intimate with me for my tastes.

"Okay," he said, looking disappointed. "But you will have a whole chicken like last time, eh?" he added with a big smile.

"Yes," I said. "I'm starving."

"Good. We have the most delicious wild chicken in all of Mexico! Come, I don't believe you've met my cook, Soco, and her daughter Mireya." He turned toward the kitchen. "Please, come out and meet my friend Jan."

The cook, Soco, came out, drying her hands on her apron, and her daughter trailed behind her. But then as Coco was introducing them to me, the young girl—who could be no more than 13 years old—did the most astonishing thing. She flew past her mother and Coco and leaped up on me, wrapping her dark brown, long legs about my middle and her arms about my neck, and she began kissing me in a frenzy all over the face.

I didn't know what to do, and I could see that her mother and Coco were as shocked as I was. They didn't know what to do either. And she was strong, and her legs were squeezing the air out of me and caused a loud fart to explode. They all burst out laughing, and it was her mother and Coco who finally got the young girl off of me. But the smile on her face, they couldn't remove. This was when I saw that Coco was now looking at me as if he, too, was going to jump on me.

"Oh no," I said. "Don't you dare!"

"Why not?" he said with a very suggestive smile. "I only wish I'd thought of that first. We're all in love with you, you know."

"Look," I said, "I'm hungry and just want to eat, so please no more of this."

"He's right," Soco told her daughter Mireya. "You can't be doing that! Leave the man alone!"

But there was something in the way this young girl kept looking at me that told me she'd made up her mind and there was nothing on Earth or in Heaven that was going to hold her back from leaping on me once again. But . . . she did keep her distance while her mother cooked and Coco served me. The young girl sat down at a table across the room and began doing her homework. But now and then our eyes would meet as I ate, and she'd smile that huge smile of hers. Nothing like this had ever happened to me. Not with Emma, and not with the girls who'd tried to de-virginize me in San Francisco. No, this was as pure a love as I'd had when I'd been a boy and my dog would run and jump up to me, giving me so much *amor!*

I ate a whole chicken and we visited for hours, and it was so beautiful and friendly and open. Then when I got up to go, here came Mireya again, and she leaped on me, once more squeezing me with her legs about my middle and wrapping me up with her arms and kissing me in another frenzy.

This time Coco went berserk, yelling at her mother to get her wild child away from me. But Soco didn't have to force her daughter off of me. Mireya let go of me on her own, stood up tall, and stared at me in the eyes without blinking. She was telling me volumes without speaking a single word.

Going out to the lake that night, I had the strangest feeling, as if all my life I'd known that something like this was going to happen to me. Like it was written in the stars long ago. Like our life here on Earth was already a long-forgotten memory in the farthest reaches of the universe. Never had I ever dreamed of such a wild, confident *amor.* But Mireya was only a child. A mere child. But still, that night it was this young Indian girl's laughing face that came to me, and I didn't wake up in a sweat, as I had when Van Housen's laughing face came to me in my sleep.

No, I was in that delicious place halfway between awake and asleep when her laughing face appeared, and she was so happy that I was happy, too. This young girl had touched my very soul! Not just my heart. And I had no idea where this was going to go, and I didn't care. Her eyes, her large laughing teeth, her strength and agility—oh, she was just like a wild young deer. I found myself laughing even as I slept.

This had never, never, ever happened to me in all my life!

In the morning I awoke with an energy and happiness I hadn't felt since I was a teenager. Oh, this young Indian girl truly had a

very powerful spirit soul! She'd taken over my dream consciousness with as much power as my Three Indian *Curanderos!* All
morning I couldn't stop whistling, I felt so happy!

BOOK THREE

MORE SOUL TALK

CHAPTER 10

Mireya

What can I say? I was in love with Jan before I ever saw him, so how could I have behaved any differently when he came in to eat at our restaurant? I leaped on him, of course, and wrapped my legs about him and squeezed him so hard that he began to fart. But I didn't care and just kept kissing him all I could. And I'd never kissed a man before who wasn't a relative, so I hadn't been prepared for the feelings that came over me as I kissed him. I became light-headed and so happy and wild-feeling that I couldn't stop until my mother and Coco pulled me off of him. I couldn't stop smiling after that, no matter how much I tried. It was like my whole heart had leaped up to live in my face. I felt such joy!

Oh, I just wanted to kiss him again and again and get that feeling of being light-headed. So when he was done eating and ready to go, I flew past everyone who was telling him good-bye and leaped on him again, squeezing him with my legs even more than before, but this time he didn't fart. His face turned white, I guess because of the whole chicken he'd eaten. I stopped kissing him and let go of him on my own this time so he wouldn't vomit, but I knew I'd marked my territory and he now belonged to me, the same as a young female deer urinating to leave her scent on the trail for the buck deer to go crazy and follow her.

But then as soon as my *gringo* was gone, my mother and Coco began yelling at me, telling me how terribly I'd behaved and if he never came back to our restaurant, I was to blame. But they couldn't fool me any more than the rabbit can fool the fox. I knew what was really going on, and I knew exactly what I had done. Both Coco and my mother were also in love with my *gringo,* just like the two fine *señoritas* at the bank who wore such beautiful clothes and had such well-defined behinds and big *tetas*. So for me, a skinny, uneducated girl, to have any chance of getting this *gringo,* who was already mine according to the stars, I had to show him a love so strong and real and full of wild passion that no man in his right heart could turn it down.

And also, this seed that Coco and my mother had so cleverly tried to plant in my head, telling me that if he never returned to our restaurant, it would be my fault . . . I would not give it the water or manure that it needed to grow. No, I immediately yanked this seed out of the fertile soil of my mind and threw it out, because I had never seen eyes so beautiful as his when he was eating his chicken. They'd danced with the joy of eating. And the way his lips moved and how he sucked the juice off his fingertips . . . was heaven for me to watch, because this is how he would also suck and lick and enjoy my strong, good body.

I hadn't been able to do my homework while he was eating. Even the words on the page danced. And then when he'd glanced my way and our eyes would touch from across the room, I just knew that I'd done the right thing. HE WAS MINE! THE STARS DON'T LIE! And that night when I went to bed, I prayed for *Papito Dios* to help me, because I knew in my Heart and Soul that I was in love and not acting foolish, as my mother and Coco tried to convince me.

"Please help me, dear God," I prayed as I lay naked in bed. "For I really don't know where it came from, but when I first saw him come into our restaurant and get so close that I could smell him, my whole body just EXPLODED, and I leaped on him before I even knew it! God, You know very well that there was nothing I could have done to stop myself from wrapping my legs around his middle and taking his face in my hands and kissing him a thousand times as fast as I could, for wild passion is normal to us young girls. And it felt so good and was so much fun that I just knew it was the right thing to do. Just like the sun knows what to do each morning when it comes up, bringing light to the world, my whole body knew that it was right for me to leap on him.

"And the beautiful feeling of his body between my legs as I squeezed and kissed him, wanting to eat him all up, was Heaven, dear God. Then that fart! Oh, it was a big one, God, and smelly, too, but I didn't care, so I just kept squeezing and kissing him as fast as I could.

"So, dear God, please help me so that no one can plant seeds in my head that I did anything wrong, because You and I both know that the heart never lies. How can it, since it is the heart that pumps Your Holy Lifeblood all through our body? My grandmother always told me that bad, confusing thoughts can only grow into plants or trees when the heart is forgotten and we allow our blood to run backward from the head to the heart. And You know that the seeds of my love for this *gringo,* a man I was in love with before I'd ever seen him, came with honor straight from my *corazón.*

"He is kind, they say. He is handsome and strong; but most important of all, he has a noble heart, meaning that just like a mother bird or deer, he is willing to give his life for his family. And I know how important this is, because I saw what happened to my beloved grandparents when our cousin Ortega with the evil eye came up from the lowlands and stole their ranch from them. God, You very well know that a girl has to be smart and know how to choose the right man for herself, and then also know how to attract him and get him to come chasing after her. Many a *burra* I have seen give her scent to the wind in just the right manner so that the male *burro* will smell of her even from far away and come screaming and screeching and running to mount her.

"Well, dear God, my *gringo* now has my scent all over him from between my legs around his middle, and my kisses all over his face and mouth and neck. So there is no way that he is not going to dream about me, because I have marked him as mine, just as much as any rancher branding his cattle with a red-hot iron. And my hot iron was my whole body, glued to him with such wild passion, as if there was no tomorrow.

"Oh, I am so happy, dear God!

"So very, very, very, very, very, very, very, very happy! No seeds of doubt or confusion are going to grow in my head! You sent him to me, dear God, and I love him; and he is mine, and that is that! GOOD NIGHT, *PAPITO DIOS!*"

CHAPTER 11

Jan

Business was booming! All spring Rochín and Pablo and I worked on building the kids' camp, and across the lake the film crew worked on the set for the Rod Steiger movie. They were building a hunting lodge and cabins for the movie while Rochín and Pablo and I worked on our outhouses and huge kitchen facilities. Both of our organizations hired local people and purchased local supplies, and the little town of Creel flourished.

The tiny one-room bank branch expanded, and one day I went in to get a loan so we could buy an old red Ford pickup truck I'd found. The two young women who worked at the bank were thrilled to see me. We visited, and they invited me to lunch. I told them yes, that would be fine, and we went up the street to eat at Coco's restaurant.

The three of us had just come in the front door and were preparing to sit down, when that young girl, whose name I now knew was Mireya, came racing into the restaurant and leaped on me, wrapping her legs about my middle once again, and took my face in her powerful hands and began kissing me in a frenzy of joy!

I was shocked. I thought she'd be at school. I hadn't realized that she came to the restaurant for lunch each day. And the two young women who were with me, Carmen and Sofía, weren't just shocked, but *flabbergasted*.

"Okay, okay," I said, trying to pry her off of me. "Please get down! Please get down, and let me go!"

Smiling that great big smile of hers, Mireya finally released me and got down.

"What is it?" I asked her. "Do you see me as a father figure? Is that why you jump on me and hug me?"

"Oh no," she said, smiling that endless smile of hers as she glanced at Carmen and Sofía. "I see you as the man I want to marry, so we can make love and have children."

I turned red. I was sorry I'd asked. Coco laughed with *carcajadas!*

"See," he said, "you never ask a child a direct question like that, Don Jan, because you will get a direct answer!"

I glanced at Carmen and Sofía, then turned back to Mireya. "Look," I told her, "you don't know me, and you're a child. These are the feelings you should be having for a boy your own age."

"But I *do* know you, Don Jan," she said, looking me directly in the eyes without flinching, or caring that there were others in the room. "Your eyes carry no evil. Your heart is warm and noble. Even the rocks and the trees sing of their *amor* for you. You are a good *hombre* who would never abandon his wife or his children." Tears came to her eyes. "And how old is the wild bird before she starts gathering grass and sticks to build her nest? And how old is the female deer before she starts urinating on the trail to attract the male buck she wants to mount her?"

I'm sure my whole face and the faces of Carmen and Sofía were now all burning red. And Coco, he was going crazy*loco* with *carcajadas*. I'd certainly been a fool to even try to give advice to Mireya. This child, this young girl, just didn't know how to be anything but direct and open and completely real. So the question was, was I (and the world) ready for such real, honest, naked love?

When Rod Steiger the movie star arrived aboard the train for the filming, the whole town of Creel showed up to meet him at the station. By now we all knew what the movie was about. It was the story of a young American boy who'd gone to Canada to dodge the military draft so he wouldn't have to go to Vietnam. And unbeknownst to the young boy, the place where he chose to hide out was the hunting lodge of an ex-colonel from the United States Army.

The company of stars and camera and wardrobe people looked like a circus from another planet as they got off the train. A couple members of the crew were black, and I guess the Tarahumara had never seen a black person, because I heard them say that they never knew that white people could be so dark. It took all afternoon for the film crew to unload their equipment and get it on the trucks so they could take it out to their site on the lake.

How Coco did it, I'll never know, but he not only got Rod Steiger, the great star, to go to his restaurant to eat, but he also got him into his private quarters so he could bathe him and trim his hair.

That evening when the famous man sat down to eat, he spotted me and asked me what I, a white guy like himself, was doing out in such a desolate place. I told him I was a Christian minister, and I was helping build a children's camp out by the lake.

"So in other words," he said, with a drink in hand and a mouth full of food, "you've come out here to brainwash these beautiful people into our uptight, racist, civilized ways, eh?"

I could see he was hot to trot, so I tried to tell him that this wasn't true—that I wasn't a Bible-carrying minister, and I didn't try to impose my beliefs on people.

"Hogwash!" he barked. "I've been on location all over the world! And I always come across you tight-ass ministers ruining the local people! When are you people going to admit that

Christianity has done more harm than good throughout the world? If I had my way," he shouted, "I'd run all you do-gooder Christians out of wherever you're doing any missionary work!"

I liked him. You knew exactly where he stood. I started laughing.

"What's so funny?" he bellowed with his great actor's voice.

"What you just said, because this is exactly what the Tarahumara do. They take a bullwhip to any minister or priest who tries to preach to them, and they run them out of their church."

"Really? The local natives do that?"

"Absolutely! They allow a minister or priest to read from the Bible, which they consider Holy even though they can't read, but not one single word of interpretation. In fact, the local Tarahumara gave the first few priests to their neighbors the Xixime, who are cannibals, so they could eat them. They'd thought the priests were also cannibals, because they'd spoken of taking of the flesh of the body of Christ at their services."

Rod Steiger burst out laughing. "I love it!" he shouted with great excitement. "Tell me more! I just love it when indigenous people defend their beliefs and way of life!"

He became all ears, and we talked into the wee hours of the morning; and I drank water and tea, and he drank *tequila* and beer. I told him that during Holy Week the Tarahumara give as much honor and respect to Judas as they do to Jesus, and that everything the white man gives them, they take, and move around to fit in with their own beliefs and spirituality.

"The Tarahumara have become my teachers," I said. Then I explained to him that if it had not had been for my working with Father Rochín for two years in setting up halfway houses in Chihuahua City, I would have never been able to accept the Three Indian *Curanderos* who'd come to me at the hospital when the doctors had told me that I'd be in a wheelchair for the rest of my life.

I kept talking, and the man was bottomless. No matter how much I told him, he wanted to know more. I began to understand how Clint Eastwood had taken the little bit I'd shared with him and expanded it into a whole new way of being up on the big screen. Great actors were like sponges. Finally, I even told Rod

Steiger about the lion eyes in the snowstorm when I was a child, and then I told him how that same mountain lion had brought me a freshly killed deer last winter when I was starving to death here in *las Barrancas del Cobre*. It was beautiful. This great actor was in awe, like a little boy—he was so excited hearing all this.

"These stories," he shouted, "they would make a great film! We need to get together and find a writer who is open enough to understand all this and do justice to these miraculous things you've told me! But not a do-gooder, narrow-minded Christian writer! We need someone who isn't afraid to—hell, I'll write the script myself! Why not? And I'll play you in the movie!"

We continued talking, and to my utter shock, he could understand the concept that for the Tarahumara, only reality that was anchored in the miraculous existed. I'd never met a person so open, and able to learn so fast.

I went back to the lake that night realizing that I'd met another Great Soul, just as I'd met in Joan Baez, Jerry Garcia, Bob Dylan, and Clint Eastwood. There were certain people you might meet just for an evening, and yet you knew that you'd be Soul-to-Soul connected with them for the rest of your life! Because, as my Three Guides were teaching me, we were all walking stars. We all were sparks from the campfires that humans had been sitting around together since before the concept of time was even conceived!

That night, once more Mireya came to me in my dreams, and we were walking on the rim of the great canyon, with wind blowing gently, making music. It was like when you rubbed your index finger on a wineglass half filled with water, and as you rubbed your wet finger faster and faster around the rim of the glass, a haunting sound occurred. The wind blowing through the great canyon was as haunting and yet gentle, only magnified 10,000-fold. I slept, smiling, with her legs wrapped about me, FEELING SO GOOD!

CHAPTER 12

Mireya

Oh, my life was now a continuous dream of pure joy, because I'd found my true love and made him mine, and now he lived inside my head and heart and soul! All day, I couldn't stop singing and laughing, and everyone could see my joy, so they, too, would laugh. It was like when a person brought this much love to the world, and then the whole world benefited, too!

Love is contagious!

Love is wonderful!

Love is invigorating!

Love is the most thrilling, exciting feeling in all the world!

And just to kiss? Oh, I'd never known that the lips had so many feelings and could excite the whole rest of the body with fire. And since this was true, then just imagine what it would feel like to finally take my man's gift deep inside, like the *burras* did with the *burros* and the cows did with the bulls and chickens did with the roosters and—OH, EVERYONE AND EVERYTHING JUST LOVED MAKING *EL AMOR!* And now I, too, was beginning to get a taste of what this must feel like, because each time I jumped on him, I came away feeling light-headed and all wet and moist. And he knew it, too, because last time I'd seen him smelling of me, even after I'd gotten down off of him.

OH, HE WAS MINE!

And ever since I'd been a child, I'd been waiting for him, searching for him through the Heavens, because I knew that he, too, came from the stars, just as I had come from the stars. So together we were destined to walk hand in hand in the night, looking up at the stars, OUR TRUE HOME IN THE HOLY ARMS OF GOD!

CHAPTER 13

Jan

The filming was done. The children's camp was complete, and we were expecting our first group of kids to be brought in from Chihuahua City by train. This was when I decided that I had to speak to Mireya and have her understand that she could no longer come racing up and jump on me. We were in the kitchen facilities at the camp. Coco and Soco would be cooking, and Mireya and six other girls would be assisting.

"Mireya," I said to her in front of Coco and her mother, "we are going to be getting our first train full of kids, and I do not want them to see you jumping on me every time you see me."

"Why not? I love you, and I don't want to hide my love."

"But Mireya, your behavior is improper. Your mother has told you this."

"Yes, I've told her time and time again," said Soco, "but she will not listen!"

"Why should I?" asked Mireya. "Everyone else is also after him. Those two women from the bank with their big *tetas* and fine behinds are after him, too, and so is Coco—only Jan doesn't like men like he likes women. I love him. He has a noble heart, and you yourself, *Mamá,* have told me that it's very difficult to find a man with a noble heart."

"That's true, Mireya," said her mother, "but . . ."

"Look," I said to Mireya, "how old are you?"

"Almost 15."

"Okay, let's say 15. You still have a lot of living to do and many young men to meet who are closer to your own age, and you'll have more in common with them."

"What? Talk of cars and clothes and all those things that aren't important. No, Jan, what I have in common with you is that I, too, come alive each night with the stars, just as I know that you do."

"How do you know this?" I said, feeling my heart leap.

"How do the birds know when and how to come together and fly north and south with the seasons? I know that we are to be together, Jan, like the moon knows the night, the sun knows the day."

"This is ridiculous!" snapped Coco. "You're a child!"

"Oh, and were you not a boy my age, or younger, Coco, when you knew you liked men and not girls?"

"Well, yes, this is true, but . . . well, you must listen to *Señor* Jan!"

"I am, with all my heart and soul," Mireya said with tears.

I took a deep, deep breath. "Look," I told her, "if you still feel this same way about me when . . . when you, well, turn 18, then and only then can you come to me and we will talk. But just talk, understand, and until that time, no more racing up and leaping on me. Okay?"

"Okay," she said with that great big smile of hers, "then this means that you will wait for me to grow up, and you won't be taken in by the big tits and fine behinds of the women at the bank?"

"Well, it's not them who are the problem, Mireya. I'm still married."

"Where? I don't see a wife."

"She lives in Chihuahua City."

"I bet she already has another *hombre.* My own mother didn't wait around very long if the man was gone. That's why I and my sisters and brother have three different fathers. The home is made by the woman. Not men, who come and go—unless, of course, the man has a noble heart and he stays with the family no matter what." Tears were streaming down her face.

"Don Jan, *mi amor,*" she continued, "I will be at your door when I turn 18. This I know deep in my heart, because I can also feel it when I leap on you, that you, too, would like to leap on me," she added with that huge, infectious smile of hers.

I must have turned a thousand shades of red and orange, because now both Coco and Soco were laughing with *carcajadas.* There was just no stopping the direct honesty of this young girl, and it was true that the last few times she'd jumped on me, I'd gotten very excited. How could I not? I was a man, and her behavior was finally beginning to take its toll on me. But now, thank God, we had an agreement, so I felt safe—at least until she turned 18.

The first two trainloads of kids came in from Chihuahua, and with my red pickup and ten logging trucks, we picked them up. Coco and Soco did a great job in the kitchen, and Mireya and the six other young women did a fine job assisting. It was a great success. The camp got national publicity, and droves of people now wanted to send their children; and the supplies we couldn't get locally came in by rail.

We had the camp running with 400 kids per week by the end of the summer. Then came news of a shooting. We were told that across the lake where the Rod Steiger movie had been filmed, Ortega, who was a second cousin to Mireya's grandfather and had brought in the people who'd built a hotel for tourists in town and another at the lookout point, had shot a small boy who was fishing on the rocks in front of the hunting lodge that had been built for the movie set. At first we thought it was one of our kids from the camp who'd stayed behind, but then we found out that it was a local Indian boy. Father Rochín and I were called in on behalf of the Indian boy's family.

"This isn't good," Rochín said to me. "If word of this shooting gets out, a lot of people aren't going to feel safe sending their kids up to our camp anymore."

"You aren't suggesting that we do nothing, are you?"

"No, of course not. We must do something. This is terrible! The boy was just fishing on the rocks like the Tarahumara have always done, way before the movie sets were ever built. Ortega is just a crazy, mean old fool. He was the one I was referring to when we first came up here and I told you Van Housen and another man basically run things in the area. So we need to be careful, Jan, very careful. These two people are very well connected."

That afternoon we drove around the lake to meet the boy's parents. They were Tarahumara. They told us Ortega had told their son he was trespassing on his land, which the boy hadn't understood because one, it was Tarahumara land; and two, the boy didn't speak Spanish. He only spoke Tarahumara. Ortega had become furious, and he'd started shooting at the boy and almost shot himself, too, because he was so drunk.

The boy was lying on a blanket on the ground up on a shelf inside their cave dwelling. Their home was a clean, spacious structure made of natural stone on the side of a cliff. Checking the boy, we found where the bullet had gone into his lower back, but had not come out in front. The bullet was still inside of him, and the boy was in terrible pain. We put him and his parents in Rochín's old blue Renault, and we drove past the town of Creel and started down the mountain to the nearest hospital, at Cuauhtémoc. But the boy died before we even got off the *mesa* with the thousand creeks.

We stopped on the side of the road, and in the light of the full moon, Father Rochín did a ceremony with the boy's parents. With tears running down his face, the boy's father threw all the money that Ortega had given them after the shooting into the creek. The next day Father Rochín and I drove with the parents to the closest municipal court at Cuauhtémoc and filed charges of murder against Ortega. Then Rochín drove on to Chihuahua City, and the boy's parents and I hitched a ride back to Creel.

Three days later the judicial police came bursting into the mess hall at our kids' camp, hit me in my injured stomach with a rifle butt, and then put me in chains that crisscrossed about my neck and went down between my legs and up to my handcuffs. They'd already arrested the parents of the boy who'd been shot and died; plus they'd arrested all the elder leaders of the different local Tarahumara villages, including my Three Wisemen *Curanderos*. My chains cut painfully into my crotch as they dragged me out of the mess hall and threw me into the back of a truck.

Mireya and her mother were screaming!

But the armed men paid no attention to them and drove us all out of the children's camp, but not toward Creel. They took an old abandoned logging road toward the rim of the great canyon. Up ahead we passed Van Housen's pickup parked on the side of the road. He was standing by his vehicle with his Safari helmet and his plaid Pendleton shirt buttoned all the way up to his neck. I made eye contact with him as we drove by. He smiled. I guess he was very happy that I was finally going to get what was coming to me.

Up ahead the police stopped at the rim of the great beautiful copper-orange canyon. It was spectacular. Over a mile deep and six miles wide, with sculptured cliffs and *mesas* that stood as monuments of creation. They got us out of the trucks and lined up the Indian leaders and the boy's parents along the canyon's rim. I could see that my Three Wisemen *Curanderos* were among the Indian leaders. Then they brought me up in front of the line, yanking the chains that went between my legs with such force that I was bleeding from my crotch and ready to scream out in pain, but I didn't. I knew what they were trying to do, and I would not hate them and would not scream in pain.

No, my boys, my beautiful boys, had endured much worse, so I was not going to give in to my tormentors. I, too, would stay centered in the Holy Light of Our Lord Jesus, and keep forgiving them, for they did not know. I would not belittle the memory of my beautiful, wonderful young boys who had taken the words of Jesus Christ to heart. The police hit me with their rifle butts and kicked me once I was down, but still I kept blessing them and forgiving them. Finally they yanked me to my feet when they saw that I would not get angry or cry out.

"Now you stupid, *sin razón Indios* will all see what happens to *un hombre* who brings false charges against one of our leading citizens!" screamed the captain of the police. "And you fools will see once and for all that this man is no Holy Man! That he has no special powers! That he's just a stupid, meddlesome *gringo* who should have stayed in his own country, instead of sticking his nose into business that he knows nothing about!

"Then after we shoot him, we will shoot all of you, and report that it was you *Indios* who killed this fine, wonderful *gringo*. How about that! I, too, can predict the future pretty good, eh? Shoot him! Now!"

The young policeman with the old-fashioned double-barreled shotgun like some of the local Indians still used for hunting came up to me and put the two barrels to the side of my head.

"God bless you," I said to him in Spanish. "I'll be gone, so I don't matter, but you will live and be wanting peace, so go with God, my young *amigo*. God bless you, my son."

"SHOOT HIM NOW, DAMMIT!" shouted the captain once again. "I don't want to hear any more of his bullshit!"

I turned and calmly faced the two huge barrels, and all the teachings of my Three Indian Healers came flashing to my heart eye. I was safe. I was home. Just as those lion eyes had led me home to safety that day in the snowstorm, I was now already with God. Right here! Forever!

I watched the young boy's index finger pull the trigger . . . and I closed my eyes and breathed, remaining at peace, detached, and ready to go to the Light with joy. I heard the two hammers snap-snap, but the shotgun didn't go off. I opened my eyes.

"GIVE ME THAT GUN!" bellowed the captain. "I told them we shouldn't use one of these old weapons! They never work when you need them to work! But the fools want me to make it look authentic that the Indians did this killing!"

He cracked open the double-barreled weapon, saw that both hammers had, indeed, hit the two shells, reclosed the double-barrel, aimed it at a small pine tree, and pulled the trigger. The huge 12-gauge exploded, cutting the little pine in half!

ALL THE HEAVENS BURST LOOSE!

The Three Wisemen shook off their chains and shackles as if they were nothing and then they turned, running to the rim. The police opened fire on them, but the bullets didn't have any effect on the Three Indian *Curanderos* as they leaped off the rim, arms outstretched, and took flight, turning into mighty eagles! The boy's parents and the remaining Indians knelt down and began to pray. The captain was fit to be tied, he was in such a rage!

"GIVE ME YOUR WEAPON!" he screamed, grabbing one of his men's automatic rifles. "Are you fools shooting blanks, or what?"

He pointed the automatic weapon at the policeman he'd grabbed it from and pulled the trigger. The gun cut loose in rapid fire, cutting the young officer to pieces.

"DAMMIT!" roared the captain. "Load up these imbeciles! We will take them to the prison! There, we have more control over these kinds of things! Up here there's just too much Indian super-stitious power for us to have control. I warned them! I told them that these kinds of things have happened to us up here before! But do they listen to me? No, they think I make it all up!"

And so the dream continued as they loaded us back up into the trucks and drove off. High above I could see my Three Holy Teachers flying overhead, screeching like the eagles. I breathed and breathed again. I had not let my boys or Jesus down.

CHAPTER 14

Mireya

Every day I grew to love my *gringo* more and more, so it was very difficult for me to stop myself from jumping on him every time I saw him. But then he had a talk with me, telling me not to jump on him anymore, and to understand that if I still felt this way about him when I turned 18, then for me to come to see him and we'd talk. But he couldn't fool me. I understood that we weren't just going to talk, because the last time I'd jumped on him I'd felt his manhood leap and want to come inside me as my legs wrapped about his middle, pulling him in tight.

And as for the young boys he said I should be with, I had no use for them. I knew the realities of life, and I knew I was a headstrong girl, so I needed a very well-seasoned man who would understand me and not run away when the twists and turns of life came our way. I was young, that was true, but I wasn't living with my eyes closed. I was paying close attention and learning from my mother and my aunts, and I'd especially learned a lot from my grandparents, too. A woman, I had learned, had to be very careful to whom she opened up her legs and invited into the warmth of her body, because it was us, the females, who carried the child.

I was so happy when my mother and I were hired to work at the camp for the kids. I got to see my *gringo* every day and see how good he was with the children, even with some of the spoiled ones who came from rich families down in the lowlands. Also, our job wasn't just to cook and serve and clean, but to keep an eye open for the safety of the kids.

Once, I spotted a rattlesnake that two girls were going to step on because they didn't know the ways of the wild. I caught the snake by the back of its head before it struck them and took it up the hill to turn it loose. This was when some boys from the camp came running up to kill the snake with sticks, but I took a stick to them, laughing the whole time. But then I was told not to beat up the kids of our camp again. I didn't take a stick to the kids anymore after that, but I can tell you, I sure had fun.

Those four boys thought they were so big and tough, but when they learned that a girl just about their same age could easily beat them all up at the same time, they were shocked. But not me. I knew what I was doing. When you had the high ground, you could leap so much higher and go so much faster than when you had the lower ground.

Also, I got to race with the kids from the camp, but even their best boy runners could not keep up with me. They were from the lowlands, and their legs were no match for us from the high country. Ever since I'd been a child, I'd been racing up and down our great canyon, leaping off cliffs and tall rocks by bending my knees and using them like springs. I was lucky and didn't have big *tetas* like those two women from the bank who were also after my *gringo,* so I had nothing on my body that bounced up and down when I ran and leaped. I became known as *la venada,* the deer girl, to the kids at the camp. I loved it!

By the end of the summer, nearly 2,000 kids had come through our camp from Los Mochis on the coast and from *la Ciudad de Chihuahua* to the east of us. Many parents came to visit, and you could see that they were very impressed with my *gringo* and Father Rochín. These two men could do no wrong. It was like everything they touched turned to gold. But then came word of the little boy across the lake who'd been shot by Ortega, my grandfather's cousin who was the second-meanest man in town, right behind the priest Van Housen with the evil eye.

My mother told me, *"Mijita,* something very bad is going to happen," as we watched my *gringo* and Father Rochín drive off to see the boy's parents.

"What's going to happen?" I asked my mother.

"I don't know, *mijita,* but I can feel it in my bones."

My mother's bones were always talking to her, like the trees and rocks spoke to me, so I knew that she knew what she was talking about. But then when we heard that the boy who'd been shot had died as they took him down the mountain, I thought this was what my mother had been talking about when she'd said that "something very bad" was going to happen.

But then a couple of days later when those armed police came breaking into our kitchen area, I realized that this was what my mother had been feeling in her bones. The damn police didn't even try to open the door. No, they deliberately knocked it down, tearing it off its hinges; then they rushed up and hit my *gringo* in his injured stomach and began kicking him in his bad back, too.

I screamed that they had no right to be so abusive and started to go after them. It was all Coco and my mother could do to hold me back. They put my *gringo* in chains and dragged him out of our dining room, across the rocks and dirt, and threw him in the back of the second truck. We watched them go down the road, but not toward town; instead, they took the old abandoned logging road toward the great canyon. Now we knew what they were going to do. They were going to execute my *gringo,* along with the Indian elders they had with them, then throw their bodies into the bottomless canyon, as they always did, so they could never be found, because the coyotes and lions would eat their remains in no time at all.

I was screaming! I didn't know what to do, and this was when Coco and my mother and all the rest of us from the camp went down to the lake's edge, and we began to pray. We'd been praying for some time when a great eagle came flying close overhead, and Coco shouted, "See! It's one of the Three *Espiritos!* He has come to let us know that they didn't kill them."

"My *gringo* lives!" I shouted.

"Yes, they all live! Their guns couldn't kill them!" said Coco. "We need to get to town and tell everyone what's going on."

"But how will we get there?" asked my mother. "They shot holes in the tires of the red truck."

The police had shot up our camp as they'd driven away, just to be mean and show us that they could do whatever they pleased.

"I'll run and get help!" I said, taking off like a deer.

I ran through the forest, leaping over rocks, and at Elephant Rock I met a truckload of people from town. We hurried back to the camp and got my mother and Coco and everyone else we could load up. We all loved my *gringo,* and we were not going to allow anything bad to happen to him and the others.

CHAPTER 15

Jan

The *comandante* and his men loaded us in the two pickups and drove back down the logging road. Every bounce sent shooting pain all through me. The chains were doing their job. They were cutting me to pieces. I closed my eyes and began to pray, trying my best to go out of my body so I wouldn't feel the pain. The people of Creel were waiting for us as we came into town. The captain and his men paraded us up and down the street so everyone could see that we were in chains and that they had the power.

Then I saw that Mireya and Soco and some other women were offering to sell *tamales* to the captain and his men. Our tormentors were all starving, I guess, because the captain made the wonderful mistake of letting his policemen stop to buy the *tamales*. This was when Josefina and her sister Carmen, two large-breasted old women, got on each side of the captain's vehicle and pulled revolvers out of their aprons, shoving them into the police captain's face, demanding our release.

"No, I can't," said the captain. "They must be taken to the prison for questioning."

While Josefina and Carmen spoke to the captain, Mireya and her mother and Coco gave us water and wet rags for our faces. The sunlight was boiling hot in the back of the two police trucks, and we'd been dying of thirst. Mireya washed my face with a piece of material she'd ripped from her blouse, exposing herself, and she was so gentle and loving and good to me.

"All right, you can take them to the prison," said Josefina, "but you be careful how you treat them. Do not abuse them, or the birds of the air will peck the eyes from your head before the next full moon."

"You can't scare me with your Indian superstitions!" answered the captain. "I can read and write! I'm a learned man!"

"So are the birds learned human beings," said the old woman, "and their message, they have already written in the stars!"

The captain laughed at Josefina and Carmen and told his men to eat their *tamales* so they could keep going. Before we had even made it halfway down the mountain, the captain and his men had to pull over. They had the runs and terrible stomach cramps. The *tamales* had done their job. This gladdened our hearts, but not for long.

That night at the old prison we were stripped and put in a filthy cold concrete basement that stank of urine and shit and had rats running around. I began to think that the *comandante* maybe had known what he'd been talking about, and the Spirit World could not help us here.

That night they tortured me over and over again; and the worst wasn't the beatings, the breaking of my legs and arms, or the pulling off of my nails with pliers. No, it was when they forced soda water up my nose and the bubbly liquid hit my brain with such force that my head EXPLODED! Finally, I began to cry. I couldn't help it, and this was when the captain began to smile, just as Van Housen had smiled at me as we drove past him.

They'd won.

They'd broken me.

I hadn't been able to hold on to my dignity, like my wonderful boys had done.

I'd lost it.

I turned coward.

I felt so ashamed. And now I was crying like a little baby, and my tormentors loved it.

But the dream continued . . . and miracles have no end. Because in the early-morning mist, we began to hear something. And we couldn't figure out what it was at first, but then little by little we realized that it was the united voice of thousands of people outside the prison, chanting and singing softly, then loudly, demanding our release.

It turned out they also had a letter from the office of the governor of the state of Chihuahua backing them up. At noon, the captain and his men came into our cells with hoses and sprayed us with cold water, then gave us back our clothes before they released us. I guess they didn't want it to look like we'd been mistreated.

I couldn't walk. I had to be held up by my armpits. Jorge and Silveria, who'd been contacted by Rochín, were with the crowd. So was the beautiful *Latina* and her big all-American husband. When Mireya and her mother saw me, they began to cry, and this time Mireya didn't race up and leap on me. No, she tenderly took me in her arms and kissed me gently and softly, and with the help of the others, guided me into the bed of our red Ford pickup truck.

I guess the picture of Mireya kissing me got in the newspapers because the following week Emma came up by train with a gun to kill Mireya for publicly humiliating her. But Emma, with all of her fine city ways, had no idea who she was meeting when she put the gun into Mireya's face at the mess hall of our children's camp, threatening to kill her.

Myself, I wasn't there.

I was at the hot springs at the bottom of the great canyon having my wounds attended to by the Three *Curanderos*. They were using herbs and roots and the hearts of certain cactus plants to take the swelling out of my broken arms and other injuries and help me heal; and also, most important, they were showing me that nothing was ever over within the Kingdom of God until it was brought into harmony, so now it was my Sacred Duty as an apprentice *mayori* to go back and revisit the day when I'd felt the presence of *la Mano Negra* across the street from me.

I did as told.

And now I invited the Soul Spirit of *la Mano Negra* to come and sit with me, face-to-face, here among the great ferns and waterfalls of the gorgeous untouched canyon.

I sat upon a rock and called in the Spirit of the greatest assassin of all, sending him/her my love-*amor,* and more love-*amor,* and . . . then here he/she was in front of me, but not in full form yet. No, he/she still looked like a shadow—a formless form, just like the Three Wisemen Healers had looked when they'd first started walking across the lake, coming toward me.

And I now understood that God had long ago made peace with the Devil, yet they both still continued to exist so we human beings could then continue to have free will and choose the Light or the Darkness. And so as an apprentice *mayori,* I indeed had a Sacred Duty to do as God would and bring about my personal peace with *la Mano Negra,* just as Jesus had done with Judas. I took in a deep breath, closed my eyes, and gave all I had to this Great Soul on the smooth river rock across from me, and . . . and . . . Mother Earth sighed with a tremor, she was so moved and happy!

CHAPTER 16

Mireya

We got to town just as the police began parading my *gringo* and the others up and down the street, showing them off like prize deer they'd hunted down. This was when Josefina and her sister Carmen put revolvers in the face of the captain, and it gave us the opportunity to offer water to my *gringo* and the others. Ripping a piece off my blouse, I wiped the blood and snot off my beloved *gringo*'s face. I loved him, and I poured water on the rag I'd made from my blouse and washed his face as tenderly and lovingly as I could.

After this, the no-good police drove off with my *gringo* and the others. Coco quickly got us all together, along with Josefina and Carmen, and the word spread like wildfire. Even the two fine young women at the bank said they would get word to Jan's good friend Jorge Ramos, the bank's president in Chihuahua. Everyone was trying to figure out how they could help. We all loved my *gringo,* and we weren't going to allow these no-good police to kill him and mistreat the others.

We went back out to the camp and changed the tires of the red truck, and all of us who could fit in and on top of the different vehicles went down the mountain. The rest of the town would go down by train first thing in the morning. We were told Father Rochín, who was in Chihuahua, was going to contact the governor's office and all of Jan's old friends from the halfway houses.

Also, we were told that an announcement was to be aired on the radio station where Jan used to work. People began responding by the hundreds and getting in their cars and trucks to come join us at the prison's gates. Just before dawn, we lit candles and began to say a rosary out loud, then to chant and sing softly. More and more people were arriving, and soon there were thousands and thousands of us . . . and our united voice was so huge and beautiful that even the flocks of crows and blackbirds joined us with their happy sounds as they flew overhead on their way to the fields!

I can tell you with all my heart and soul that that morning in front of the prison, I learned that *Mañana es otro milagro de Dios* is by far our most powerful expression in Mexico. Because this morning as we all stood together in prayer and the sun—the right eye of God—came up on the horizon, it was the most spectacular experience of my life. I truly believe that if they hadn't released my *gringo* and the others, the very walls of the prison would have come tumbling down. So great was our united power! So earnest were we in prayer! So full of *amor* were we all for my *gringo* with the noble heart and the dead boy's parents and the Indian leaders!

When I saw him, I almost died. They had tortured him beyond belief. He couldn't walk. And his face was all swollen, and his nose was bleeding and twisted. We found out that they'd rammed soda bottles up his nostrils. I began to cry. I loved him so. Couldn't they see how good he was? But then I realized that this was why they'd done what they'd done. They could see his goodness, just as the ones who had crucified Our Lord Jesus had also seen the goodness in Him, too!

With tears running down my face, I took him in my arms and kissed him tenderly as we put him into the bed of the truck on some blankets. All the way back to Creel, I gave him love and comfort, singing gently to him, my love, my hero, my saintly man with a noble heart. Those poor fools at the prison—they were the exact same kind of people who had crucified Our Lord Jesus; and I hated them and wished them a cruel, long death.

A few days later a crazy woman came running into our kitchen at the camp with a gun in her hand. She was well dressed and very beautiful, and I had no idea who she was. I was visiting with the other young girls who worked in the kitchen. We'd finished our work and were taking a break.

"You dirty little whore!" she screamed at me in front of everyone as she came racing across the large room, shoving a big revolver into my face. "He's my husband! How dare you be having an affair with him, you dirty, stupid Indian whore! I'm going to kill you, if you ever so much as look at him again!"

I had no idea what she was talking about. I was a virgin. I hadn't had an affair with anyone. "Who are you?" I asked. "And what are you talking about?"

"Don't lie!" she shouted. "I saw your picture with him in the paper. You've made me the laughingstock of all of Chihuahua!"

"Oh, you mean the *gringo*," I said, laughing. "No, I haven't had any affair with him yet, but it is true that I do love him."

"You can't love him!" she yelled. "He's my husband! And if you ever go near him again, I'LL KILL YOU!"

Well, I can tell you that I wasn't going to live in fear of her any more than the deer lives in fear of the lion. Sure, the deer knows that the lion is out to get her and that he wants to kill her and eat her, but still the deer doesn't live in fear. I've watched deer all my life, and I can tell you that they live happy lives and play in the meadows and attend to their young with love and patience. So not for one minute was I going to allow this woman to plant the seed of fear in my heart.

I LEAPED AND YELLED RIGHT BACK AT HER, but ten times louder than she'd shouted at me!

"WELL, THEN KILL ME!" I screamed at her. "GO AHEAD AND KILL ME RIGHT NOW! Because I will never stop looking at him with my eyes full of love! We all love him! Not just me! My mother, Coco, and even the trees and the rocks! Will you kill them all, too?!"

At this point the woman who claimed to be my *gringo's* wife began to lower the gun, but I grabbed her hand and kept the revolver pointed at my heart, yelling, "DON'T STOP NOW! COME ON, DO IT! KILL ME! And see if this will bring him back to you! No, you had your chance! You were married to him, and yet not once did you ever come up here to share his dreams and sorrows and joys! Not once did you come up here to hear him sing to the stars and trees! You say he is your husband, but what proof do you have? A ring on the finger doesn't make you a wife! A piece of paper doesn't do it, either! It is here in the heart where the union of a man and woman is made! The rest is all just a bunch of unimportant farts! So go on, shoot me, then shoot my mother and Coco and all the town who loves him, too!"

"But you've been sleeping with him! You've been—"

"No, she hasn't!" my mother shouted at the woman. "She is my daughter, and yes, she's been in love with him since the first day she saw him, but she's only a girl! That's all!"

It was Coco who now came forward, and he took the gun away from Emma. She left, screaming that she'd be back—that this wasn't over and for everyone to keep their hands off her husband, because he was legally hers and they had a child.

"KEEP COMING!" I shouted after her. "And prove that you even exist! For all I can see, you are no more than a smelly old fart making noise in the wind!"

"Mireya!" said my mother. "Do not provoke!"

But I'd already said what I felt, and it felt good, because I was so mad at her that I could have strangled her until her eyes popped out of her head. She hadn't come up here like a woman who loved her husband and wanted to know how he was doing after the terrible beating he'd received in the prison. No, she'd come up here because our picture had gotten in the newspaper. This had embarrassed her in front of her friends in Chihuahua City. What kind of wife was that? It was no wife of all, but a stupid old cow in love with her own self and how she looked to the world.

She had no heart, and certainly no soul. She was all big *tetas* and a well-defined rear end and so full of her great looks and all her fancy makeup. How could I possibly have fear of such a lost human being?

No, my love for Jan was as pure and true as a mother bird or deer ready to give her life for the one she loved. This was life. This was living. This was being true to my heart and soul with my whole being.

The woman left, saying it wasn't over and that she'd be back, but I didn't care. I was sure of my world and my *amor,* so I had no fears whatsoever, just like the deer. In fact, this was now what everyone called me, *la venada*—the deer—and I liked it, because deer were not just fast, but strong and very loving and agile, too, just like me!

CHAPTER 17

Jan

I was down in the bottom of the canyon at the waterfalls when we received word of the incident between Mireya and Emma. It was said that the townspeople were very impressed with Mireya's bravery and high intelligence. For the first time the talk about town was that it must truly be written in the stars, as Mireya had been saying all along, and we were destined to be together. But I wasn't paying attention to this talk. I'd been thoroughly tortured by men who'd known what they were doing, and it was taking all the knowledge of my Three Indian *Curanderos* to help make me well.

They were giving me special herbs and roots and using the hearts of certain cacti to rub on my body. They were keeping me in a state halfway between asleep and awake, which they explained to me was the Realm of the World of the Miraculous. They told me it would take at least two years to heal my wounds in normal time, but in this state of "no time" that existed halfway between being awake and being asleep, my healing would take less than one full moon.

"This is where we live," said the shorter of the Three Wisemen *Curanderos,* "in this Holy Place between asleep and awake. This is why we still look good and strong, yet we are over 200 years old by Earth time. And this is also why you were able to see us take flight that day when we ran and leaped off the great canyon's rim, for in our reality, we just dream something, and . . . we are what we dream."

I inhaled deeply, held, then blew out. This was a big one, yet so simple. "Is this also why the shotgun didn't fire?" I asked my teachers.

"Exactly. You were in the Womb Center of Creation, where all is a Flow of Peace and Harmony, so no weapon can exist or function in this Sacred Holy Place. Only Love and Harmony and Peace can exist within this Flowing Current of Creation. You did well. You are learning as fast as we knew you would."

"You knew I'd be a fast learner?" I asked.

"Of course. There is no past, present, or future when you are with God. All is right here forever, right now, in Eternity. So when a person unites with God, in our Womb of Creation—or Kingdom of God, as you Christians call it—then this person can also instantly know all there is to learn."

It began to rain gently, softly, and I drifted in and out of sleep . . . yet I wasn't really asleep. I could still hear their Holy Voices going on inside of my head, and they were speaking about water. About raindrops coming down from the Heavens and joining other raindrops gently coming down between the rock walls of the great canyon; getting caught in the winds; and falling, falling, landing on the leaves of the great trees and giant ferns, then drip-dropping off the jungle of leaves and trickling over the rocks, then flowing together with other raindrops, as we—all of us—became little streams of water that got larger and larger as we went cascading over the numerous waterfalls and finally joined in with the larger stream that united into a huge, roaring waterfall that shook the earth herself as it cut through the great canyon and went out to the lowlands and then to the sea, only to then return to the Heavens from which we all came.

I could now clearly see that I was being told that I, a human being, was water. And water couldn't be hurt by kicks or bullets. So the Three Wisemen *Curanderos* were explaining to me in Singsong Voices that together we were the little waterfalls nearest us, gathering and flowing together as we went downstream, joining other waters, and then went over the huge waterfall, bursting into mist and sound and droplets of new rain! This was why I'd heal in no time at all. I was water. We were all water that came down from Heaven, and to Heaven we'd return.

The days passed and the dream continued . . . and each night blessed us with a canvas of studded stars and shooting comets with great, long tails of light so bright they lit up the sky! Our whole world was full of magic and the beautiful fragrance of luscious jungle wildflowers!

I began to see, to feel, to understand with every fiber of my being, that all my Three Wisemen *Curanderos* were teaching me, a part of me had already known. That this Sacred Holy Knowledge was already deep inside of me, of you, of all of us. That we human beings knew everything once we let go of all we thought we knew and were once more in the Holy Water Flow of Creation, because then all was Love and Harmony and Peace . . . so, of course, down deep inside we already knew everything there was to know, and from this Sacred Place, we could do anything instantly, including two years' worth of healing in one full moon.

I slept.

I was at peace.

I was with God Almighty.

And so, of course no weapon could function at this Holy Place where I now lived. How could it? All fear was gone, and when all fear was gone, then gunpowder only worked as fun, happy fireworks for kids to love, like on the Fourth of July.

Oh, I could now see that this was the Holy Place I'd been going toward, ever since I'd seen those lion eyes as a boy. This was Our True Home, a Place of Joy and Laughter and Peace.

And so I drifted in and out of sleeping, resting, dreaming in this Holy Place; and all was Safe and Warm. And this was what I'd seen in the lion eyes the day that she had led me home to safety in the snowstorm. This was also how I'd known that I'd be safe even as I'd watched the young soldier's index finger press the trigger of the double-barreled shotgun.

Calmly, I'd watched.

Detached and with no fear I'd watched, because I'd been in this safe, warm Holy State of being with God, our True Home, the Kingdom of God, so I had no fear as the young soldier's finger had pressed on the trigger. And of course the hammers had gone click-click, but the weapon had not exploded. How could it? Weapons of destruction had no function in the Kingdom of God.

This was what Jesus had known as they'd crucified Him, and I was now learning, too. My Three Wisemen *Curanderos* truly were the same Three Wisemen of the Bible who'd come forth from the Spirit World to give instruction to Jesus. I now knew this with every fiber of my being, as we rained down from Heaven, then went drip-dropping off the leaves of the beautiful, luscious jungle.

Raindrops were we.

Raindrops coming down from Heaven and joining together into little streams, then into a great big huge river of such force that we, you and I, were the rain that had carved the Copper Canyon, ten times larger in volume than the Grand Canyon of the United States, and not one canyon and instead Eight Sacred Canyons all coming together in THE MUSIC OF THE LAND AND WATERFALLS OF OUR ONGOING CREATION!

SACRED WERE WE!

SACRED WERE WE, AND SACRED WAS OUR BELOVED CANYON!

The weeks passed and the dream continued . . . and Father Rochín came to see us several times, and he, too, could see my Spirit Wisemen Healers. He told us that Ortega had filed charges against us for trespassing, just as he'd accused the boy of trespassing when he'd shot him. Then Rochín told us that a young attorney friend of his, Juan Lopez, had been going through records, and he'd found out that Ortega did, in fact, own the property where the movie had been filmed.

"But Rochín," I said, "that doesn't make sense. That land has belonged to the Indian *ejido* forever."

The word *ejido* referred to land held in common by a designated group of people, so if this was true—that Ortega owned this *ejido*—then he probably also owned tens of thousands of acres, land that other, different groups of Indians had owned and been living on for thousands of years.

"This is what my friend told me that the records show," said Rochín.

"But how can this possibly be?" I asked, still having a difficult time believing what I was being told.

Carlos Rochín shrugged. "This we haven't been able to figure out yet, but I do believe that this is just the tip of the iceberg. Get well, Jan. We need your help. The Indian leaders now see you as a True Force of the Spirit World, and with your help, we can meet with the leaders of each village and see about making a Miracle happen. Because this is what will be needed if we are to make a difference."

I inhaled deeply, held, then blew out. I'd been in Mexico long enough to know all the red tape a person had to go through to get anything done. The Spirit World was very simple and easy to understand compared to the world of laws and rules and government.

"But won't the judicial police be waiting for me the moment I come out of the canyon?" I asked.

"You tell me," said Rochín, laughing. "You are the one who has become a *mayori*."

I laughed. This was a good one. I, the *gringo* who couldn't seem to do anything right, was now supposed to be the leader! This was ridiculous!

Time passed. The Dream World continued, broadened, expanded, and deepened. My whole past life began slipping, sliding, passing before me; and little by little, my Three Spirit Indian Healer Guides would take each of my past situations in my past life, and no matter how terrible, they'd instantly turn it around like magic before my Heart Eyes and Soul Eyes. I'd now see it as the most perfect and important and needed ingredient to happen to me on my ongoing Spiritual Journey in order to make me who I now was, A GLORIOUS, WONDERFUL HUMAN BEING! And so I now saw that all of our past lives were preparation for the life we were living at this Present Holy Moment of Right Here Forever!

I wasn't special.

No, I was the norm of what we could all be.

For instance, I now completely understood that the night the big car had hit Chato and me and sent him flying and rammed my motorcycle and me under the other car had been a blessing, because then the Three Indian Healers had been able to come to me in the hospital, and I'd learned, without a shadow of doubt, that we Humans were not just of body but of Spirit, too. And not just a little bit of Spirit, but Totally of Spirit once we opened up our Heart and Soul Eyes!

It was also during this time, when I had been in the hospital, that the mountain lion of my childhood had come EXPLODING into me, taking up residence in my Heart and Soul, and she gave me the power to know that I wasn't going to die. NO, I WAS GOING TO LIVE!

Then shortly after, the Three Large Butterflies had come dancing past my eyes. I'd then seen the dried-out-looking garden outside the hospital turn into a luscious, beautiful green garden. So I could now see that no experience, no matter how awful, was ever a mistake, but instead was a lesson, preparing all of us, no exception, for Our Life's True Spiritual Journey!

I could now see that the torture I'd received in prison had also been no accident, but a wonderful gift given directly to me by the Holy Creator, so I could witness firsthand the Miracle of thousands of people Uniting in Song and Heart and Love-*Amor!*

Oh, I was so lucky!

In the U.S. more than 200 young people had come to see me off, and now down here in Mexico IT HAD BEEN THOUSANDS! And their heartfelt voices had united with such POWER that the walls of the prison began to tremble; and now down here in the bottom of this great canyon, surrounded by ferns and waterfalls, I was healing miraculously with herbs and cactus hearts and natural spring waters. Why? Because I'd become Holy Water. And so Miracles were, of course, coming to me in a steady flow, coming, coming, coming down from Heaven and drip-dropping off the leaves and rocks, feeding Our Very Souls.

Oh, I'd been so blind!

Because I now saw that even the boy who'd jumped out of the window in the Haight-Ashbury district of San Francisco had, indeed, taken flight with his Soul, as his body plunged to its death. Because I now remembered that he'd been smiling a beautiful Mona Lisa kind of smile. It was as if he'd finally discovered the secret to all living when he'd leaped, thinking he was an eagle and could fly; and that leap had LASTED AN ETERNITY, taking him through all of his past life experiences, as I was now doing with my Three Spirit Guides!

Little by little, with their guidance, I was going back over my entire life and discovering an abundance of Miracles, and I was now seeing that my biggest recent Miracle was not that the old shotgun had misfired. No, the biggest one was how so many people had assembled at the prison gates in such short Earth time. OH, THE FORCE OF SOULS UNITED WAS WHAT HAD BROUGHT THE WALLS OF JERICHO TUMBLING DOWN!

I could see now that it took Unity of Heart and Soul for Us Human Beings to enter Eternity, just as Unity of Heart and Soul was what had taken the boy who'd leaped out the window into that Mona Lisa time zone. I now began to see and understand what had also happened to me when I'd first come down to Mexico and I'd gotten sick.

I'd had typhoid.

I was dying.

There was nothing the doctors could do for me that time either. I'd just married Catalina, and her father gave us the number of a prayer group to call so they could send their blessing.

Catalina called but couldn't get through because of a tornado, and then the phone had rung and it was the Oral Roberts Prayer Tower from the United States, and they were doing a group prayer of more than a million people. Catalina gave them my name, and they said that she should tell me to prepare myself for a Miracle. I'll never forget, I'd opened up my Heart and Soul with every fiber of my Being, and within minutes I could feel the Power of their COLLECTIVE PRAYER COME BURSTING INTO ME! And in no time at all, my sure death disappeared, AND I WAS HEALED!

I'd forgotten all about that incident.

All over Chihuahua the phone lines were down, yet we'd received that call from the Prayer Tower. Oral Roberts, my Three Indian *Curanderos* explained to me, was one of them, and this incident had been most important so I could see that this was exactly what happened to all of us Human Beings when we went into Soul Time—then everything, no matter how large or small, was Sacred and Holy and Perfect and necessary for us to experience for our Spiritual Journey into the Living Eternity of Soul Reality! Then they added that the worst always became the best, if we kept faith, so this was still only the beginning for me.

Well, they must have seen the terrified look that came to my face, because THEY BURST OUT LAUGHING WITH *CARCAJADAS!*

Laughing and laughing and giggling, and I awoke laughing, too.

"No, no, no!" said one of them. "This doesn't necessarily mean you will be tortured even more than last time. In fact, this last torture would not even have happened if you'd kept faith and not gone into fear. We were there and ready to help you. We were those rats at your side in your cell, but you couldn't see our beauty and you pushed us away in repulsion. That was when you became available to your fear and their torture."

I could not fathom what they were saying. This was totally beyond me. "Are you saying," I asked, "that if I had kept my faith, I would have been able to see you as those rats, and Miracles would have continued coming my way, like that shotgun not firing, and I . . . I would not have been tortured?"

"Exactly."

"But how is that possible?"

"You tell us," said the taller one of my guides. "You've learned much. You now know that this is your dream, and you have the same powers within you that we have. What would have happened if you had kept your faith? Tell us."

"I don't know."

"Yes, you do," continued the tall one, who usually didn't speak much. "Remember, you are the man who saw our lion eyes at a very young age with calmness and wonder, so this was why the great cat saw you with equal calmness and wonder."

"Remember," said the shorter one, "everything you see outside of yourself is your own—"

"My own dream," I said. "So this, then, means that if I hadn't become fearful, then . . . then they would not have seen me? Is this what you are saying?"

"Stop playing small," said Miguel. "Forget the legs that keep you rooted to the earth as you run, and spread your ANGEL WINGS AND FLY WHEN YOU HIT A HILL AND THE GOING GETS TOUGH!"

I took in a very large breath, then exhaled. This was what Miguel had told me time and again when he'd been teaching me how to run. "Then is it that fear can only see fear?"

All Three Sacred *Curanderos* smiled.

"Go on," said Miguel.

"And Love can only see Love."

"Go on," repeated Miguel.

"And in the world of the Miraculous, all there is, is Love and . . . Harmony and Peace," I said, "and so, of course their shotgun couldn't fire, and they also could not have tortured me if I hadn't gone into fear."

The tears were streaming down my face. I now saw it all so clearly. Yes, this was it. And I'd also lost faith and gone into fear the day those two cars were chasing after Chato and me, and I'd also gotten frightened when they'd stripped us of our clothes and thrown us into that basement full of shit and piss and . . . rats.

I now saw it!

Yes, yes, yes! I could now see! I wasn't blind any longer!

Those beautiful large-eyed rats had, indeed, been there to help me!

They'd been my Three Holy Healers! And when Chato and I had gone around the great statue of Francisco Villa in Chihuahua City on *la Avenida de la División del Norte,* I had seen Villa smile, becoming alive—so surely he would have come down mounted on his great horse with all his mighty powers and crushed those two big four-door cars like flies, if I hadn't gone into fear!

It was fear all through my life that allowed terrible things to happen to me!

It was fear that caused our problems all over the world!

AND JESUS CHRIST HAD HAD NO FEAR, EVEN AS THEY CRUCIFIED HIM!

This was what He had come to planet Earth to teach us: HOW TO BE FEARLESS so we could then all pass through THE NEEDLE'S EYE OF CREATION INTO THE WORLD OF THE MIRACULOUS!

The tears continued pouring down my face. We were, indeed, the Sacred Holy Raindrops that came down from Heaven, gathering on the leaves of the jungle of life, uniting in Spirit and drip-dropping off the leaves of experience and collecting on the rocks of adversity as we poured down with SUCH POWER AND ABUNDANCE THAT WE CARVED STANDING MONUMENTS, LIKE THIS GREAT, HOLY COPPER CANYON!

We human beings were the Waters of Creation!

We were the Living Spirit of the Three Wisemen, just as much as Jesus had been in His Holy Soul Time!

We were Sacred Holy Water as we Dreamed into Sacred Eagles and took flight off the rim of Our Great Mother Canyon!

Dreams were we!

Living Dreams in this place within Our Kingdom of God half-way between being awake and asleep!

My mind dissolved!

Disappeared!

And now I was Total Heart and Soul, and I saw it ALL SO CLEARLY!

It was like layer after layer was finally coming, coming, coming off me.

All along Carlos Rochín had been right when he told me that for the Tarahumara, Reality had to be anchored in Miracles or they couldn't see it.

I giggled.

I laughed.

And the world I'd known all my life was gone! Dissolved! No more!

Now everything all about me was singing with Love and Abundance in a World of Miracles!

I remained at the hot springs down deep in the Sacred Canyon-Womb of Creation with my Three Spirit Healing Guides for well over a month's travel of Our Mother Moon, and they continued to instruct me in Spirit as my body healed!

Heaven was here, at the bottom of this great canyon, among the tall ferns and waterfalls and whole cliffs full of flowers. Heaven was here on Earth as We, You, and I, rained gently in the afternoons.

This was when Rochín came back to see us in the canyon and told us that he and Juan Lopez, the lawyer, had found out that *all* the Tarahumara lands had been legally stolen away from them. Millions and millions of acres.

"And . . . and there is nothing we can do about it," he added.

I laughed. "Rochín," I said, "where is your faith? Did you forget that in our dreams we can do anything?"

He took in a deep breath. "Yeah," he said. "I guess I have forgotten. It's so tough to keep the faith with all those piles of red tape and laws on top of laws."

"Well, yes, of course, but aren't laws also dreams?" I said, laughing even more. "Dreams of man trying to bring order to the world? Eh, so who's the Doubting Thomas now? Loosen up and laugh, Rochín; laugh, and see that it is already done! COMPLETED! FINISHED! AND WRITTEN IN THE STARS!"

He burst out with *carcajadas.* "Hello, *Señor Mayori!*"

"Hello, my friend and teacher!"

We looked into each other's eyes, and I saw in Carlos's eyes what I'd seen in the lion eyes of my youth. All fear and doubt were gone. He had a look of total calmness and neutrality. And I must have had the same look in my eyes, for we now kept looking at each other with so much pure love-*amor* that it brought tears to our eyes. United Raindrops were we, just as raindrops were that Sacred Fearless Place that the lioness and I had reached in the snowstorm that day so long ago.

"Then it is done," he said.

"Yes, then it is done," I said. "Now only the details need to be worked out."

We wiped the tears from our eyes, and hugged like there was no tomorrow, because, truly, *Mañana es otro milagro de Dios* was NOW HERE, WITH US, FOREVER!

Laughing with *carcajadas,* Rochín and I looked all about us, and as far as the eye could see there was Sacred Holy Beauty. The rocks, the cliffs, the ferns, the flowers, the waterfalls, and the piece of Father Sky high above us. Our Mother Earth was, indeed, Heaven, and we were deep down inside her Sacred Womb!

Yes, a million times yes, we knew that somehow, some way, we'd get back all this beautiful land for the Tarahumara, because the Tarahumara loved this land, and they would keep it beautiful and sacred for thousands of generations!

It was beyond their comprehension to think in terms of development and profit, because how could you develop or improve upon anything that was already perfect and wondrous?

We came out of the canyon united with all the Holy Sacred Powers of Our Lord Jesus Christ within us. How could we not? The Three Holy Wisemen who'd counseled Jesus were the same ones who now gave us counsel, too.

We would turn the tide, *con el favor de Dios!*

We would part the seas, *con el favor de Dios!*

How could we not? WE WERE WATER AND ONE WITH GOD, and once more we could feel Our Sacred Mother Earth sigh and give a little tremor of pure joy and happiness!

BOOK FOUR

REALITY

CHAPTER 18

Mireya

When my *gringo* came out of the Womb of Our Sacred Grandmother Canyon, people began to say they could no longer see him, because the Holy Light that radiated from him was so bright. He'd truly become a *señor mayori*, meaning a person who now lived equally in the World of the Spirits, as did the Three *Espiritos*, who'd helped heal him. But I had no trouble seeing him, because *mi amor* was as pure and bright with Light, as his Light was of Spirit. Love, after all, didn't have to be learned, but came with each child as Bright and Holy and Strong as the Light of the Stars above.

All summer when our camp was full of kids, I got to see him every day. It felt to me like we were almost a married couple. So when I saw him come back from the bottom of the canyon, I almost made the big mistake of jumping on him, but then I remembered the promise I'd made to him, and also that he was still not completely well yet.

We talked, but it was very difficult for me. I wanted to kiss him to pieces! He gave me a book called *Uncle Tom's Cabin*. I'd never read a book before. This was the first time, and it was so beautiful! I felt so close to this black girl and her way of life. I began to count the days until I turned 18, so I could have this man make love to me like I knew he would, because he was so gentle and good.

Of course that old shotgun hadn't been able to kill him at the canyon's rim. Our Great Canyon was Sacred and full of Beautiful Spirits and all of Our Ancestry. So how could guns kill goodness? When could weapons ever destroy that which we all had inside of us that connected us to Our Holy Creator, just as this book *Uncle Tom's Cabin* showed me so well? Even the people of the evil eye didn't like to see the world as they saw it. That was why eventually our distant cousin, who stole my grandparents' ranch from them and shot the boy at the lake, one day finally hung himself from a tree looking over Our Sacred Canyon. He, like Judas, could find no rest inside his Heart and Soul. And our Heart and Soul was the Holy Place where we human people really lived. Not in our bodies, but here inside us where we had the Kingdom of God, as Father Rochín told us.

So it was no surprise to any of us when my *gringo* one day found a black glove and two empty bullet shells on his pillow, and the following day we received word that the *comandante* of the police, who'd arrested and tortured my *gringo,* had had his eyes shot out of his head. Mexico's greatest assassin had shot the eyes out of the police captain so he'd be blind and lost for all eternity.

I loved it and spat on the ground in his memory, but my *gringo* told me to forgive him, too, and not be so hard, because it would only harden me inside. I could understand what he said, but for me, I still liked to spit on him. It felt good. No one was going to hurt my *gringo,* and no one was going to ever get me to live in fear.

The story of *la Mano Negra* leaving two empty shells and killing the police captain spread like wildfire, and this was when I also learned that Father Rochín and his friend Juan Lopez had gone through records down in the town of Cuauhtémoc and they'd found that all the land the Indians lived on wasn't theirs. The land of the *ejido,* where the boy had been shot, belonged to Ortega (who was still alive at this point). Not one of us could understand this. These lands had been owned by the Tarahumara for thousands and thousands of years. Did this, then, mean that records were more important than reality? Did this, then, mean that Emma was really my *gringo's* wife?

Oh no, this could not be. There was something very wrong with all this. The land belonged to the people who lived on it and worked it, and a man and a woman belonged to each other here in the heart. I would not let any of this confuse me. After all, I knew what I knew as sure as the sun came up each day. And besides, my *gringo* and I were now taking long walks together, and he was educating me.

For instance, he explained to me that I wasn't an ignorant, uneducated girl from the mountains, as some of the kids had told me at the camp. He explained to me how intelligent and smart I was and how much knowledge and education I had. He explained to me how the Tarahumara Indians were some of the most highly intelligent and well-educated people he'd ever met.

Little by little, I began to see the world differently than I'd ever seen it before. Like I'd never understood how cruel it was of us people who lived in town to look down our noses at the Tarahumara and refer to them as Indians without reason. My *gringo* was a good man. He wanted to bring light and understanding and love and peace to all people, even to those who had tortured him.

This was very difficult for me to accept. I still hated them for what they'd done to my beloved Jan, and I was glad when we found out that *la Mano Negra* had shot the eyes out of the captain's head. Now no one would dare bring any harm to my *gringo. La Mano Negra,* whom Jan had serenaded on his radio show and spoken to in our canyon, had now come over to his side, just as the Three Holy *Curanderos* had explained to him that Darkness always did when shown Respect, Love, and the Holy Light of God.

It was now said that even Ortega and Van Housen would not dare to raise a hand to my *gringo.* His becoming a *mayori* had not impressed them, but having the eyes shot out of the *comandante*'s head while he was being protected by all his men had sent a very strong message to these two, whose blood ran backward from their hearts. Now my *gringo* was not just protected from above, but from below, too.

I laughed. This was a very good way to live life, I thought—to have not just the hand of God protecting you, but also the black hand of the Devil!

CHAPTER 19

Jan

I was shocked.

My first day back at our kids' camp, I found two empty bullet casings on my pillow. What did this mean, that *la Mano Negra* had already done his/her deed? Then why was he/she even bothering to tell me? This was no warning to cause me fear, because the act had already been done. The following day we received word that the captain of the judicial police who'd arrested and tortured me had had both eyes shot out of his head, and he'd been surrounded by his men, yet none of them had seen or heard anything until it was too late.

I hate to say it, but it felt very good to hear this news. Now the most infamous assassin in all of Mexico wasn't threatening me, but instead protecting me. Rochín and I talked about this turn of events, and we began to speculate that maybe *la Mano Negra* was an *Indio* or maybe a *Mestizo,* and he/she had gotten on our side, because she/he had found out that we were now trying to return millions of acres to the Tarahumara. Still, I told everyone at the camp that we had to be careful, because once more *la Mano Negra* had entered my living quarters without being seen by anyone.

That winter it didn't snow very much, and I could drive the old red Ford back and forth between town and the camp. Then came spring, and Holy Week occurred during the following month. It was the biggest festival of the year for the Tarahumara. We got together with all the elders of all the different *ejidos* of the Tarahumara. It took days. Father Rochín spoke first—through six different interpreters, because of all the different dialects—and he explained what it was we'd found out about the ownership of their lands.

It became a huge emotional turmoil of misunderstanding in the translation, because how could any sane person explain the reality of legal ownership to people who only recognized the miraculous? It was decided that the Tarahumara would first do their annual Holy Week, because only then would they have the Sacred Powers with which to understand and overturn all these evil-doings of darkness.

As always, Holy Week began with the fermentation of huge *ojas,* big pots of homemade corn beer that smelled to the high Heavens. Father Rochín and I were both invited to stay for the evening services, which no white person had ever been allowed to witness. The great big drums began at sundown, with four men to each one. The rest of the men got loud and drunk and began to circle the church counterclockwise—dancing, shaking rattles, and beating smaller drums.

The women and children remained on the huge, tall orange boulders that surrounded the church and watched the men. Then at dusk the women quickly came down off the boulders and joined the ranks of men, circling the church clockwise, and with screeches of joy, they stole the huge penis, which the men carried to signify Judas!

Jesus was represented by a large colorful cross decorated with flowers. Judas was represented by a monstrous 18-inch black-and-red thick penis, because according to the Tarahumara, it took a lot of guts to go against the Light of Creation and sacrifice yourself to the Darkness, as Judas had done.

This was when the screams of laughter began and everyone started having a very good time. Because if the women could end up with Judas's penis at the end of the weeklong celebration, then for a whole year they could make love with whomever they pleased and as often as they pleased! But if the men ended up with Judas's penis, they were the ones who could then make love with whomever they pleased. It became a glorious war between the sexes, with such wild *carcajadas* and screeches of joy that it filled the entire valley with sounds of happiness!

By the third day of the celebration, thousands of Tarahumara had come in from as far away as Batopilas and even the desolate Rain of Gold canyon. Now it was a great joy to see even the young girls wrestling for Judas's big penis among themselves with such screeching, unbridled laughter! But the cross of Jesus was not forgotten. And He, too, was being carried around the church counterclockwise by the men and given full honor and recognition as the women went clockwise around the church, laughing and giggling as they rushed in to grab hold of Judas's huge penis from one another.

As for me, I wasn't shocked anymore, and I'd begun to laugh, too, because I could now understand why Mireya felt so comfortable with her sexuality. Truly, it seemed so natural for all these young girls and boys to be so open and happy and joyful about sex.

On the fourth night, Rochín and I were driving back to our camp when it hit me like a ton of bricks.

"Rochín, the story of the Bible never stopped! Joseph Smith was right!"

"You mean Joseph Smith of the Mormons?"

"Yes, he was right! The story of the Bible never stopped and will never stop. You saw how everyone was begetting everyone tonight, like everyone used to beget everyone in the Bible!"

"Are you suggesting that we become Mormons and have many wives?"

I laughed. "No, I'm not suggesting that. What I'm saying is that you and I are up against our own Judas, just as Jesus was up against His own Judas, and so it's not up to us to pass judgment on our contemporary Judas."

"You're making reference to Ortega and Van Housen?"

"Exactly. Both of them. So it is for us to pray for them, and most important, for us to open up our eyes and see that they are doing their own Holy Work just as much as we do ours. In other words, we can love these men. It was my love, after all, that I believe even brought *la Mano Negra* around."

Tears began to flow down Carlos Rochín's face, but no, he wasn't sad. He was joyful, because just as the Tarahumara gave equal honor to Judas, so could he now give equal love and honor to Van Housen. I pulled over, and Rochín and I walked down to the water's edge. All the Heavens were full of stars, and . . . the darkness between the stars . . . didn't feel overwhelming anymore.

"Thank you," I said to Rochín, "for having brought me to this untouched Heaven on Earth, *amigo.* I've learned so much, and I feel such peace."

"Thank you," he said, "for helping me see life in such a loving, good way, *Señor Mayori.*"

And so we prayed together, thanking God, the Holy Creator, for this great opportunity presented to us, and it felt real and good and wonderful!

CHAPTER 20

Mireya

This summer, my mother, Coco, and the other assistants and I had to work even harder in the kitchen at our camp for kids, because now each week we had a new shipment of kids come in from either Chihuahua City to the east or from Los Mochis to the west. People with big cameras like the ones they'd used for making the *gringo* movie came in and photographed us, and they once got a picture of me smiling with my big horse teeth. I looked so beautiful! How could I not? I was in love, and this November I would turn 18 years old!

Then the summer was over, and the fall came and Father Rochín and my *gringo* began going down to Chihuahua City. It was said that they were talking to the ex-governor of Chihuahua, whose wife was good friends with my *gringo* and Father Rochín. They were trying to set up a meeting with the president of Mexico to get the lands back that had been stolen from the Tarahumara. I wondered if they could also get back the ranch that had been stolen from my grandparents, but I said nothing of this, because I could see how busy my *gringo* and Father Rochín were.

And besides, land wasn't really what I was dreaming about. I would soon be 18, and it seemed as if everyone had forgotten what I'd promised to do on my birthday, November 29. But I hadn't. I was preparing my wedding clothes and sewing by hand little red and yellow flowers into the pillowcase that I'd need for that special day. Because the way I saw it, once I went to *mi amor,* I was never going to return home again. I'd be his woman, his wife in the eyes of God, even if we didn't get a paper from the court.

Oh, I was so happy and all excited that I'd wake up in the middle of the night and go outside to see the stars, and I swear that the stars would wink at me, wishing me their best.

And, also, I wasn't a little skinny girl anymore. I'd actually gotten nice-sized titties in the last two years, and my ass had filled out a little bit, too. I knew this because after I bathed, I'd turn and look at myself in the mirror, and I liked what I saw very much. I was sure I wouldn't disappoint Jan. Every day I was filling out more and more, and after a few children, I'd be a fully developed woman with a nice round, warm body. Oh, I could hardly wait! I was so excited to squeeze him to me without any clothes between us!

"Thank you, thank you, thank you," I'd say to my *familia* of stars. "I can hardly wait—I'M SO EXCITED!"

And I swear that my star *familia* answered me with a series of shooting stars streaking across the Heavens, with all the others smiling and dancing and singing.

CHAPTER 21

Jan

When summer camp started, Carlos Rochín and I could no longer work long hours with Juan Lopez going through the records. So our young lawyer took over alone, and we concentrated our efforts on the camp, which had grown immensely since the year before. Then something happened. Juan stopped returning Rochín's calls, and when the priest went down to see him, Juan informed him that someone had broken into his office and stolen all the copies of the records we'd accumulated.

"I believed him, Jan," said Rochín when he returned from his trip, "until a couple of days later when I saw him driving a beautiful new car. Where had he gotten the money? He was as poor as a church mouse. They got to him, Jan."

"Yes, it looks that way," I said.

"Of course. No one broke into his office. He turned over all the records that we'd accumulated on the logging companies and Ortega. Now they know in full detail what it is we're attempting to do, and they have the money and power to keep sabotaging us before we can reorganize well enough to present a case."

I nodded. I completely agreed with Rochín. "So, my friend, let us go to the water's edge and pray for a miracle."

We went down to the lake and began to pray, and two weeks later we were informed that the mother of the president of Mexico, Miguel de la Madrid, wanted to come to our camp to see what it was we did. We now had kids from some of the wealthiest and most powerful families in Mexico coming to our camp, and their parents were amazed by how much their kids learned about respect and life in just a week's time. We weren't amazed. *Las Barrancas del Cobre* was a magical place!

Of course, Van Housen heard the news, as did everyone else, so he immediately contacted the archdiocese and tried to take over. The day *Señora* de la Madrid arrived, the whole of Creel was beaming with excitement. We'd been told that she was coming in a private railroad car with six of her lady friends and their personal servants and bodyguards.

Van Housen looked like a poster of godliness. He'd put away his Safari helmet and Pendleton shirt, and he was dressed in his very best priestly attire. He had the archbishop contact the grand old lady, so he was sure he could brush Father Rochín and me aside and be her sole escort during her stay in Creel. When the train pulled into the station and the grand old lady and her group got off, Van Housen did the tactful maneuver that Rochín had told me about. Quickly he stepped right in front of us, blocking Rochín and me from her view, and turned on the charm.

Rochín's face caved in, but I merely closed my eyes, said a little prayer, then reopened them, just as I'd done when I was a boy in the snowstorm and saw the lion eyes. Miracle of Miracles, the wise, tough old lady saw through Van Housen's deceit and told him to get out of her way, that she'd come to see Father Rochín and the American who sang like an angel, even with his broken Spanish.

But Van Housen was not to be undone, and he made the grave mistake of trying to impose himself on her. Instantly, she lost all patience and threatened to have him removed by her bodyguards if he didn't remove himself from her presence. Van Housen turned on his heel and left.

I thanked all the stars above for the president's mother's great courage, and she and her entourage stayed with us for a week. It was fabulous, and before she left, she gave Rochín and me her card and told us to call her personal secretary, Pierre Benoit, if we ever needed anything.

When the summer ended, we closed the camp, and Rochín and I began going through records again. We found out that Ortega and the logging companies not only owned well over two million acres of the land the Tarahumara had been living on for untold generations, but they also owned hundreds of thousands of acres that had belonged to the federal government. This was beyond all credibility. No wonder the judicial police had come after us. On paper Ortega and the logging companies owned half the state of Chihuahua, which was so huge that people referred to it as the Texas of Mexico.

"But how is this possible?" I asked Rochín. "To steal land from uneducated Indians is one thing, but to steal land from the federal government is a whole other ballpark."

"You're right. This has to be an inside job," said Rochín. "The highest levels of government had to be in on this one. Ortega is just a puppet."

Father Rochín confessed to me that he'd been smelling a rat for years. "I'd always found it very suspicious how every year the Tarahumara were only given a handful of cornmeal for the forest that was logged, but now we can see that Ortega had federal help. This is the only way this huge operation could have taken place. I mean, we're talking about people in power all the way up to the presidency. We're going to have to be very careful when we contact the president's mother. These aren't just drug lords we're going to be up against this time, Jan. These are the pillars of the nation of Mexico!"

I could see what Rochín meant.

"We need to inform the Indian leaders of the gravity of this situation as soon as possible," Rochín continued. "And we need to be very careful. This isn't just Ortega and Van Housen that . . . that we'll be battling."

When we drove to visit the different Tarahumara villages and talked to their leaders, we were told that for years they were given a blank piece of paper every year and told to make an X and put their thumbprint on it; then they were given their handful of cornmeal. Suddenly we understood, because the documents on record showed page after page of the Indians signing away the rights to their lands with X's and thumbprints.

"So then the Tarahumara signed blank pieces of paper that were later turned into official documents of land ownership," I said.

"It looks that way," replied Rochín, "but something is still missing. How did Ortega and the owners of these logging companies make contact with the federal people? I know them, and none of them have the sophistication, brains, or education to have come up with such an elaborate scheme and then present it to the—" Rochín stopped speaking.

"It was Van Housen, wasn't it?" I said.

"Yes, of course. He, through the archdiocese, is the only one who had contact with people at a high federal level. Now, sadly, it all suddenly makes perfect sense," Rochín said. "Sure, this is the reason the archdiocese only wants Van Housen up here in Creel. Over the last few years alone the records show that they've logged millions of board feet of some of the finest lumber in the world. They've charged the Indians for the logging roads, the trucks, and the sawmill equipment. This is how they justified the Tarahumara share as only a handful of cornmeal."

Carlos Rochín's eyes filled with tears. "I had always believed him. I'd always thought that no matter how cruel Van Housen was, he was doing what he did out of the principles that he upheld. It never entered my mind that . . . that . . ." he broke off. "Then this means our archdiocese only wants Van Housen up here, not because more Indians attend our services, but because he has given the church millions of dollars. OH, I CANNOT BE A PRIEST ANY LONGER!" he yelled. "I can't! I can't! I, too, like Francisco de Vaca will relinquish my faith!"

"Wait! Hold on! You don't have to do that, Rochín!"

"Jan," he said, "this isn't all of it! Some of my . . . my very own family own the trucks these logging companies use. So this means that my very own nephews and cousins, whom I brought up here to the lake to get close to nature and God, saw this untouched forest and got together with Van Housen and Ortega and—OH MY GOD! MY GOD, HELP ME! I don't want to turn bitter and lose faith, dear Lord!"

I helped Carlos Rochín to lie down, and I went down to the lake's edge to pray. I, too, needed God's help. So much had happened in the last couple of months that at times I just didn't know what was real anymore.

I was praying and beginning to feel better when I heard a loud whistle. I glanced around, expecting to see a human being, but I saw no one. I heard the whistle again, then I saw three large, bright yellow-orange birds with black wings. They whistled once more, and I smiled. They looked so beautiful and full of joy as they hopped from branch to branch. I'd never seen birds like this before, and I now remembered that during my first year up here, I'd seen many types of birds I'd never seen before, especially the woodpeckers. Some were as large as parrots, and their underwings flashed of fluorescent green and red as they flew from tree to tree pecking them clean of beetles and other insects.

"Hello," I said to the three large birds.

"Hello," they repeated back to me with the tenor of an actor's voice.

I smiled, laughed, and remembered how at first the Indians had not been able to see me, or at least hadn't given my existence any importance, until I'd begun to play my guitar and sing to the beautiful night. Only then had they gathered on an outcropping of rocks to hear me, and the children had come close to me. It had been one of the greatest joys of my life!

The three birds turned into my Three Wisemen Healers, and together we built a small fire, and I went and got my guitar and began to play at the water's edge, feeling the warmth of the little fire and my *amigos'* hearts.

"Big fire, white man far back," said Miguel. "Little fire, Indian up close. We have come to tell you that our Holy Sacred Grandmother Earth herself will guide you and Father Rochín through this one, because it is in returning all this Sacred Land back to the Tarahumara that it will be saved for untold generations. All over our planet our Holy Grandmother wishes for us to return to our original native ways before it is too late. So sing, *mayori,* sing and play your music and make our Grandmother happy, here in her heart of hearts."

And so I sang and played my guitar all afternoon and into the night, and the Three Holy Wisemen of Jesus stayed with me, replenishing the little fire with wood and giving me warmth of heart. I was still singing when the dawn began to paint the eastern sky in color, and this was when I saw that Mireya, her mother, Coco, and a whole group of Indians had gathered on a nearby outcropping of rocks and were listening to me.

My cup runneth over with love! And I instantly knew that Rochín was truly not supposed to relinquish his faith. On the contrary, he had to go *deeper* into his own faith. We were surrounded by God's *amor.* The dream was continuous, and those beautiful orange birds who had whistled to me like human beings had, indeed, been the Three Wisemen *Curanderos* who had come to me at the hospital and shown me that miracles were our daily bread. Both Rochín and I had to go deeper and deeper into our faiths, just as Our Lord Jesus had done 2,000 years ago, even as they'd crucified Him.

The world was still turning, and the love of God was still glowing. This was when I heard a SCREECH, and I looked up and here was a Great Golden Eagle above me. I smiled, remembering the shaft of eagle feathers and lion claws that had been presented to me by the Three Indian Wisemen.

PARADISE

CHAPTER 22

Mireya

The summer passed and the fall came, and in a few weeks, I, Mireya, the happiest woman in all the world, was going to be 18 years old! But then it began to snow so much that Jan couldn't drive into town from the camp anymore. So the night before my 18th birthday, I prepared my boots and winter clothes, and in the dawn of the morning, I perfumed my body, tied flowers in my hair, left a note for my mother, and set out on foot for the camp.

It was cold and snowing, and the going was difficult, but I didn't care. I felt strong, warmed by my burning love. Twice I saw deer hiding from the storm underneath a grouping of trees. I smiled to them, waving hello, and continued on my way. It was midday when the wind picked up and I began to have real difficulty. The snow was so deep that it had gotten up over the top of my boots, and my feet were wet and cold. I knew that if I stopped to rest, I'd freeze to death, so I had to keep going no matter how exhausted I was. Then in the blowing snow, I lost my way, and if it hadn't been for the outcropping of rocks that looked like an elephant, I don't know what I would have done.

It was beginning to get dark, and I was so tired that I couldn't lift my heavy, waterlogged boots anymore, and I fell down. I began to cry. My perfumed body, I was now sure, smelled awful! And I'd lost all the flowers I'd tied in my hair. Oh, I was sure that I would look more like a wet rat than a healthy, beautiful young woman by the time I came straggling into our camp. But what could I do? So I kept going and going no matter how tired I was, and I walked directly up to Jan's cabin, which was deep in snow.

It was a terrible struggle to make my way the last few feet to his door. I knocked, trying my best to straighten up. When he opened the door, I saw the shocked look on his face. I guess I looked even worse than I thought I did. But I still tried to smile as best I could.

"It's my birthday," I said to him. "I'm 18 years old today, and I still feel the same way about you, Jan."

"What?" he said, as if not remembering what I was talking about. "Come right in. Did you walk all the way from town?" he asked.

I got mad. "Well, yes, of course!" I yelled. "I told you that I'd be at your door the day I turned 18!"

He continued to look at me like he still didn't know what I was talking about. But then I guess he did remember, because he now said, "Oh yes, I said you could come to me when you turned 18, so we could talk. Come, let's get you over by the fire. You must be freezing."

"Oh no, I'm not cold," I said, lying. "My love for you has kept me warm the whole way. But I would like to take off my jacket and wet boots."

When he helped me take off my jacket and boots, I began to tremble like a leaf. In truth, I was so cold and tired and weak that I could scream. In my rush to get out of the house before my mother awoke, I'd forgotten to bring any food with me.

"Mireya," he said, "my dear child, you're freezing cold. Did you really walk out the whole way from town without snowshoes?"

"Y-y-y-ess!" I said, trembling all the more and rubbing the icicles out of my hair and my dripping, red, swollen nose. "In town it wasn't snowing very much. I had no idea the wind would pick up."

"My God, it's a miracle you didn't die. Here, come by the fire, but I think you're going to have to get out of all the rest of those wet clothes."

I couldn't talk anymore, I was shaking so hard. I just nodded yes, and he brought a blanket-*serape* and held it up to give me privacy so I could take all off my clothes. Now I could feel the warmth of the fire on my naked body, and I took the blanket and wrapped it about me.

"Would you like some hot soup?" he asked.

"Y-y-y-ess! Y-y-y-ess!" I said. I was losing my voice and still shaking.

He brought me a bowl of soup. I was so hungry that I used both hands to reach out for the bowl, and the blanket-*serape* fell away and I was naked, with the light of the fire dancing on my body. I saw his eyes open wide as he stared at my nakedness. A gleam came to his eyes, and in that instant, I knew that even though I didn't look my best, he was very happy with what he saw. Seeing that, I ate with a joy and hunger I'd never felt before and didn't care one little bit that I was as naked as the day I was born.

But then after I finished my soup, I covered my body back up with the blanket-*serape* because I could see that he was getting very nervous.

"Mireya," he now said to me in a tone of voice that I didn't like, "yes, I do remember that I told you to come to see me when you turned 18 if you still felt the same way about me, but, well, I . . . I don't want to take advantage of a young, innocent girl."

"Are you saying that I am innocent because I've never been with a man?" I said. "This is ridiculous! Innocence is when someone doesn't see, with both of their eyes wide-open. My mother, she had us children with three different men, and good advice she always gives us, but then she never takes her own advice. I'm not innocent, Jan. I'm by far one of the most experienced women

I know because of all I've seen and had to do to make my way in the world.

"I met Emma, who still claims to be your wife, and by the look of her, I'm sure that she'd been well *toreada* by innumerable men, but does this give her the wisdom to no longer be innocent? Innocent, *she* was," I said in a strong voice, "when she pointed the gun to my face, thinking she could turn the tide of my love for you. No, Jan, I am not innocent! I am a well-thought-out woman who walked through snow and storm to lie down with you in our bed for the rest of my life if . . . if you'll have me."

"Oh, Mireya," he said, "I just don't know if I can even perform. Those chains they had between my legs and kept yanking cut my private parts to pieces."

"Let me see," I said, reaching out to take off his pants.

He backed away, laughing. "Oh, Mireya, I just don't know if I or the world is ready for such a blunt, direct, honest love as yours. Truly, I feel so inadequate. And, also, I've never been that successful with women."

"Does God have any trouble being loving?" I asked.

"Well, no, of course not."

"Well, then, we will ask God to guide us, as He guided me to you through the snowstorm today when I thought I could not take one more step, I was so cold and tired."

"Oh, Mireya, Mireya, Mireya," he said, "please understand that Father Rochín and I are both in great danger, and I don't want you to get involved."

"Jan, *mi amor*, did you forget that the old shotgun wouldn't fire when they had it pointed at your head? Did you forget that their bullets had no effect on the Three Spirit *Curanderos* as they ran and leaped off into the canyon? Why are you of such little faith when it comes to love?"

As I said this, I let the *serape*-blanket fall from my body. I was done talking. I was now going to have him. I reached into the bag of clothes I'd brought and slipped on my beautiful white wedding dress, the one I'd sewn little yellow and red flowers on, just as I'd sewn them on our pillowcase.

"You're so beautiful!" he said. "You're an Angel, Mireya!"

"YES!" I screamed. *"¡UN ÁNGEL DEL AMOR!"*

And I leaped on him, wrapping my legs about his middle, kissing him as fast as I could, like I'd always done. But I was bigger and heavier now, and he fell over backward on the floor, but I didn't get off of him, because for the first time, he began to kiss me in return.

I laughed with joy!

I wasn't wearing any underwear . . . and OH, OH, OH, OUR KISSING BECAME HEAVEN ON EARTH as I felt his member EXPLODE, wanting to come inside of me! Oh, oh, oh, I'd been waiting for this for nearly five years, because even before I'd met him, I was in love with him, and now he was finally mine, just as it was written in the stars!

God was with me!

God was with us!

And Jan never had any difficulty with his private parts, and all night we made *el amor* again and again, and twice we heard the scream of his mountain lion scream along with us! No doubt about it, God loved *nuestro amor!*

CHAPTER 23

Jan

What can I say? I'd been married twice before, so I'd thought I knew a few things about marriage and women, but I quickly found out that I knew nothing about love compared to this innocent young girl. She was intuitively knowledgeable about love and intimacy far beyond anything I'd ever imagined! Not just in tirelessly lovemaking day after day, but in our conversations about Life and God and Harmony and Peace, and all the Joy and Fulfillment that can be found between a man and a woman that I'd never known anything about.

She became my Love-Teacher, and I became her Love-Student, and the gentle openness with which she spoke and taught me was profound.

Her grandmother, not her mother, had truly spent a lot of time with her and taught her so much about *amor* when she was a little girl. They'd worked side by side in gardening, in cooking, in tending to livestock; and her grandmother had told her all about the magic side of Life and God and the Miraculous Wonders of Living *la vida* as they'd worked side by side.

Little by little, I began to understand that Mireya was singularly the most profoundly intelligent and learned human being I'd ever met outside of the Three Wisemen *Curanderos*. And when I gave her information about the outside world, as I'd been taught by my Harvard University mail course, she instantly understood all religious and political implications by bringing everything I told her about the outside world right back to her relationship to God and Mother Nature.

That is, she instantly realized that Rochín hadn't had to renounce his faith when he'd become disillusioned, but on the contrary, he had to go deeper into his faith to find his answer. Even my story of *la Mano Negra* didn't seem strange or frightening to her. And she didn't see the logging companies and big hotel chains as a big threat either.

"People run these large businesses, right?" she asked.

"Yes, that's true," I said.

"Then, Jan, just talk to them about their children and their grandchildren and their grandchildren's children, and show them how they have already ruined our coastlines with their hotels and developments, and explain to them how this will happen here, too, if they don't do things differently. So it's not about saying no to them, Jan. It's about saying yes and yes and yes, just as it is yes and yes and yes between the stars and the darkness and *nuestro amor.*

"Everything is round and smooth and beautiful and perfect already. Just look around at the rocks and flowers and waterfalls and see how they are always saying yes and yes and yes to each other through the changing seasons. So these big businesses must realize that they, too, must say yes and yes and yes with the changing seasons, or their own children and grandchildren's children will be the losers, like what happens with the drug lords. Poor greedy men—in the end they lose everything."

I laughed. What else could I do? For Mireya no problem existed in the world. All was good and possible and beautiful and already perfect. All we humans had to do was relax and dream and understand how to get the most love and joy out of our wondrous living. But there was one thing I told Mireya that she couldn't grasp, which was when I tried to explain to her how my first job as a young minister had been in the Haight-Ashbury district of San Francisco.

"But how could kids be so lost?" she asked. "Having all that sex, couldn't they see that it would never lead them to love? True Love comes from the Heart, here inside. Not from this hole between my legs and this rock stick between your legs. What happened to the wisdom they received from their grandparents?"

"That's it," I said. "They had none. Or more precisely, they stopped believing in their parents' and grandparents' way of thinking."

She laughed. "How can that be? The fawn doesn't stop believing her mother deer, and the baby rabbits don't stop believing in the whole family of rabbits."

I just didn't know what to say. "Look," I finally said, "I guess this is the big question that civilization must ask itself, because what you read in *Uncle Tom's Cabin* about racism and hate is the very reason, I guess, why young people stopped trusting or believing in the values of their parents and grandparents."

Tears came to her eyes. "Oh, Jan, this is so sad, because when children stop believing in what their parents and grandparents tell them, then they are all lost people. Not just the kids." She wiped the tears from her eyes. "Oh, we must pray, Jan. I feel so very sad for all these lost families in those United States. We must go to the north and help these poor people find trust and love in their parents and grandparents once again."

I took Mireya in my arms. My God, I was learning about what it meant to be a true Christian from a girl who'd never been inside a church or read one single word from the Bible!

"Yes," I said, with tears streaming down my face, "let us pray."

"Yes, *mi amor*, because without the good, loving advice, particularly from grandparents, then an entire *familia* becomes lost," she said. "Parents can't do it all. They are still caught up in the

troubles of their own living. Oh, I would have no life or understanding if it wasn't for my grandparents, who taught me how to
see beauty and wonder in everything. In the coyote, even as he
steals your chickens. In the rabbit, even as he eats of your garden.
For all is about sharing, and knowing that there is enough for us
all, because God, in His Infinite Wisdom, gives us Daily Miracles
through the changing seasons. So this is why it is easy for me
to know my way, because I trust life to always be beautiful and
as smooth and easy to handle as the smooth, round river rocks
who've had so much rushing water pass over them. This is the
Spirit World of God for us—living water passing over us until we,
at last, are as smooth and round and happy and whole as river
rocks."

"All this your grandparents taught you?"

"Yes, of course, as I am sure that your grandparents taught
you."

"No," I said, "I never even got to know my grandparents very
well."

"Why?"

"Because we moved to California when I was very young."

"You moved," she said, "without taking your grandparents
with you? How is this possible?"

"Well, you see, my dad died, and my older brother, a brilliant
engineer for IBM, had a very high-paying job out in California, so
my mother—"

"Your mother moved for money?"

I started laughing. What else could I do? Her world was so different from the world I'd grown up in that all I said made no sense
to her. "Oh, Mireya, Mireya, someday I will take you to the United
States. To California, to San Francisco and San Jose, so you can
even see the places where I set up the two coffeehouses."

"Really? You will take me? I have never even been down the
mountain past Cuauhtémoc, not even to our *Ciudad de Chihuahua!*"

"Yes, we will fly in to San Francisco, California, and you will
see the Golden Gate Bridge and the Haight-Ashbury district and—"

"Fly? In a plane? Me?"

"Yes."

"And there's a whole bridge that's made of gold?" she asked.

"No, no, that's just what it's called."

"Why, if it's not gold?"

"I don't really know, maybe because it's painted an orange-golden color, or maybe because it's the gateway out into the great Pacific Ocean. Anyway, you will see firsthand where a whole generation of lost young souls came to San Francisco, I guess, in search of trying to find their way back into seeing life as . . . as you see it, Pure and Miraculous and Beautiful and full of Love and Goodness."

"Of course," she said, "there's no other way to see this Great Paradise that God has given us, because every day is *otro milagro*—another miracle!"

I stopped talking. Her entire face was glowing with joy. I felt so blessed, so happy, so lucky, to have met this incredible woman. Oh, how I wished I could take this "natural woman," like Carole King had so wisely sung about, and have her meet King and Joan Baez and Jerry Garcia and Bob Dylan and Clint Eastwood and Linda Ronstadt and all the rest of them, so they could celebrate her, just as I was now celebrating her. She was my guide, my teacher, and I, who'd thought I was too old and worldly and jaded for her, was her simpleminded student.

It was in our second week together that we decided to leave the high country and hike down into the bottom of the canyon, where it would be warm and sunny. And this would also be the perfect place for us to do our Indian-Ceremony Wedding of the Sacred Blessing in Uniting a man and woman before God. We would do this by the hot springs and the small waterfalls where the Three Holy Wisemen *Curanderos* had done their Miraculous Healing of my broken-up body. It *was* truly Miraculous how even my twisted, broken arms and legs had healed so rapidly; and my nails, which had been pulled off with pliers, had grown back.

I made snowshoes for Mireya, and the day we left the high country, it looked like it might begin to snow once again. We

could see that a big storm with dark, formidable clouds was coming in from the north, but we had no fear. We were with God, the
Holy Creator and Ruler of the Whole Universe! And not just our
tiny Mother Earth!

CHAPTER 24

Mireya

A blanket *de amor* came down from Heaven and covered Jan and me with such private, warm goodness that each day was wonderful, and the nights were even better. The magic that my grandmother had told me existed between a man and a woman now filled our Hearts and Souls with such Great Abundance that no matter how cold and windy it was outside, we were warm and happy in our Hearts and Souls, because this was where we now lived, in our Heart-Soul.

We slept on the floor in front of the fire, and I loved the way the Light of our Little Holy Fire Danced on our naked, gorgeous bodies. Skin-to-skin we lived and made *el amor* most of the day and night, then slept together like newborn puppies with our legs and arms wrapped about each other. I never knew that the smell of my *hombre*'s body would become an intoxicating perfume and his feelings would become my feelings and his dreams would become my dreams. And oh, did we eat mountains of beans and squash, and deer meat that my love's lion brought to us and put on the porch, just as house cats bring mice to the person they love.

Then it looked like the weather was going to clear and we'd be able to go to town for supplies, but my bones spoke to me, as my mother's and grandmother's bones had always spoken to them, and told me that a big storm was going to hit us, which then meant that we'd get even more snow. I told Jan. He believed me. Quickly he made snowshoes for me from young tree branches and the hide of the last deer the lion had brought in for us. The next day we could see that dark clouds of the storm were coming our way from the north.

"We won't make it into town," Jan said to me. "So our best chance is for us to get off this high ground and go down into the bottom of the canyon."

I screeched with delight. I was so happy! It had always been my dream to spend my moon of honey with my True Love down in the Paradise of Our Sacred Canyon. The canyon was only a mile deep, but the trail to go down had so many twists and turns that I was told it was well over a ten-mile journey to get to the bottom of our beloved Grandmother Canyon.

The storm was coming in fast by the time we put on our snowshoes and walked out of the camp and around the lake to the canyon's rim. We had to go back toward Elephant Rock to get to the place where there was a trail to take us down into the canyon. The going was difficult, and we were pretty tired by the time we got to the great canyon's rim. Looking down into the enormous canyon and across to its great orange-red walls on the other side, we could see snowdrifts piled up on the flat ledges.

An eagle SCREECHED, and we started down the steep, dangerous trail. More than once, even I, who am as agile as a deer, almost slipped off the trail's edge, falling thousands and thousands of feet. But I didn't fall. I'm quick and strong, and each time I was able to get hold of a rock or tree branch, *con el favor de Dios*—with the favor of God.

After a few hours, I could see that Jan still didn't have all his strength back, so twice I carried his pack for him, especially over dangerous, steep twists in the trail. Then finally we were past the snowdrifts and getting down into the warmth of the great canyon, which we locals called the vagina of Chihuahua. Oh, it was such a luscious, beautiful vagina to see and feel and smell, once we began to enter the green tropical jungles at the bottom of the Copper Canyon. Here, it was warm, and songbirds and the sound of waterfalls filled our ears with joy, and butterflies and wildflowers filled our eyes with wonder. We'd been so cold up on the rim. No wonder the Tarahumara had their winter homes in the bottom of the canyon. Oh, it was Truly Paradise to come up to a series of little waterfalls cascading over rock and joining up with the main river, which was around the bend to our left and quite a ways away.

That afternoon we bathed in the hot mineral springs where Jan had bathed when he'd been with the Three Holy *Espiritos* to heal his broken body. Before dark we gathered flowers from the numerous wild plants that grew year-round in the canyon, and we made headbands of flowers and woven ferns. And then by the edge of a beautiful little waterfall, we stripped naked as the day we were born and faced each other Heart to Heart, traveling into each other's eyes, the Gateway to Our Souls, and we asked God to Join us and Unite us in His Holy Sacred Love of Abundance and Joy for all. Because my grandmother had always explained to me that there was no scarcity in the World of God. Scarcity only existed in the world of humans who were disconnected from the *amor de Papito Dios.*

Jan and I locked eyes, and took turns speaking to God as we placed our right hands on each other's Heart Area. Oh, I was so happy that I began to cry, and once more I thanked God for having gifted me this wonderful man. THIS WAS MY DREAM COME TRUE!

The days came and went, and we lived in a Blessed World of Magic, exactly how my grandparents had explained it would be for me when I finally married. My grandparents had also married down in the bottom of Our Sacred Canyon. For weeks Jan and I stayed down in the depths of the canyon, Uniting Our Love deeper and deeper into Hearts and Souls and Bodies with all of our Lovemaking.

The days became weeks, and Our United Dream continued . . . and the weeks passed, giving us a journey through a full moon, and every day we swam under the waterfalls and then sunned ourselves on the large, flat, warm rocks near the hot springs. We were a man and a woman in Love and living off the land, and as happy as the birds in the trees and the deer in the meadows. We'd found Heaven on Earth, and we were just as pure and whole as Adam and Eve. In fact, that was exactly who we were, because the story of the Bible, my grandmother had told me, had never ended, and we, too, were here, right now, glowing in God's Light *de amor.*

One day I told Jan I wished for us to pray for all those poor lost young people he'd known in San Francisco and San Jose. Oh, it truly hurt me deeply inside to imagine all those young people telling Jan that life was all about drugs and skin-to-skin sex, so it really didn't matter who they were taking into their bodies as long as they were having plenty of sex.

It hurt me to imagine all these young people being so lost, especially when Jan told me that whole rooms would be full of people having sex right beside each other. We prayed, and I don't really know if our prayers helped anyone, but I know it made me feel better, because I now understood that these hippie youngsters, as Jan called them, hadn't had a wise old grandmother to instruct them. And everyone needed instruction. Even the little *burro* had to learn how to use his lips and tongue so he could eat the cactus plants without getting so many thorns in his mouth that the juices of his mouth didn't dissolve the thorns in a few days.

This was why, different from the *gringos,* who breed a male *burro* to a large female horse so they can get big mules, in Mexico we breed a little stud horse to a donkey so we can get more sure-footed little mules. You see, it is the mother who teaches the young, so a mother horse will teach her offspring to only graze on grass, as horses do; but the mother *burra* will teach her offspring not just to graze on grass, but how to eat brush and cactus and even cardboard and trash, and also how to walk among the rocks and cliffs as agile as a goat and go a week in the hot sun without water. This was why at our camp that first year I was able to beat up those four big bully boys who were harassing the girls. I took a stick to them and had them down and crying in seconds. I was raised by a *burra* mother and grandmother. Not by a tall, well-fed horse mother and grandmother.

Jan and I continued to make *el amor* all day and all night long. I just couldn't get enough of Jan inside of me. I felt as large and wide-open as Our Sacred Canyon. Every day was an adventure. Every day we fished; trapped quail; dug up roots; picked wild berries and spices; and lay on the flat, hot rocks to sunbathe after we'd been in the hot springs. OH, IT WAS HEAVEN ON EARTH! IT TRULY, REALLY WAS! And yet more than once Jan would get a worried look and want to talk to me. But I didn't want to talk. I just wanted to keep living and loving and eating.

"Please," he'd say to me. "It is important for you to understand."

"Understand what? Happiness? Or that we live in Heaven?"

"Come and sit down," he'd say to me, indicating a flat rock alongside him.

"Okay," I'd say, but I already knew that what he was going to tell me wasn't at all important. How could anything be important when you live with God?

"Mireya," he'd say, "maybe I'm not the man you think I am. Those chains they put between my legs the day they arrested me and then kept yanking . . . well, I just don't know. Maybe I'll never be able to give you children."

My whole heart went out to him. He looked like a little boy, he was so unsure of himself.

"Jan," I said, "I love you here in my heart. I adore you. No matter how you are, you are my beautiful *hombre* and perfect husband."

"But Mireya, you're so young, and you'll surely want children, and I don't know if . . . if I can do that."

"Jan, can't you see that Our Love is Pure and True and the Heavens above rejoice when they see True Love and come down to Mother Earth and help us? You know that. All this is already written in Our *Corazón* and in the Stars in Heaven."

Tears ran down my face like rivers, because I could see that he was so worried. "Jan," I continued, "*Mañana es otro milagro de Dios* isn't just a saying for us. It is our foundation for all living. God is helping us to make love, and God will bless us with a child. How can this not be? God is always here with us, even at this very moment. No love between a man and woman can exist without first *el amor* of Our Holy Creator. Now no more talking. Kiss me," I said. "Kiss me and make love to me again. I'd been waiting for and dreaming of this for so long that my bones ache with my want of you deep inside of me, *mi amor!*"

"Mireya, Mireya," he said, "yes, I fully agree that God is with us, and I do want to keep making love with you, but . . . there's more that you need to know," he said, and he now told me the story of Chato and the other boys who'd been shot down and the others who'd been hung in their cells. Tears came to his eyes, and once more I saw the depth of my *gringo*'s Love and Noble Heart.

"Jan, did they die happy?" I asked. "Of course they did, because they were experienced in the world of drugs, and they knew what they were doing, yet they chose to go to the Light in the name of Jesus. And this is exactly the same case with me. I, Mireya, with all my Heart and Soul, know what I'm doing, *mi amor,*" I declared, with my own tears once more pouring down my face. "And I'd rather die a thousand times by torture and bullets than live without the fullness of your love penetrating deep into my body, so I can always know the meaning of being a woman with her man.

"Jan, I'm young, but, remember, I do not live with my eyes closed. Everyone in town knows what you and Father Rochín are doing, and we know that even as we speak, the priest Van Housen and his evil eye are gathering all the forces of Darkness that he can find, but do we in town stop eating? Do we stop laughing? Do we stop living? No, of course not. Because to stop living and loving is to give away *nuestro poder*—our power—and this we can never do.

We were born to live, and live we will do just like the deer, living with joy and playing in the sunlight with complete love, even as the deer knows that the great jaguar and mountain lion are both after her.

"I love you, Jan. You are my wonderful *gringo,* and you know in your heart that you want me as much as I want you, and now please no more talking. We've done that. And now," I said with a burst of laughter, "I am jumping on you once again!"

I came off the boulder and leaped on him as we rolled into ferns by the waterfall. What can I say? It is every girl's dream to find her perfect love, and I'd found mine, but I'd never realized that once a woman's yearning had been touched by having her man deep inside her, there was no turning back. No, to sleep, to eat, to make love and share with each other our most intimate secrets of life was a complete, full life in itself.

It was as if time stood still and the days and nights ran together as one great continuous feast of joy, and not just of body, but also of Mind and Heart and Soul. Jan now read *Uncle Tom's Cabin* to me again, and I cried for that girl. She truly was so much like me.

The day we decided to come out of the canyon's bottom and go into town, it was a strange experience, because I had come to feel as if we were the only two people in all the world. It took us all day to climb out of Our Sacred Canyon, and at each turn, I'd stop to look back, feeling like we were leaving our True Home. The tall red cliffs glistened like copper. The luscious green jungle got smaller and smaller the farther up we climbed. When we got to the top, we saw that all the snow was gone and the meadows were green.

Had we been gone for the whole winter?

Was it springtime now? We didn't know. Truly, time had stood still for us.

We were walking toward town when we saw the first human being we'd seen in all this time, and I don't know how to explain it, but I became all embarrassed. Could this person see what Jan and I had been doing all this time, being so happy and naked and making *el amor* day and night, kissing and licking and feasting of each other? Oh, I hoped not. How could I ever again look people in the eyes without screaming at the top of my lungs to show them how happy I was?

A truck stopped and gave us a ride into town. When I saw my mother and Coco at the restaurant, I screamed out at the top of my lungs!

"I'M IN HEAVEN!" I screamed. "I'M SO HAPPY!"

It was now my *gringo* who became embarrassed and didn't know what to do. My family all started laughing, and I went to the kitchen with my mother to make something for us to eat, while Coco and the rest of *mi familia* visited with Jan. I was so hungry! It seemed like I was now starving all the time. My mother told me I'd been gone for nearly two months, but she didn't reprimand me. No, she was wonderful. That afternoon after we'd eaten, she hugged me and we cried together. She said she knew exactly what I was feeling. She, too, had once felt this way.

"So you and Jan must be very careful," she said, making the sign of the cross over herself, "because the world gets jealous and finds ways of destroying anyone who's so full *del amor.*"

"We'll be careful, *Mamá*," I said.

"Good, and did you two do your Indian ceremony of marriage before God and the Mother Moon?"

"Yes."

"Good."

The next day Jan and I were driven back to our camp, and we found that Jan's cabin had been broken into and everything of value taken. Pistols, knives, and cooking stove, as well as a very expensive over-and-under 12-gauge shotgun; an antique .30-30

Winchester; and the two revolvers that Villa's wife, Luz Corral, had given Jan in an old wooden chest, calling him the *gringo Pancho Villa* of the people. Also, the robbers had pissed and shit on our bed.

Instantly I felt not fear, but outrage! Jan suggested we go down to the water's edge and pray. But I couldn't pray. I was too angry!

"Mireya," he said to me, "this is what they want, for us to be so angry that we will lose our love. We need to pray, not just for us, but for them, too. Only in this way can we keep Our Paradise of Love on Earth."

"Okay, I'll pray with you, but I need help, *mi amor,* because I'm so angry I could kill! Look at our bed. Look at the beautiful pillowcase I embroidered with little yellow and red flowers—they shit and pissed on it," I added, with tears running down my face.

"Yes, I see, and it's awful, but you must realize why they did this. They're jealous of our love, Mireya. They wish they had such a love. We are winning. I can feel it. They truly want to join us, but they just don't know how to do it yet."

The winter passed and the spring came, and this time when Emma came up threatening to kill me, I was ready for her, because Jan and Father Rochín had found out, as they'd been going through records, that Emma had never recorded her marriage to Jan, as she'd told him she had. And I knew why she hadn't done it, because at that time Jan had nothing, so she hadn't wanted to commit herself to a man who only wore Levi's and T-shirts. It was only after the banker Jorge and his wife, Silveria, had opened up the restaurant with Jan and she'd seen the money pouring in that she'd taken their marriage seriously and . . . this was when she'd made sure to get pregnant so she'd have a hold on Jan.

She could fast-talk all she wanted, but I could add up one and one and figure out why she had done what she had done. My grandparents always said that it was what a person did that counted, not what they said, and her actions were always full of only herself. It made perfect sense to me that such a person would never register her marriage, so she'd be available for a better situation if it came up. She had no understanding of the Greatness and Wonder of this man with a Noble Heart.

So this time when she found both Jan and me in the kitchen at the camp, she immediately began screaming that I could no longer deny I was sleeping with her husband.

"Not just sleeping!" I yelled, running up and getting in her face. "We make love day and night, and he isn't your husband! You lied! You never registered the marriage, because at that time Jan was poor and you had all those rich friends, and you really wanted someone with money! You never cared about Jan or all the good things he was doing! You just cared about how you looked to all of your rich friends in Chihuahua. You knew that half of them were in love with him, so this is why you decided to get him first.

"Just look at you and all that makeup and that fine hairdo. It must take you hours of looking at yourself in the mirror to paint and fix yourself up. You love *you* and no one else; and you were never, never, never his wife! Even the last time you came up here, you didn't ask about Jan and his injuries. No, you were just worried about how you looked to your friends. You have no heart or soul. You are a lost, blind, lonely old woman; and I pity and feel sorry for you!"

She probably only heard half of what I told her, because she was also screaming at me as I was screaming at her. But finally she'd heard enough of what I'd said to sit down and begin to cry. She said she'd lost her home and didn't know what to do and needed Jan's help. And Jan, like a typical man, went to go to her to give her comfort—but I, who'd grown up knowing the way of the rattlesnakes, leaped forward, blocking his way, and this was when I saw the knife in her hand.

The treacherous woman had planned to cut my *gringo* open like a *mango* when he got close enough to her. I slapped her across the face so hard that I knocked her out of the chair; then I forced the knife away from her, and I would have choked her until her eyes popped out of her head if Jan and my mother hadn't pulled me back. Oh, she was as dangerous and sneaky as the priest Van Housen himself, and we could never let our guards down with these kinds of people for a minute!

The things that Jan and Father Rochín were now finding out in the records were astonishing. All the mineral rights and old gold mines of the Tarahumara had also been stolen, even beyond the lands that had been taken away from them. And some of these old gold mines—like the one in the Rain of Gold canyon, which had been abandoned during the Mexican Revolution of 1910—probably still had gold, particularly considering the new type of mining they did by tearing down the whole mountain and making it into a deep, ugly godforsaken hole.

Jan and Father Rochín didn't know what to do. Huge multi-billion-dollar corporations were just chomping at the bit to get ahold of this land that the Tarahumara had been living on for untold thousands of years.

But I didn't have any problem now. I knew exactly what to do, and I got hold of Emma by the hair and dragged her out of our kitchen and threw her out the door, kicking her in her soft, jellylike ass!

"Now," I said, "if you wish to see Jan and me, or just Jan alone to ask for help, you knock on our door and wait for the door to be opened for you. Then you say 'Good day' to both of us, and talk to us with respect and honesty."

She was shaking and crying and trying to get herself together. My mother got a washcloth and took it outside to her. The black mascara on her eyelashes and the white cream on her face had mixed together with her red lipstick, and she looked like a clown from the circus.

Emma took the washcloth and began to wipe her face, and little by little, her shaking stopped. I saw no more problem in handling these big companies than I saw in handling Emma. After all, my *gringo* and I were in Love, and all of Heaven rejoiced when they saw True Love on Mother Earth and came down and gave us guidance and power and Daily Miracles!

CHAPTER 25

Jan

After weeks of struggle, Carlos Rochín and I finally felt prepared. We thought we had figured out what to say and how to say it, so we called the number that the elegant, brave president's mother had given us to reach her private secretary, Pierre Benoit. Miraculously, he didn't brush us off and instead said that he and the president's mother had been expecting our call—that only last week she'd had a dream about our camp and the wonderful work we were doing with the kids. We told him that we would like to come to see her. He said he'd talk to her and get right back to us. Within the hour he called us back and said she could see us the following week.

Rochín and I took the bus from Chihuahua to Mexico City, and the whole way we talked and planned. We didn't have proof, but we'd figured out that this huge robbery of land and natural resources could not have happened without the full knowledge and approval of the secretary of the interior, the secretary of agriculture, and also the secretary of defense. So this, then, meant that the three closest people to President de la Madrid himself were involved; or more precisely, the three most powerful departments of the nation, right next to the presidency, hadn't just allowed this to happen, but had actually helped in the execution of this act and then the cover-up.

And it was common knowledge that the heads of these departments had been close friends of the president long before he'd taken office. So how could Rochín and I present this matter to the mother of the president without sounding like we were implicating her own son? This was the dilemma that Rochín and I had been working on for weeks. Then the answer came to Rochín just a few days before we made the phone call.

He'd been at a function of his family's, and he'd seen how close and friendly his younger cousins and nephews were with each other, these same men he'd taken up to *las Barrancas del Cobre* as young boys. Now they were in their late 20s and early 30s, about ten years younger than Rochín, but of an entirely different generation and mind-set than his.

"Jan," he told me after the family function, "I was standing there sipping my glass of wine and listening to their conversations about money this and money that when it dawned on me that it's not the heads of the departments of interior and agriculture and defense who have done this incredible swindle. It is their sons and nephews, just as it is my own younger cousins and nephews whom I took up to the lake to show them the wonders of God, and who, instead of respecting those wonders, turned it all around for their own money scheming and profit.

"So, my friend, if we handle this just right, we can get *Señora* de la Madrid to understand that we are not pointing a finger at her son or his *compadres* he brought into office with him, but to their spoiled, rich sons and nephews. And these boys must be disciplined like the spoiled boys they are, for the benefit of all of Mexico and future generations. What do you think, Jan? I don't want this situation to blow up in our faces."

"Yes, I agree that this is an explosive situation," I said. "But even if we convince her of our position, how can she, a woman, inform her son without these spoiled sons and nephews getting wind of it and . . . and I don't know, Rochín. It's like we're sitting on a box of dynamite."

"Well, then, *señor mayori*, call in your Spiritual Powers, because we need to move on this situation, and now. It's not going to be easy for de la Madrid to turn this thing around even if he does get on our side. The swindle was done very cleverly, within existing laws. So I suggest that when we talk to his mother, we let her know that this same thing happens in every country, even in the United States, so this is an opportunity for *nuestro presidente* to clean up his own cabinet and show the world how civilized and good and honorable Mexico really is."

"And all this came to you while you were sipping wine and listening to your nephews' and younger cousins' conversations?" I asked.

"Well, no, that was actually only the seed," replied Rochín. "It didn't all come to me until that night when I was sleeping, and then suddenly, like in a flash, I understood the whole thing. You know, it's like what you've told me happened to you when you saw those lion eyes in the snowstorm and you suddenly saw everything differently."

"Yes, I wasn't afraid anymore, and the whole world changed."

"Exactly, I was listening to my nephews and younger cousins, and instead of being upset with them or disappointed, I simply listened and heard their joy and excitement over money matters, and it was then that I saw and understood the entire situation. It wasn't their fathers who'd done this. It was these young men, so I then saw that there is a small hole through which we could present this to the president's mother without sounding like we are implicating her son's closest friends. It will work, I'm sure," he added, laughing.

I joined in his laughter. "Hello, *señor mayori* yourself, Rochín. It seems that you, too, are now glimpsing the future."

"I guess I am," he said, with a beautiful Mona Lisa kind of smile.

In this frame of mind, Rochín and I took the bus to the capital of Mexico, and we were escorted to the private apartment of the president's mother. It was a whole series of elaborate, immense rooms, as large as a mansion and all within the *palacio del presidente*. *Señora* de la Madrid was happy to see us and wanted to know how the camp was doing. She told us that her visit to our kids' camp had been one of the highlights of her year.

"So what can I do for you?" she asked.

We didn't quite know how to begin. Father Rochín finally decided to lead the way, and he explained why he loved *las Barrancas del Cobre* and why he considered it one of Mexico's greatest natural treasures.

"At the site where Jan and I built the camp is the exact location where I had the vision to become a priest," he said, "and devote my life to bringing the Light of God to the youth of Mexico, who are our future. And this is why we've come to talk to you, *señora*, about our youth. You see, *señora*, youth needs to be given vision and freedom and yet reins or . . . or it is easy for youth to get lost, and if not with drugs, then with greed and false power."

"Father Rochín," she spoke up, "I enjoy hearing what you have to say, yet I feel you are dancing around the real issue that you two came to see me about, so let us not waste any more time, and please be frank with me."

Rochín turned and looked at me. I nodded, closed my eyes, said a little prayer, and sent them both all my love and energy and goodwill.

"*Señora*," he said, turning back to the president's mother, "what Jan and I have come to tell you is that millions and millions of acres of *las Barrancas del Cobre* that the Tarahumara live on and have been taking care of for thousands of years have been stolen from them and are now on the verge of being developed by foreign monies with the help of individuals within our own political power."

She didn't flinch or panic. No, she simply said, "Go on. I'm listening. I saw the beautiful thing you two are doing with that camp."

This woman was a gift to the world! When Van Housen had stepped in front of Rochín and me back in Creel, at first I'd thought it was all over for us, but then I'd prayed . . . and she, a Mexican woman and a very devout Catholic Christian, had possessed the insight and guts to tell the tall, imposing priest to remove himself or she'd have her bodyguards remove him.

What confidence!

What bravery!

What a great woman!

And here she was, not flinching or panicking again. I was in complete awe of this beautiful, elegant, gracious lady!

Rochín continued, laying out the whole thing. The Rod Steiger movie and the story of the young Indian boy who was shot in the back while fishing on the rocks where he and his father and grandfathers had always fished, and then how Ortega accused the boy of trespassing.

"The boy died while Jan and I and his parents were taking him to the hospital in Cuauhtémoc," continued Rochín. "We helped the parents file murder charges against Ortega, and instead of justice being done, a few days later Jan and the Indian leaders and the boy's parents were arrested by the judicial police, and Jan was almost tortured to death."

She turned to me. "This is all true, Jan?"

"*Sí, señora,* but for me the really important thing isn't that we were arrested and I was tortured. The thing that stays with me is how the very next morning thousands of people assembled at the prison gate, and even through the prison walls, we could hear them saying the rosary and then chanting and demanding our release. For me, *señora,* this is the Beauty and Spirit *de México.* This is why, I, too, like Father Rochín, devote my life to helping *la gente del pueblo*—the common people—just as Our Lord Jesus did 2,000 years ago. The story of the Bible did not end with the Jews, *señora,* but is still going on with us here today, with the two most powerful and common expressions of all of Mexico: *Mañana es otro milagro de Dios* and *con el favor de Dios.*

"This is what we instill in the kids who come up to us in *las Barrancas del Cobre*—a deep respect for life and land and God and each other. That morning, *señora*, as the sun was coming up, I had hope in *mi corazón* no matter how thoroughly they'd beaten me and tortured me, breaking my ribs and twisting my legs and arms until they broke and pulling the nails from my fingers and ramming soda bottles up my nose that exploded the bubbly water into my brain. I didn't know if I'd live, *señora*, but one thing I did know for sure, and that is my love for my life, here in this country where I've found my Soul in every person I come in contact with. This is my second home, this land created by God with such Natural Beauty and Spirituality."

I was crying and she was crying, and Rochín was crying, too. She called Pierre to her side. He'd been sitting across the room, listening to everything.

"Come," she said, "you must be part of this."

"By all means," replied Pierre. "It will be my honor."

"Go on," she said, turning to Rochín and me. "So what do we do?"

Rochín inhaled deeply, glanced at me, then exhaled. This was it. This was the tricky one that we'd been talking about for weeks and had continued to discuss as we'd come to the capital by train.

"*Señora*," he said, "what I am about to say next, we do not have proof of, but . . . and please do not take offense . . . this acquisition of millions of acres of Indian land and hundreds of thousands of government land could not have been done without the help of the secretaries of—"

". . . of agriculture and interior," she said.

"Exactly, but I do not believe that it is your son's old friends who did this, *señora*. In fact, I don't think that they even know about it. It is their sons and nephews, young men who never had the chance to go up to *las Barrancas del Cobre* at an early enough age so that they, too, could see the Holy Beauty of the land and come to know the True Spirit of the Soul *de México*."

"I agree entirely with Rochín," I said, with tears pouring down my face. "Because if these sons and nephews had experienced the Miraculous Beauty of *las Barrancas* in their youth, they wouldn't forever be admiring Europe and the United States, but instead see Mexico and its indigenous people as the LIVING SOUL OF GOD!"

The great woman reached out and took my hand. Tears poured from her eyes. "On the radio, I heard you talk like this," she told me. "You truly are *un Mexicano de corazón y alma.* If we could only see the world through your eyes, we'd have such a wonderful world! So, yes, I agree that this is why we must get this land back to the Indians. We must preserve the natural beauty of this Sacred Place. We do not need another Cancún or Acapulco, and we need to do this right away. Before my son goes out of office. But . . . but this will not be easy. I cannot just go up to him and say any of this. We must plan and organize so he can experience the Miraculous like I did when I was up there with you for a week.

"I will think on this matter," she added. "I am glad you came to me. You have my support. Just give me a few days, and Pierre will get in touch with you. Thank you. Do not fear. Some way, somehow, we will get this done. Our sons and daughters must be taught that Mexico is not for their own greed and gain, but a Sacred Holy Land for us to protect and preserve for future generations!" She stood up. "It is with great pleasure that I have come to know you two fine men. And, Jan, yes, *mi casa de México es su casa!* We are proud of you! Your *corazón* is in the right place!"

"Thank you, and I'm proud to be here, *señora,*" I said.

Outside the *palacio del presidente,* Father Rochín knelt down and gave a prayer of thanks. I joined him, thanking God, the Holy Creator, for His ongoing, CONTINUOUS DREAM OF LIVING, BREATHING MIRACLES!

As soon as we got back to Chihuahua, Pierre Benoit called us. He informed us that next month in Chihuahua City there would be a gathering of the governors of the states that bordered the

United States and that the president himself would be presiding. Pierre told us to meet him in Chihuahua, along with the Indian leaders, and that somehow, some way, he'd set up a meeting between us and the president.

"But no one must know anything about this," he added. "Because you do not have any appointment with the president."

"But he does know about us, doesn't he?" I naïvely asked.

"No, of course not," said Pierre. "If he did, then so would his secretaries of agriculture, interior, and defense. You just show up, and . . . and pray."

"Okay, we now understand," said Rochín. "Not a word to anyone."

"Exactly. Not one word, or this whole thing could backfire."

"We will pray," I added.

"Please do. This is what the president's mother is now doing across the way at our national cathedral."

I could just picture the great, elegant old lady across the open square from the president's palace, at the national cathedral, praying for a Miracle, because this was, indeed, what was needed—*¡UN MILAGRO DE DIOS!*

CHAPTER 26

Mireya

When *mi amor* and Rochín came back from Mexico City, there was something very different about both of them. You could feel it. You could see it. You could smell it. And when we now made love, *mi amor* would begin to cry, saying that he was so happy. So very, very, very happy! That all his life he'd dreamed of this, but never really imagined he'd ever have it.

Hearing this, I also cried; but different from Jan, I always knew I'd have this great a love. And so our lovemaking wasn't wild anymore. It was now as gentle as the summer rains when the flowers don't close up and the deer and rabbits don't go to hide under trees and brush. Gently, gently, we made love six, eight, ten times a day . . . and it was so good and smooth and fulfilling that I, too, would have tears of happiness come to my eyes.

We were going to have a baby. I could feel it deep inside of me. Oh, I was truly the happiest woman in ALL THE WORLD!

But still, no matter how much I tried to teach Jan how to make *tortillas,* he couldn't make them, and we'd laugh our heads off.

Miracles Jan could do, but making a handmade corn *tortilla* was beyond his earthly skills, and oh, there was nothing in the whole world that smelled and tasted better than a handmade corn *tortilla* off the hot *comal* and eating it with a little salt and homemade butter. My grandmother always told me it was the simplest of things that brought joy to a woman once she was well mounted day in and day out, feeling fulfilled and happy deep inside.

Then it was time for Jan and Father Rochín to go down the mountain with the tribal leaders and Our Three Holy Wisemen. He asked me if I wished to go, and I said no, because I could see that he had a lot on his mind; plus, I'd never been off our mountains before. I wished him well, and told him that my mother and I would be praying for him five times a day, for the five points of the human body. Oh, I so wished for God to protect my *gringo* and Rochín and the others, but also, I knew they were in good hands with Our Three Wisemen, the same ones who'd guided Jesus when He'd been on Earth doing His Holy Sacred Work.

CHAPTER 27

Jan

Rochín and I didn't want to draw attention to ourselves, so we didn't go down the mountain by train from Creel. Instead, over a three-day period, we drove down to Chihuahua City with the Indian leaders in pickup trucks and cars. We assembled at the original halfway house, the one with the huge chandelier. The day of the event, Rochín and I couldn't figure out how to dress. Should we go out and buy the proper clothes? But our Indian leaders were dressed in sandals; loincloths; long, colorful shirts; and straw hats or wrapped headbands. Rochín and I decided that we'd look out of place with our Indians if we tried to dress up, so we finally decided to just remain in clothes we always wore, which for me were Levi's, a T-shirt, and sandals; and for Rochín it was basically the same thing, except he wore cheap slacks instead of Levi's.

And so we went to the big old elegant hotel in downtown Chihuahua where the event was being held. Everyone was dressed in suits and neckties. We looked completely out of place. The lines were long, and the police and army personnel were searching everyone before they were allowed inside. Rochín and I didn't know what to do. For over an hour we'd been talking to the different gatekeepers and people in authority, showing them the president's mother's card and trying to get in, but we made no headway.

Then Our Three Sacred *Curanderos,* who were with us, just looked at each other, smiled a Mona Lisa kind of smile, and our Collective Dream continued as they started walking past the long lines toward the entrance. Rochín and I followed them, and why the police, who were stopping and searching everyone, didn't stop us, I'll never know, because we just walked past them as if we were all invisible. Then we were inside the hotel without a pass or anything. And to further Our Miraculous Situation—like magic— Pierre walked right up to us.

There were hundreds and hundreds of people all around us, going every which way, and incredibly, we just went around a corner and Pierre was coming down the staircase toward us.

"Good," he said. "I'm glad we found each other. Perfect. And I'm especially glad you didn't dress up and that the Indians came in their natural dress."

We introduced him to the different Indian leaders. He took each one's hand very respectfully, then started laughing.

"What is it?" asked Rochín.

"I had no idea what to do until this very moment while shaking hands," he said. "It's like a brilliant, wise spirit has leaped into me! Come! Follow me quickly! We don't have a second to lose! I was becoming concerned when I couldn't find you, but this is even better!"

I glanced at Our Three Holy Healers. They smiled, and we followed Pierre through the crowd, around the side of the building and past a large garden.

"Here," he said, "see that staircase? The president and I and a few others will be coming down those steps in just a few minutes, and we will turn left and walk by here into the ballroom of the hotel, where we will meet with all the governors and their people. You just stand here, facing this way, and say nothing and do nothing. Just watch us come down those stairs and walk past you; and the president, a very intelligent and curious man, will see you and see how you're dressed, and it will touch his heart. He'll think of Benito Juárez and Zapata when they came to the capital. He'll ask us if any one of us knows who you are, and then I will say that yes, I do, that you are the men who built and run the camp for children that his mother visited earlier this year, and that these are your Indian friends who work with you.

"He'll be intrigued, because his mother spoke so highly of you two, and he will want to know what you are doing with the Indians at the hotel. I'll say that I don't know, but I'll find out, and this is how we can get to the president without any of his cabinet knowing what this is all about. This is a godsend," he said, laughing again. "I can't believe how this is all working out so well. IT'S A MIRACLE!"

Rochín and I glanced at each other and then at Our Three *Curanderos,* who were once more smiling that quiet little Mona Lisa kind of smile.

"Yes," agreed Rochín, "it is a Miracle!"

"Now don't move," Pierre told us once more. "Stay right here, facing that . . . that staircase and say nothing to anyone and do nothing. Just stay right where you are. I'm so excited! This is going to work!"

"Okay," I answered. "Here we are, and here we will remain."

"Perfect," he said, and turned, running across the way and up the stairs.

We waited and we waited some more, and then I had to pee really badly, but I didn't dare leave. Ever since I'd been tortured and dragged with chains wrapped under my crotch, I haven't been able to hold my pee. Suddenly some armed guards took up positions at the top and the bottom of the staircase. We could hear talking and laughter, and the talking and laughter grew louder and louder; then de la Madrid appeared at the top of the staircase with a whole entourage.

Instantly, as he started down the stairs, he noticed us, and he stopped talking for a moment, then continued his conversation. We did nothing. We said nothing. We just stood together, watching him. When he got to the last step of the staircase, he stopped and took a long look at us. Then just as we'd been told he would do, he must have asked about us, because this is when Pierre stepped in close to him, and he whispered in the president's ear. And de la Madrid must have liked what he heard, because he smiled at us as he continued across the room. Then they were gone, having gone into the spacious ballroom.

A few moments later, Pierre returned and told us to meet him at midnight in the lobby of the hotel, explaining that the president wanted to personally meet with us and our Indian leaders. Then he gave us 13 presidential passes.

"These," he said, "guard with your lives!"

Once we were outside, Our Three Holy Indian Healers began LAUGHING WITH *CARCAJADAS!* We joined them. Everything had been of Miracles! Our Whole World had gone into a steady stream of the Miraculous!

IT WAS DONE!

IT WAS FINISHED!

IT WAS WRITTEN IN THE STARS AND COMPLETED!

We ate at a taco stand and lay down on the grass in a park. We were lying there and half napping, waiting for our meeting with the president at midnight, when the largest meteorite I'd ever seen came shooting across the sky, lighting up the whole night. It was so bright and huge and close that I thought it would hit Mother Earth, but it didn't and just kept going with its long bright tail until it was out of sight. Rochín and I both glanced at Our Three Indian *Curanderos* at the same time. All three were grinning ear to ear, feeling very proud of what they'd just caused, giving us a sign even in the Heavens!

"Well," I said to Rochín, "I guess we're in good hands."

"The best," replied my friend, making the sign of the cross over himself. "The Holy Hands of God live in these Three Blessed Elders."

And so with our 13 passes, we went to see the president at midnight, and to our utter amazement, he didn't get the least little bit defensive when we told him about his own cabinet. Instead, miraculously, he saw this as an opportunity to do something of greatness with his old friends before they left office. There was food and the finest of wine for us to enjoy, but neither I nor the Indians ate such rich foods. Father Rochín did eat and drink a little bit.

De la Madrid became as excited as a little boy and wanted to know all about *las Barrancas del Cobre.*

"Is it true that our canyon is ten times larger than the famous Grand Canyon of the United States?" he asked.

"Yes," I said, "but it's eight different canyons instead of just one. This is why our canyon has so many beautifully carved *mesas* and ridges, showing us the age and different stages of the development of our planet, teaching us how water, just like the human heart, can carve even the hardest of stone. It is the natural wonder of this magnificent canyon that inspires the kids who come to our camp. For a young boy or girl to see and give witness to such grandeur and natural beauty that's already made perfect by God is a mind-altering situation."

"Yes, this is what my mother told me," the president said. "That you two men give meaning and vision to our children in just a few days."

"It is not us," said Rochín, "but the voice of God speaking through the Great Holy Wind of the Music of Our Sacred Canyon.

In fact, the Tarahumara say there are eight canyons because the eighth sense is our sense of music."

"Truly, our eighth sense is music? Well, then, this canyon is a national treasure that must be saved for the future generations *de todo México* and the world!" declared de la Madrid.

"Exactly," said both Rochín and I at the same time.

IT WAS A MIRACLE! De la Madrid, the president of Mexico, was totally for the Tarahumara, whom he understood would protect *las Barrancas del Cobre* for Eternity, and he was willing to go up against his own cabinet heads if necessary. But then he also warned us that there was only so much he could do at the federal level, and the repercussions that we might experience on a local level would be very difficult for him to stop. It was 2 A.M. before he bid us good night and told us that our meeting had been one of the finest moments for him of his entire presidency!

Going down in the elevator, I just kept looking at Our Three *Curanderos.*

They'd done it! They really had!

Everything had gone so smoothly!

The Miraculous had, indeed, become Our Living Reality!

CHAPTER 28

Mireya

I don't know how to explain it, but my female instinct quickened when I saw how happy Father Rochín and *mi gringo* were when they got back from having seen the president of Mexico in Chihuahua. They thought everything was going to go well now, but I just knew deep in my bones that we were in for some terrible times. This was not a time to celebrate, I told them. This was a time to look for snakes under every rock and bush and know that we'd stepped squarely into the world of the evil eye.

But my poor *gringo* didn't see it this way, so when a logging truck came around the bend going too fast and almost ran us off the road and over a cliff, he refused to believe that it had been done on purpose.

"Jan," I said to him, "you must understand that you and Father Rochín have stirred up a hornets' nest, and things are going to get much worse. Not better."

"Who is now the person of little faith?" he asked, laughing.

"Jan, listen good," I said. "I have faith that God is with us and we have a chance of getting all this land back to the Tarahumara, but . . . but we must also not forget the ways of the world and sleep with our eyes closed. In fact, in the old Indian way, we must now move every night so no one can ever know where it is that we bed down for the night."

And that very night my bones screamed out to me! I woke Jan up, and we sneaked out of our cabin and went down to a little cave by the water's edge to sleep.

We never heard them. All we know is that when we awoke to the screams, it was my mother and Coco and the others who were screaming and trying to remove the huge rocks that had been put in front of the door of our cabin, which was engulfed in flames. I rushed up to my mother.

"*Mamá*," I said, "Jan and I aren't in there! We sneaked out of our cabin in the night!"

She broke down crying, and so did my two younger sisters. They'd all thought that we were trapped inside and had burned to death. We sat down together and watched the cabin burn, and it was beautiful how the flames leaped so high up into the star-filled night. Coco took hold of some of the burning logs with a shovel and dragged them away from the cabin and started making coffee and cooking breakfast. We all started laughing with *carcajadas*, and soon we were joined by our neighbors and some of the Tarahumara and we had a *fiesta* going. I sat with my *gringo*, and we held hands and felt very close as we watched our beautiful home burn in glorious, great leaping flames.

"Well, well," said Jan as we sipped a delicious cup of coffee made with Mexican chocolate, "I now know more about building, so I can build an even better home for us next time."

"And I can help," I told him. "Then this next *casa* will be all ours."

It takes a very long time for a log cabin to burn. We were able to cook on the coals for three days. And the Mother Moon, she was so beautiful and easy to see now that we had no roof over our heads.

Then later that week, in my sleep, my husband's great mountain lion came to me and took me for a run through the forest, and then together we leaped into our beloved canyon. My uncle Oscar was in the dream, too, and he was shouting with such rage, and normally he was so peaceful and quiet.

The next day we found out that my uncle had been driving his truck when he spotted some of his truck-driver friends and four policemen drowning five Indians on the other side of the lake near where the *gringo* movie had been filmed. Oscar braked and leaped out of his truck and rushed down to the lake, shouting at the top of his lungs for them to stop! Then with the strength of a mighty mountain lion, he ran out into the water and knocked his friends and the policemen aside and pulled the sacks off the Indians' heads and untied their hands, which had been bound behind their backs.

"I know you men!" he shouted at the truck drivers. "You are good, decent men! This isn't the kind of thing you do! And you policemen, you're better than this. Where are you from? Chihuahua City or an entirely different state? Be smart; open your eyes and see that they bring you in from other places so you will do their dirty work without any remorse. These Indians have done nothing wrong. In fact, it is they who are in the right, and our local leaders who hired you are the thieves and killers who should be drowned in the lake."

"But we have our orders," said one of the cops. "They told us that these Indians aren't Christians, that they're cannibals, and we should baptize them in the lake until they die so we can save their immortal souls."

"Who told you that, the priest? Father Van Housen is the biggest thief in the whole area. Believe me, those are all lies. If they weren't lies, then why didn't they have you arrest them so they could be put on trial? No, they sent you here to do their dirty work in hiding, so if anything goes wrong, they can blame you. Be careful or it will be you, the new cops, who will get your eyes shot out of your heads, as happened to the police captain. You heard about that, eh?"

With frightened eyes, the four young policemen nodded.

That night the whole town met at Coco's restaurant, and my uncle Oscar retold his story about stopping the truck drivers and policemen from drowning the Indians. We were all so proud of him, because normally he was so quiet and easygoing, but now he was a lion in the name of justice!

"I don't know what got into me," Oscar said, "but suddenly I had the strength of a thousand men!"

"I know," I told him. "Last night I dreamed of you, Oscar, and a mountain lion running through the forest, and together you two leaped off the canyon's rim."

"That's right," he said. "I had the same dream, and when the lion and I leaped into the canyon, we had no fear because we turned into mighty eagles. And in the morning when I awoke, I was all different. It is like all the fears I've been holding back inside of me, ever since the day I was stark naked on the anthill, are gone. I'm free, and that is why I was able to scream like a lion and rush down upon those policemen and my fellow truck drivers and yank the Indians from their grasp. I was fearless, and it felt so good after all these years of being frightened."

He took a big breath. "I'm going to do everything I can do to get our family's ranch back. Our cousin and his people never bought it. They never gave us any money. So it is still ours!"

We all agreed with him, and I took Jan's hand, caressing it. This was so wonderful. My husband's mountain lion was now visiting all of us. This was what happened in a *familia*, my grandmother used to always tell me, and this is what also happened between a man and a woman when they were truly in love. Our Spirit Guides United and became the Power of *nuestra familia*, and in our Dreams we could do anything, so then everything we Dreamed was now not only possible, BUT ALREADY DONE AND WRITTEN IN THE STARS!

CHAPTER 29

Jan

Mireya and I decided to build our new, larger cabin on a little knoll closer to the water's edge. It would be colder here, but we were now two bodies instead of one, and much warmer when we slept. This was when my banker friend Jorge Ramos sent word that he needed to see me.

Two days later I went down to Chihuahua City to meet him at his bank. He was glad to see me and suggested we take a walk in the park.

"What I have to tell you, Jan," he said, "I could not tell you in my office. It's not just the . . . well, our powers of government that you are up against, *amigo*. It is the largest international hotel chains of the world. You and Rochín think that Ortega is just a puppet for our secretaries of interior, agriculture, and defense— well, I want you to know that these secretaries are just puppets for these large international monies. These corporations well know they have polluted and ruined the most beautiful parts of our coastlines in Mexico, so they now realize they must move into the interior to keep up their insane margin of profit, and what place is more inviting and beautiful than *las Barrancas del Cobre?* So what I am telling you, my friend, is that these people are even more dangerous than the drug lords who came after you a few years back. Myself, Jan, I suggest you leave this one alone," he added.

"But, Jorge, we now have the backing of—"

"Yes, yes, I know. You have the backing of President de la Madrid, but what can a president really do, Jan? He was put in office by the people of money and power who really run this country, just as they do in the United States and all the rest of the world. Look, Jan, Silveria and I truly respect you and what you are all about, but understand this, with the halfway houses I could help you locally organize people against the drug world. But this time, *amigo,* it is our good, law-abiding citizens who will come after you. Because, Jan, you must realize that it's not against the law to develop untouched land. And the fact that these lands were stolen from the Tarahumara *Indios* has very little meaning to the world at large and to these international corporations, because, let's be realistic, if we go back far enough in history, all lands were stolen from someone at some time."

I said nothing, and we continued walking through the park, looking at all the young mothers nursing their children and older kids playing on the playground equipment. I had no idea what to say, but something deep inside me also knew that this wasn't a time to lose faith and back down. No, this was a time for me to dig deeper into my Heart and Soul and not back down, but instead realize that all of us can really walk on water alongside Our Lord Jesus if we don't look down.

"Also, Jan," said the banker, "remember how they went after your boys when they couldn't get to you last time? Well, they will do this again. So be very careful of those you love, because my wife and I both fear for you, Jan. We really do, and your ex, Emma, has made it her crusade to get you and this beautiful young Indian girl we've heard so much about."

For the first time my heart gripped tight with terror, and I knew I had to get back up in the mountains as fast as I could. Mireya's life was in danger. But then I took a couple of deep breaths and realized I could never get back in time to make a difference and . . . I further realized it was my own fear, here within me, that opened the doors for the danger to come into Mireya's life and become a reality.

"Excuse me," I said to Jorge, feeling my lion powers come bursting up inside of me, "I appreciate everything you have told me, and I know you are being a sincere friend when you tell me all this, but . . . and I say 'but' because I am erasing all you've just said to me . . . I am not allowing one ounce of fear to come inside me and plant any seeds of doubt within me and my Kingdom of God. No, I am going to look at all you have told me straight in the eye, Jorge, and tell you that we can all walk on water alongside Our Lord God Jesus when we don't lose faith and look down.

"In fact, this is the greatness of Mexico, her people's unrelenting faith in God and that each day *es otro milagro de Dios*. I feel it in my bones as I look at all these beautiful young mothers nursing and playing with their children here in the park. And it is them and their children's children whom I fight for in the name of Jesus Christ. At this very moment as we speak, Mireya is safe, and anyone who is sent to do her any harm will be brought down by THE MIGHTY HAND OF GOD! This I do Know in my Heart and Soul! That all is well and perfect in THE EYES OF GOD!"

Jorge said nothing and just smiled, looking at me. Then he gently placed his right hand on my shoulder and said, "I now remember why our restaurant was so successful. You, my friend, have a presence that lets people know you truly walk with the Lord. I will remind Silveria of this fact. She has been very worried for you, because it is now some of our closest friends who are out to get you. These sons and nephews of the three secretaries have many friends throughout Chihuahua, and their talk is so vulgar that, well, it repulses Silveria and me, but what can we do?"

"You tell me," I said. "What can you do, Jorge?"

He started laughing. "You're right. I could speak up, and yet . . . oh, I only wish I had your faith, my friend. When we heard of the two empty bullet casings left on your pillow, we rejoiced.

You have done wonders, so who is to say that wonders won't continue for you? After all, you are *el Torero del Diablo!* The man who openly invited *la Mano Negra* to bullfight on his radio show, and see what's happened? The great assassin came to your aid." He laughed again. "But then I guess this makes sense, that even the darkest force of the drug lords is now your helping hand, because it is your halfway houses that have helped some of their *own* children and grandchildren get off drugs."

He shook his head, laughing with *carcajadas.* "Oh, the twists and turns *de la vida* never fail to amaze me! Still, be careful, Jan, and with this one, I suggest you pray not just to God, but to the Great Devil that lives within *la Mano Negra,* too."

Hearing this, I flashed on how the Tarahumara gave honor to Judas as well as to Jesus during Holy Week. He was right; according to the Tarahumara, we had to give recognition to both the Light and the Darkness for us to be in Harmony with Creation, for ultimately both were of God. Didn't it say in the Holy Book that Lucifer, meaning the bearer of light, had been God's Greatest Angel? Yes, I could now see why my Three Healers had me make peace with *la Mano Negra.* This was the new world consciousness that was brewing. Total inclusion. No exception.

Getting back to Jorge's office, we decided to have lunch together. It was a very fancy restaurant. He seemed to know everyone. He introduced me to a few of his wealthy friends, and from the way they looked at me, I wondered if these were the very people I was now up against.

The following day when I got back to Creel, I found out that the four young policemen who'd tried to drown the Indians at the lake had, indeed, been on their way to our new home site, where Mireya was alone working on our cabin, when their eyes were shot out of their heads.

The whole town was speaking of nothing else! *La Mano Negra* was now for sure our ally, too! Mireya and I went to the water's edge, and we prayed for the Souls of those ignorant young policemen. We could hear their cries of sorrow. We asked the Spirit World to accept them, for they hadn't known what they did any more than the men who'd driven the nails into Our Lord God Jesus's flesh.

After that, I brought out my guitar, and Mireya and I sang some old songs of the '60s that I'd taught her. And the night and the stars rejoiced, and the trees and rocks and water of the lake joined us. IT WAS BEAUTIFUL!

Jan, circa 1980.

Jan and Mireya
at campground, 1979.
Mireya is 15.

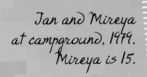

Mireya at 17.

Joaquin's naming ceremony, 1991.

Mireya's mother, Socorro; and grandmother, Maria Concepción.

Mireya with Tarahumara shaman.

First group of campers at Creel.

Tarahumara women.

Jan wrestling.

Jan with Robert Heyder.

Pharisee dancers.

Tarahumara visiting
Mesa Verde ruins. 1987.

Tarahumara runner.

Tonio Rivas, Elder, mayori.

Jan and Tarahumaras on Sacred Buffalo Rug with Lakota tribal Elder, Denver, 1987.

Natural History Museum, New York.

Jan, Mireya, and Joaquin with Southern Ute tribal leaders.

Joaquin, Aaron, and Jan.

Tribal ceremony in cave.

Jan finally accepted to become a Spiritual Grandfather Leader.

CHAPTER 30

Mireya

It was no longer a secret. Everyone and their sister and brother knew about the robbery of the Tarahumara land, and that my *gringo* and Father Rochín were in partnership with the *presidente de México* to get this Beautiful Sacred Land back to the Tarahumara. In fact, it was now being said that the president would be coming to Creel in his private helicopter to look at our kids' camp and fly over the canyon to see its spectacular beauty.

We were all so excited. The Sacred Doors of Heaven had opened up for us, the nobodies of Mexico, and overnight we had become somebodies! But this still didn't stop the shit from "hitting the fan," as I found out the *gringos* like to say in the United States. I love this saying. It's so real and understandable, because if shit hit the fan, it really would fly and get over everyone, even on the person who threw it. Oh, what a thought! I was learning English, and I'd asked Jan to teach me all the swear words and juiciest sayings first. This, and singing songs, was the only way to learn a foreign language, because it was "big-daddy fun"!

Anyway, we knew the police would no longer come after us to do the dirty work of their bosses. Not after the police captain and these four new young policemen had gotten their eyes shot out of their heads. So now Ortega, who was half-drunk most of the time, took it upon himself to do his own dirty work. He began hitting every Indian he saw walking along the side of the road with his truck. He began to carry a shotgun and would take shots at anyone he thought was against him, which, I guess, meant almost everyone.

Then we found that we weren't the only ones who were having problems now that the "shit had hit the fan." All of Mexico knew what was going on, because it was now common knowledge that two of the nephews of the head of the department of, I think, interior had gone after their uncle, trying to kill him, and they'd been arrested by the personal guards of the *presidente*.

Laws had to be changed, Jan told me.

Presidential decrees had to be made.

The very foundation of the national political structure of Mexico had to be altered to undo what the spoiled, rich sons and nephews had been able to do under the existing laws of the president's predecessors Luis Echeverría and José López Portillo, two of the biggest modern crooks and thieves of Mexico!

Jan and Rochín were invited to personally go to Mexico City to meet with de la Madrid and his cabinet members, to make sure they understood what needed to be done, because once this was completed, then hopefully it would be irreversible by future administrations.

The mentality of the nation was at stake, Jan kept telling me.

A whole new way of looking at commerce was in transformation.

And Jan explained to me he could now see these seeds of change that were growing in Mexico had been planted back in the '60s in Haight-Ashbury in San Francisco, with the music of those idealistic kids.

These were the types of things Jan and I spoke about when we now slept under the stars and looked up at the Heavens, Our True

Home, as the Tarahumara liked to say. It was so beautiful being in love with my great *gringo* and becoming educated about the ways of the world. Each night we ended our prayers with the eye of understanding that the time had come for us, *la gente,* the people, to UNITE AND HELP HEAL OUR MOTHER EARTH, OUR GREAT GIVER OF BEAUTY AND ABUNDANCE FOR ALL!

Or, as Jan told me that Harry Truman (which means a True Man) had said when he'd been President of the U.S.: "The buck stops here!" We, too, were now saying as a United-People-All-Over-the-Mother-Earth that "the buck stops here," because come "hell or high water," the abuses of the past stopped here, and we were taking full responsibility, just like this Harry True Man had said. Oh, I liked this Harry! He must've had big ones, meaning balls in English!

CHAPTER 31

Jan

Rochín and I were in Mexico City, in the beautiful hotel room that Pierre Benoit had gotten for us, when there was a knock at our door. Rochín was in the shower, so I opened it. It was a messenger from immigration, giving me a paper to sign that told me to go to the office of immigration at 8 the next morning. I assumed it had to do with my new passport, so I thought nothing of it. All day we'd been working with Pierre and the president's staff on maps and boundaries and legal descriptions of the great canyon so no mistakes would be made.

I slept well that night, and in the morning after breakfast, I went down to the immigration office before going to the presidential palace. I was taken to a private office, and to my shock, there was Emma, with three armed men and one man in a suit. They closed the door behind me, bolting it, and Emma told them that yes, this was me, her husband, and she fully agreed with the charges. I was a subversive and should be deported immediately.

"You heard what your own wife has said," said the man in the suit. "Sign here, and you have ten days in which to leave the country, or if you don't sign and agree to this, then . . . you will be arrested and taken into custody immediately," he added with a smile.

I looked at Emma. She, too, was smiling and as beautiful as ever, but their smiles were not Mona Lisa kinds of smiles. Theirs were smiles of final conquest and deep satisfaction. There was nothing I could do. If I didn't sign and they arrested me, it would be hours before Rochín would sense that something was wrong. By that time, I could be hundreds of miles out of Mexico City in the back of an unmarked police car and on my way to my death.

The man in the suit now reached over and patted Emma's hand very affectionately. Emma returned his gesture of affection.

"Okay," I said, "I'll sign."

"Very intelligent of you," said the man.

Getting to the presidential palace, I told Rochín and Pierre what had happened. Instantly my friend's face filled with fear, but Pierre remained cool.

"You know," he said, "maybe this is a blessing in disguise. You and Rochín have already done all you can really do to help us, so maybe it is best for you to leave the country as soon as possible, Jan. But I suggest that you not wait for the ten days. I suggest you leave immediately, but let us know where you'll be in the United States so as soon as we finalize this matter or . . . the government of Chihuahua is changed, we can contact you and you can return."

"But this governor just took office this year," Rochín pointed out. "It will be five years before there's a change in government in Chihuahua."

"I cannot talk about this right now for obvious reasons," said Pierre, "but both of these matters will be finalized very quickly and in the very near future."

All week I'd been very impressed by this young man, Pierre. His mind was razor sharp, and he was instantly ready to take thought and put it into action. There was no confusion going on inside his mind, heart, and soul. All was smooth within his Kingdom of God.

"How about Rochín?" I asked. "Should he go with me?"

"I don't know," replied Pierre. "What do you think, Rochín? Do you feel your life is also in danger?"

"Somewhat," said Rochín, "but certainly not as much as Jan. My family doesn't approve of what I'm doing, and yet we are family, so I'm sure they will protect me."

"Okay, then that's it, Jan," Pierre told me. "You better leave right now. Don't even wait for the morning train. You must understand that you are basically now free game, as you *gringos* say, until you are across the border. Also, where do you think they will expect you to cross the border?" he asked.

"At Juárez, going into El Paso, Texas," I said.

"Then I suggest you don't cross there. They might have a little party waiting for you. I tell you," he added, "I used to think the old-timers were exaggerating when they'd tell me that the danger of working for a president would always be from within and not from outside forces, but I now see they were right. Look at your own country, Jan, and see what happened to John Kennedy and then to his brother Robert. We laugh when you Americans believe your newspapers that always try to solve the problem by putting blame on some crazy individual. Ever since Lincoln was shot in the theater, you Americans have been putting your heads in the sand, thinking that your political system is so noble and clean. Here in Mexico we don't put our heads in the sand and hide from the obvious truth. Every child knows how crooked our government is. De la Madrid's predecessors Echeverría and López Portillo would have reeled you two in with beautiful promises, then thrown you to the dogs, telling the public how much they admired you and had tried to protect you, but . . . well, things just happen and now you've disappeared.

271

"Jan," he added, "I say all this to you so you'll realize that even though you have the president's protection, the wheels have already been set in motion to have you killed." He stopped and took a deep breath. "*Señora* de la Madrid instructed me to always be completely frank with both of you and ensure your safety throughout this matter. So I say to you, Jan, go with God, and go immediately.

"*Señora* de la Madrid is my inspiration. I'd gladly give my life for her or her son. They are the first decent people to come to the presidency of Mexico in a very long time, and they are setting up a system to ensure that the horrible abuses of power, as had become commonplace for so long, don't happen again. Go! We'll take it from here."

That very night we left our hotel room without luggage, and passing through the lobby, we noticed—as we'd expected—that two men were watching us. We went into the bar, ordered drinks, and I went to the bathroom and Rochín went to the phone booth. Then independently, we both went out the side door to the street and got in a taxi, and we were gone.

We traveled all night by bus back to Chihuahua, and how this happened, I don't know, but when we got off the bus, Our Three Wisemen *Curanderos* were waiting for us. They immediately told me that it was best if I didn't go into town or take a taxi—that Mireya was waiting for me in Cuauhtémoc, and we should get started on foot right away.

"On foot?" I said. "That's well over a hundred miles."

"Yes, very close," said the shorter one, laughing.

I hugged Rochín good-bye and took off with the Three Old Wisemen. We walked all day and night . . . and then shock of shocks, who was with Mireya, waiting for me in Cuauhtémoc, if none other than Emma herself. I couldn't believe my eyes. Was I going crazy, or what?

BOOK SIX

MIRACLES

CHAPTER 32

Mireya

Ever since I was a little girl, I'd been taught how to deal with rattlesnakes and all other kinds of danger, so when Emma came to see me—this time without a gun—I was very cautious. She told me Jan was in great danger, and she was on her way to Mexico City to help have him deported. They would give him ten days in which to leave Mexico, and in that time he would have an accident; or if that didn't work, then they would be waiting for him at the border, and he would be arrested and disappear. Hearing this, I began to listen to her in earnest, but still I didn't trust her.

"Look," I said to her when she was finished, "I don't trust you. Why should I? First you come up with a gun to kill me, then you come back with a knife to cut Jan open. I don't believe I should trust you any more than I'd trust a rattlesnake that's coiled and ready to strike."

"I couldn't agree with you more," said Emma, "but believe me, it's different this time, Mer—"

"Mireya," I said.

"Mi-re-ya?"

"Yes, that's right."

"The difference this time is that I didn't bring a gun or a knife. I brought Jan's children. They're in the car. Both of them. So I've come as a mother. Not as a wife. And I might be, well, half-crazy and jealous and . . . and as you said, overly worried about what people might think about me, but I am not blind or stupid. I've seen some of the kids who have come up to your camp, and the results. They are better behaved, and they talk about nature and God and family in a whole new way, so when things get settled— which I'm sure will happen, knowing Jan as we both do—I'd like my children to come up to the camp and get to know their father, who, you well know yourself, is a wonderful man. And you're right, I couldn't see that when I had my chance.

"I worked at the governor's offices and knew nothing but all these rich, powerful people. My father and mother raised us with no money, and . . . well, the point is, I'm going to Mexico City to help the department of immigration deport Jan, so I need to know which hotel he and Father Rochín are staying at. Then, when he gets back to Chihuahua, you must have someone meet him at the train depot and have him secretly escorted out of town immediately, and brought up here so we can help him get safely across the border. Does all this make sense? Are you beginning to trust me?" she asked.

I looked into her eyes. "Let me see the children," I said.

We went out to her car, and both children were asleep. A boy about six and a girl about four. Jan had told me that he'd heard that Emma had borne a second child, and she'd claimed it was his, but he didn't know if this was true. He'd never seen the second child. To me, both children looked a lot like Jan. My heart was moved.

"They look like angels," I said. "What are their names?"

"Jan and Jamie," she told me. "I'd like to leave them with you while I go to Mexico City, if that's all right with you."

I looked at her. She was like a completely different person, and . . . and I remembered how Jan always told me that people were all basically good, and it was just that sometimes they get sidetracked away from God. In San Francisco, over and over he'd seen the worst become the best, and here in Mexico he'd seen it, too, with boys like Chato and many of the others.

I took a deep breath. This was very difficult for me, and yet more and more I was beginning to believe in this world that Jan told me so much about, and . . . also, it wasn't much different from the world I'd been raised in on the *rancho* of my grandparents when I'd thought that I had all a child could possibly want. I'd been free as the birds in the sky and the deer in the meadows. It was a wonderful world that *mi gringo* lived in.

"Yes, you can leave your children with me," I told Emma, and saying this, a great joy filled my heart, and I hugged her and gave her the name of the hotel where Jan and Rochín were staying, without any fear or worry. I felt whole and round and complete as a river rock, and so happy to take care of my love's children.

Emma and I took the children inside, and she explained the situation to them, telling them that I was their father's new wife, so I was their second mother. She hugged them and kissed them, reassuring them that everything was all right, that she'd be back in two or three days. Then she left, telling me she had to hurry to get to Mexico City.

For three days I took care of Jan's two children in Cuauhtémoc, and then Emma returned and told me she'd been with the officials when Jan had come to the office of immigration and signed his papers of deportation. She also said she'd never had a chance to talk to him privately, so he knew nothing about our situation. And it was true, because when Jan came in with Our Three *Espiritos* and he saw me with Emma, I could have died laughing—he looked so shocked.

Jan and I spent the night together making love. I took him into me again and again, wanting to make sure I was pregnant so I, too, could have beautiful children like he'd had with Emma. I never let him sleep. I kept him going and going with every trick my mother and grandmother had taught me that a woman had to know so she could keep her husband strong and happy. Then in the morning I had to let go of him and see him drive off with Emma and their children to the border.

I had no passport and spoke almost no English, and Jan and I hadn't gotten married in the court system, so my presence would have just drawn attention to us at the border. I waved good-bye to them, and my eyes filled with tears. They looked like a *familia,* and I wasn't a part of that picture. Yet I understood the situation, so I had no confusion. They had to get to the border as quickly as possible, and they were not going through *Ciudad Juárez* to El Paso, which was the closest crossing. No, they were going to take back roads and enter the United States through Arizona instead of Texas.

My eyes continued crying, yet my heart wasn't breaking, because I knew that Soul to Soul Jan and I were United in Our True Love no matter how far apart we were body to body. A Human Being wasn't just of body, but of Spirit, too, like Our Sacred Three *Espiritos* who were guiding Jan through Life.

I loved my *gringo,* and watched the car get smaller and smaller as they disappeared into the great vastness of the wilds of Chihuahua, headed for Arizona. They would be staying with Jan's brother in Los Gatos, California. He would call Rochín when he got there, and Rochín would get word to me. My eyes continued crying, but I didn't feel lost or scared. No, I felt calm and strong and ready to go on with my life, even while *mi amor* was away from me.

CHAPTER 33

Jan

Emma and I took turns driving, and in no time we got to the Arizona border, just south of Tucson, and passed through with no problem. I'd told both Pierre and Mireya that I'd be at my mother's house at our estate in Los Gatos. Emma and I continued driving day and night across Arizona and up through California.

I would never forget as long as I lived the look on Mireya's face as I got in the car to drive off with Emma. She hadn't looked scared or worried. No, she'd looked so strong and confident and kind of detached and all-knowing. It was a lot like the look I'd seen that day in the lion eyes when I was a boy, yet . . . there'd been more. Much more. And I guess this was Our Love and the completion of our all-night lovemaking. It was like I could still feel every inch of my body attached to her, and it felt good and warm and wonderful!

It was late afternoon on our fifth day of driving when we came into the San Jose basin. I'd called my brother from Santa Barbara, just north of Los Angeles, to tell him that we were on our way, but I hadn't explained the situation to him. He was an engineer, so I thought it would be best to explain things to him face-to-face once we were there. Part of me wanted to drive by Willow Glen to see where I'd set up our first coffeehouse, but then just outside of San Jose we drove by the huge pickup place where the farmworkers waited each morning to be taken to the fields. I'd worked side by side with many farmworkers in the fields the summer before I'd become a minister. In the fields is where I'd begun to get to know the Mexican people. It had been nearly 15 years since I'd been here. The freeway system was all different. I'd never realized how freeways could cut a city up and change everything.

Twice I got us lost, but finally we were on Highway 17, on our way to Los Gatos across the valley. There were high-rise buildings where once there'd been nothing but prune orchards. We passed Los Gatos and started up the pass through the mountains on the way to Santa Cruz on the coast, and here was our turnoff, Black Road and Bear Creek. My heart filled up with feelings. Right up ahead was where the gigantic redwoods started and I'd seen the lion eyes. Suddenly I missed Mireya so much! The lights were on in the main house of our family compound when we drove up through the huge trees.

"This is it," I said to Emma, "the place where I grew up."

My mother; my brother, Leon; and his wife, Joann, came out to meet us, and instantly I saw a change come over Emma. She took my hand in hers as if we were husband and wife and turned on the charm. She spoke English, so she had no problem telling my mother and brother and his wife that she was my wife and these were our children, and she'd heard so much about them. It was incredible.

All the ride up from Mexico and across Arizona and up California, Emma had kept a respectful distance from me, and I'd thought we understood each other. But now all that was gone, and she was saying that yes, we were tired and wished to bathe and put our children down so we could go to bed together. This was the old Emma I knew, so I knew I was in for trouble.

That very night, I gave Emma and our children the bed, and I slept on the floor, but it was difficult, especially when she undressed. She was so beautiful. I turned and faced the wall so I wouldn't have to see her and I could think of Mireya.

I remembered that, in the old Indian way, Mireya had given me a piece of her clothing that she'd worn so I could smell it when we were apart. Smell was the strongest and most basic of all our senses. This was why dogs smelled each other and marked their territory with their urine. Cats did, too, especially mountain lions. I brought out the piece of clothing of hers that Mireya had given me. Her well-used unwashed underwear. And I smelled it and instantly, like magic, I was at peace and completely with my love and able to go to sleep without any confusion or worry. And in my dreams, Mireya and I were down deep in the canyon by the waterfalls, and we were among the ferns and wildflowers, making love again and again. IT WAS WONDERFUL!

Over the next couple of days I tried to explain to my mother and brother my situation—that Emma and I weren't married; that we'd never been married, because she hadn't filed our marriage papers; and that I was married to a young Indian woman named Mireya.

"But these are your children, aren't they?" asked my mother.

"Yes, I think so."

"You think so?" She was getting very upset.

"Yes, I think so, but a man can never be too sure with a woman like Emma." I tried to explain to them how Emma and I had first gotten together. But it didn't work. My mother got her purse and hat and went to her car. Leon followed her and then came back by himself.

"She says she'll be going to the beach house."

"The one in Santa Cruz?" I asked.

"Yes," said Leon. "She goes down there when she gets upset, and walks along the cliffs. It calms her down, she says. Don't worry, Jan. She'll be back in a few days, I'm sure."

But when she hadn't come back in a week, I could see that my brother was climbing the walls.

"We need to talk," he finally told me one afternoon. "Away from the main house, down in the shed."

"Okay," I said, and I followed him out of the main house and down the road to the toolshed, feeling like a little kid who was going to be reprimanded.

"Please, sit down," he said to me once we were inside. I sat on a pile of lumber. "Jan, you're my brother, and . . . and Mother and I don't understand your life at all. Joann and I got married right after she finished college, and we've been married ever since, and I go to work every day and she keeps house, and we have a life that Mother and our kids can depend on and that makes sense.

"What happened to you, Jan? I don't get it. First you become a minister, which Mother and all of us thought was very good, but then you left your congregation and went to the streets, riding a motorcycle at night. What was that all about? And then you went to Mexico and got involved with these lost, lowlife kind of people . . . and now you say you're married to an Indian woman, instead of this beautiful half-white woman; and the president of Mexico is backing you up in a land dispute of millions of acres, and yet other people are trying to kill you.

"Jan, look at it from our point of view. Does any of this make any sense to you? I mean, if even one-tenth of what you tell us is true—getting run down by a car and a shotgun put to your head that doesn't fire, and you say it wasn't a misfire, that you're doing God's work and God is helping you—it would be unbelievable. Jan, Mother honestly thinks you need to see a doctor. I'm your brother, and I agree with her and think you need help. And quickly!"

I started laughing. He was right. From his and my mother's point of view, I was totally crazy, even if only a tenth of the things I'd told them were true.

"You think this is funny?"

"No, I think you're right, and you love me," I said.

"Love you? What's love got to do with anything I'm saying, Jan?"

"Everything," I answered, "because, you see, back in Mexico I was living by myself by a lake, and I was cooking by fire and heating my cabin by fire, and I started remembering how you taught me how to build a fire up at our meadow. I was a little kid, and we'd sit there and say nothing as we watched the fire burn, and it felt so good, because you loved me. And you still love me, brother," I added, getting up to hug him. "And that's everything!"

"No, don't you dare hug me!" he yelled, leaping away from me in terror. "That's no help! We've got to keep our feet on the ground, Jan, and look at this thing straight on, without any of all that touchy-feely crap that you're always pushing! Our dad wasn't like that! Our mother still isn't! What happened to you? How did you get so lost and screwed up, Jan? You've got to get your head on straight and stop chasing rainbows. Don't you remember what I told you? People are just basically no good, so the best a man can do is clean out a space for himself and his loved ones, and let the whole rest of humanity go to hell, which is what they're doing anyway, one way or another. Those are the facts, Jan! That's reality! And it's about time you faced it!"

"Let's go up to the meadow tonight and build a fire together," I suggested.

He shook his head. "Jan, you're not listening."

"Yes, I am," I said. "I've listened to you, brother, very carefully, and I thank you for your concerns and worry and for our mother's concern, too."

"But you're not going to take anything I've told you seriously, are you?"

"Well, it's not that I'm not going to take what you've told me seriously. It's that, well," I said, putting my hands in my Levi's and rocking back and forth on my feet, "I've seen things and experienced things that are so far beyond what you tell me that I just know that—"

"That what? That I don't understand what life is really all about? Is that what you're saying?"

"No, not really. But I do believe that you'd have to come down with me to *las Barrancas del Cobre* and see with your own two eyes—"

"Like you used to tell me to go with you to San Francisco where all those lowlife hippies and drug addicts hung out. No, thank you! I've got a life! I'm not searching! I'm a God-fearing Christian, and I know that two and two are four! I'm not all mixed up with one woman who has my kids, but married to another woman— and an Indian, to boot!"

"Why are you so angry, Leon?"

"Because you make me angry, dammit!" he screamed. "Joann and I were happy, and everything was making sense; then you come back to stay with us for how long, I don't know, and . . . and you're my little brother, and I care for you, but . . . but . . ." He began to cry.

"Let me hug you, Leon. Come on, let me hug you."

"NO, DON'T!" he yelled, backing away, but then he stopped. "Well, okay. Okay. But just a little."

And so I took my older brother in my arms and held him close. He'd gotten so small over the years, and I'd become so much taller and larger. I held him close until he began to let go, take big deep breaths, and relax. Then he was crying freely.

"All my life I'd been scared of . . . of losing control," he said. "I just don't know how you've done all the things you've done, Jan. And people love you. I was there the day all those kids went to the airport in San Jose to see you off to Mexico. I heard them talking. They loved you, Jan. They admired you. What is it, Jan, that I've missed seeing all my life? I just don't get it."

"It's simple, brother," I said. "All you need is to see that people, all people, have the Holy Spirit of God within them, so they are basically good and doing the best they can. Jesus said it all when He said, 'Forgive them, for they do not know . . .' And truly they don't know until they accept Jesus Christ."

"But you've told me that these Indians down there aren't Christians."

"Was Jesus a Christian?"

"Well, yes, of course. What kind of question is that, anyway?"

"Think about it, Leon. He called Himself the Son of God. He never said He was a Christian."

"Well, no, of course not. He was Jesus, for christsakes!"

"The Tarahumara accept Jesus because He's a Miracle Maker, and Miracles are the basis of all their reality, so they're not Christians, but they are true followers."

"Wait! Hold on! I don't get it! Are you saying you can be a follower of Jesus Christ, and still not be a Christian?"

I took a breath, then gently said, "Do you remember when Jesus's disciples asked Him where He'd been when He was gone for those three days before He was resurrected? He told them He'd been to see His other people. Well, Leon, I believe those other people are the Tarahumara and many other tribes all over the world, because the more and more I don't preach, but instead listen and observe, I've learned that many indigenous people already have the basis of Jesus's teaching within their Own Spiritual Beliefs. They just use different names and different stories. This is how I am able to see the Spirit of God in everyone. I listen. I watch. And I don't jump to conclusions."

"Then you're telling me you really think people are basically good Christians all over the world and everything is okay?"

"Yes, as a Christian I know this . . . with all my Heart and Soul!"

"Well, if I thought that, I guess I would see everything differently, but I can't, Jan. I see so much bad and evil on the news and in the papers and all around me and—"

"Stop reading the papers and watching the news, and take a walk at night through the redwoods and look up at the stars, and realize how really small all the bad is compared to the Infinite Beauty and Goodness that surrounds us."

"I wish I could, Jan, but—"

"We'll walk tonight together, Leon," I said. "I remember how we used to do that when we were kids."

"Yeah, we did, but I was bigger and taller than you back then."

"You still are, in my eyes," I said. "You will always be my big brother."

"Then you don't think I'm a coward to have stayed so close to home all these years?"

"Of course not. There are many paths to God."

That night we took a walk together after dinner through the huge, gigantic redwoods, and we climbed up on the ridge from which we could see the stars. Then we built a fire and said nothing for a long time, and then for the first time in my life, I felt able to tell my brother about the lion eyes I'd seen in the snowstorm when I was a boy. He was totally mesmerized, and he didn't question or belittle what I had to say. No, he was open to the wonders of living life, and . . . even to the Miraculous. It was the finest time I'd ever spent with my big brother.

CHAPTER 34

Mireya

For the first few weeks Jan was gone, it was very difficult for me. I felt like my heart had been ripped out of my body, especially at night when I had such a hard time going to sleep. But then something very interesting happened. Three Indian women came to me, complaining that Van Housen was paying them close to nothing and then selling their dolls and purses and other items at his store at the train station for a lot of money. And when they complained to him, he insisted that the materials he purchased and supplied them with so they could make their dolls and wares were very expensive, so he really wasn't making much profit, especially with the expensive rent he had to pay for his store. The women asked me to help them find out if this was all true, because they worked very hard for long hours and hardly made any money.

Myself, I instantly became suspicious because of how he'd helped steal the land from the Tarahumara. So I asked my mother and Coco to find out about renting a place across the way from

Van Housen's store; then I got on the train by myself for the first time in my life, and I went down to Chihuahua City alone. It was scary yet very exciting.

Getting off the train, I walked the whole way to the huge outdoor marketplace, and I found that I could buy all the makings for dolls and purses very cheap. Jan had left me some money, so I took all the money I could afford to and bought the things the women would need, choosing colors and fabrics that would be very pleasing to the eyes and to the feel.

The women were thrilled when I came back and showed them what I'd purchased. I told them the priest had lied, and the materials I had bought were not expensive. Then I told them that Coco and my mother had also found out that the rent for a store at the train station was very reasonable. I told them that if they wished, I could open my own store, and I'd pay them five times more than Van Housen paid them. They were thrilled and immediately agreed to go in with me.

Coco and my mother helped me rent a place directly across from Van Housen's store. For as long as I could remember Van Housen had the only store at the train station where the tourists came in. And also, he'd run off all the street vendors, telling them they needed a city permit to sell their items within the city limits. But Creel wasn't a city and had no city limits. It was just a train-stop station.

Well, at first we only sold refreshments and sweet bread at my little store, so Van Housen thought nothing of it. Then my women began filling my store with the finest dolls and purses and other wares they'd ever made. Van Housen came rushing over, shouting at me, trying to intimidate me. But I was ready for him, so I leaped at him, screaming like I was really crazy. He was so surprised that he went pale and turned and ran. We all started laughing, and within a few weeks we were getting almost all the business from the tourists who came to our train-stop station. Van Housen just wasn't the force he'd once been. We didn't fear him anymore.

Also, the Holy Spirit of God was now with us, because my three Indian women and their families came to me the night Van

Housen and his men were going to burn my store down. They told me they'd been forewarned in their dreams, and, of course, I took their dreams seriously because I knew that dreams were true.

I got hold of my uncle Oscar, and he and six of his truck-driving friends were there with us, too, when Van Housen and his men came to do us harm. We came out of the darkness with shouts and clubs and drove them away, telling the old priest that the saints from Heaven had come to warn us and that he was going to become sick and die if he didn't stop his evil ways. Oh, it was so much fun to see them all run in fear. The tide was changing in our direction. The forces of good were gathering and helping us at every turn.

Then we got word that, Miracle of Miracles, the stolen lands had officially been transferred back to the Tarahumara and that President de la Madrid was coming to see us in his private helicopter. This also meant that my *gringo* could come back home to me—now an experienced businesswoman. I had expanded my store and was thinking of opening up another that would sell handmade furniture and mirrors and other household goods.

The word had spread to *la gente* all over *las Barrancas del Cobre* that I was an honest person who paid very well. Now I didn't have to go looking anymore. All day I had a string of people coming in to show me their wares, and Van Housen would stare at me from afar like a lost old man, but he never came near me again. The poor fool had lost his heart and soul so long ago that now he had nothing left within himself to nurture him in his old age. A soul and a heart full of love and well-being was what gave the Tarahumara the foundation with which to live in good health past a hundred. And it was said that to the degree that one accepted their spirituality at the age of 78—the most perfect age for a human being—to that degree they could live in perfect health past 100, just like Our Three Sacred Healers.

When I was told that my *gringo* was on his way home, MY HEART SOARED! It had been 3 months, 5 days, 12 hours, and 20 minutes since I'd last seen him. OH, I WAS SO EXCITED, I COULD SCREAM—SO I DID. I SCREAMED, RUNNING DOWN TO THE TRAIN

STATION SO I COULD LEAP ON HIM AND SQUEEZE HIM TIGHT TO ME, WITH MY LEGS WRAPPED ABOUT HIS GENEROUS MIDDLE!

CHAPTER 35

Jan

It was three months to the day after I left when I received word that the governor of Chihuahua had suddenly resigned, and all of the acreage in question had been successfully returned to the Tarahumara. It was now safe for me to return to Mexico. Pierre had truly known what he was talking about.

But Emma wasn't so sure she wanted to go back. She wanted me to consider for us to get back together and make our home in the United States. My brother and his wife, Joann, were on her side, but I said no, that I was returning to Mexico to be with Mireya. Besides, my mother never once came back from Santa Cruz to see Emma and me and her grandchildren. And I knew Leon had spoken quite well of me to her after our talk in the shed, but still, I guess, everything she thought about me was written in stone, so she was not going to give an inch.

The day Emma and I packed and were ready to go, I asked Leon if maybe we shouldn't drive by Santa Cruz so my mother could at least say good-bye to her grandkids.

"I don't think that would be a good idea," he said. "I spoke to her about that, and . . . well, she bluntly said that she's a devout Christian, and as such, she has no eyes for you and yours, that you've made your own bed."

Tears came to my eyes. I now understood why my mother would leave me at school if I was just ten minutes late. She'd become a hard-hearted woman, I guess, ever since our dad had died. "Tell Mother I love her," I said to my brother. "And that I will pray for her."

"I will."

My brother and I hugged one last time, and then Emma and I were back on the road with our two children. I'd gotten to spend a lot of good time with little Jan and Jamie in the last three months, and I'd come to believe they were really mine. Mireya had told me they both looked a lot like me, but I guess I'd just been too suspicious to be sure.

All during the drive back, Emma kept attacking me verbally in front of the children, telling them how I'd ruined their lives. Before we crossed the border, she'd destroyed all the good feelings I'd developed with my kids. Then as if this wasn't enough, she had me sign papers deeding over to her the two properties I owned in Chihuahua. I gladly signed the papers. Emma was beginning to remind me a lot of my mother. Both were very angry women who thought they were all alone in the world. They had no basic faith in God, even though both claimed to be devout Christians.

Rochín was waiting for me at the Hotel Presidente when we got to Chihuahua City. He wanted to know what time we'd crossed the border.

"Earlier today," I said. "About eight hours ago."

"This is the exact same moment when . . . when Mexico City received the largest earthquake they've had in modern times, Jan. They report that the whole capital has been devastated!"

It was September 19, 1985, three days after Mexican Independence Day. Two old coffee-drinking friends came up. Rochín and I had always liked to have coffee at this grand old hotel when we were in Chihuahua City.

"I knew you were back, Jan," one of them said, laughing uproariously. "First the governor mysteriously resigns, and then an earthquake!"

I joined in his laughter. "I had nothing to do with the earthquake."

Everyone now BURST OUT LAUGHING WITH *CARCAJADAS*. Then Rochín took me aside and caught me up on the rest of the news. All the millions and millions of acres had been returned to the Tarahumara, plus all the mineral rights, and in a couple of weeks the president and his mother would be coming to see us in Creel in his private helicopter. Then he added that Jorge Ramos and several of his friends wanted to meet with me, but I told Rochín that I first had to go and see Mireya.

I couldn't believe what I saw when I got off the train in Creel. In the three months I'd been away, Mireya had gone toe-to-toe with Van Housen, beaten his ass, and now owned two fine-looking stores at the square where the train stopped. We hugged and kissed, but she couldn't stop talking—she was so excited!

"Three Indian women came complaining to me while you were gone," she said with that great big smile of hers. "They said Van Housen paid them close to nothing, then put their dolls and purses and other items in his store for high prices. They asked me to look into the matter and suggested that I open a store and help them sell the things they make directly to the tourists.

"I got on the train all by myself, Jan," she said with joy, "and went down to Chihuahua City alone. I was scared, but so excited. I walked across town to the open market and used part of the money you left me to buy the materials needed, and they were cheap. Van Housen had lied to the Indian women. Then I got

Coco and my mother to help me rent a place directly in front of Van Housen's store.

"You'd be so proud of me, Jan!" she shouted. "At first we only sold a couple of trinkets, arts and crafts, but then the word got out that we were paying five times more for the dolls and purses than Van Housen did, and everyone started bringing their things to us. My store became a great success overnight. But then Van Housen caught on, and he came to my store, and he thought he was going to scare me, but I leaped in his face with all my power—plus, well, a pretty little decorative machete in hand, too—and he ran.

"Oh, the women laughed, they were so happy. Jan, we are making so much money. It's wonderful! I'm glad you're back. How did it go? Did Emma behave herself, or did she try to win you back once you were across the border? Be truthful, eh? Tell me what happened. Did she take you to bed?"

"Mireya, how could she possibly try to even lure me," I said, "when all I do is talk about my great love for you day and night?"

"Oh, Jan, you really know how to say the right thing just at the right time, don't you, *mi amor?*"

"Did it work?"

"Yes," she said, leaping on me and wrapping her legs about my middle.

Our cabin out at the lake was done, so we immediately drove out so we could start making up for the lovemaking that we'd missed in the last three months. She was fantastic! She'd taken Life, *la vida,* by the horns with Faith and Joy and Confidence while I was gone, and she'd done Wonders! She was definitely the Most Powerful Woman I'd ever known, yet her Heart was Tender and Warm and Open to God's Miracles.

CHAPTER 36

Mireya

It was difficult for us to truly understand what had really happened with the earthquake in Mexico City, because there was no earthquake here at our *Barrancas*. All I knew was that Jan was back with me, and we were happy.

The Tarahumara decided to do a *tesgüinada*. *Tesgüino* was the name of the corn-mash beer that the Tarahumara made for Holy Week. At a *tesgüinada,* the Tarahumara gather to forge important relationships with one another through joking and trading, and they wanted to do one in honor of Jan and Rochín and the president of Mexico for helping them get back all their lands and mineral rights.

For weeks the Tarahumara came in on foot from all over *las Barrancas del Cobre* to participate in the celebration, preparing for the arrival of *Señora* de la Madrid and her son. But then we received word that the president and his mother would not be coming to Creel—that there was still so much unrest in the capital because of the earthquake and two cabinet members resigning that it was best for them to keep things kind of quiet about the Indian lands being returned to Tarahumara, because then wild, dangerous rumors would begin, with people trying to understand what had gone on behind the scenes.

The main thing we had to understand was that *Señora* de la Madrid and her son were fine and sent their best and that Pierre Benoit would personally come up to see us and stay with us for a few days. My mother and Coco prepared a great feast for Pierre, and I made a special room for him in one of our dormitories. Jan and I spent a couple of days with him. He wanted us to take him down into the canyon to see the waterfalls where the wildflowers and great huge ferns grew year-round.

Jan warned him that the going would be difficult, but he told us not to worry, that he kept his body in excellent shape. Well, what can I say, Pierre was the first non-Indian, besides Jan, I ever saw start to cock his ear this way and that way as we climbed lower and lower into the Great Sacred Canyon.

"Is that music I hear?" he finally asked. "Or is it just my imagination?"

Jan, Rochín, and I all laughed. Then when we explained to the Indians who'd come with us what Pierre had said, they, too, started laughing with loud *carcajadas!*

"Why so much laughter?" asked Pierre, laughing, too.

"Because you are probably the first white person, besides Jan, who's ever cocked his head trying to hear the voice of our beloved canyon, and we are all overjoyed with *gusto*. You see, it is both," said Rochín. "It is your imagination, and it is also music."

"It almost sounds like a whole symphony," said Pierre, "as I tilt my head this way and that way."

"It's the wind passing over the canyon, and then sweeping into certain tight crevices," said Rochín.

"Yes, but what I hear is much more than that," said Pierre.

"You are right," said Jan. "It is also the Soul of Our Sacred Canyon."

I'd had enough and laughed. "OH, ALL YOU MEN ARE SO LOST! Why do you think that Our Great Canyon is called the Vagina of

Chihuahua? She is a woman with her legs wide-open and making passionate love with the wind and rain and all the Souls of Our Ancestry! SO HER CRY IS HER GREAT *GUSTO* OF MAKING *AMOR!*"

Even my husband, Jan, turned red-faced. "My wife," he said, "she knows no way to beat around the bush. She's always blunt and straightforward."

They all burst out laughing; and we spent a fantastic, wonderful week down in the bottom of the canyon, and this was when Pierre explained to us what was going on in Mexico City. He told us that every government in the world was basically run by a group of families, and that half the time these families were at each other's throats over money and political power and that the general public knew nothing about this.

De la Madrid and his mother were some of the finest and smartest and best-connected people who'd ever gotten into the presidency, because, like the Kennedys of the United States, they had their own money, so they didn't owe a bunch of favors to a lot of people, meaning they could then do what was best for the nation as a whole. And hopefully Salinas de Gortari and Fox Quesada, who each had money of their own, would be able to continue this new system of true democracy of which de la Madrid had planted the seeds.

What Pierre told us made a lot of sense to me. And now I liked this *gringo* saying of the True Man President of the U.S. even better. "The buck stops here" cut through all the horse manure and bullshit! Oh, I loved English! It was juicy!

When we came out of the canyon, the *tesgüinada* was just getting started. This one was not being held by the church. No, this one was being done at the cave of the uncle of Calitxtro, the president of the San Ignacio *ejido*. His uncle was the greatest living *mayori* of the whole area. He'd also been a student of Jan's Three Spirit *Curanderos*.

The cave was immense. It easily held more than a hundred people inside and another couple of hundred outside its huge entrance. Jan explained to Pierre that it was a great honor for them, being white men, to be allowed into the cave to give witness to the celebration. Pierre said the cave was greater than any castle he'd ever seen in Europe.

Fires were lit, illuminating the entrance of the cave; and the great, huge drum began to echo out over the land at dusk. The men started drinking the foul-smelling beer and dancing in circles to the slow, steady beat of the drum, going into a hypnotic state halfway between dreaming and being awake. The women, of course, didn't need to do this to go into their own hypnotic state, because of their bloodletting every month and their experiences of child birthing—so they sat dressed in colorful clothes, and the children stood by them.

Jan and Pierre were the only white people in the whole place. Rochín and I were almost as dark of skin as the Tarahumara, so we didn't stand out. Then began the Holy Voices, the Natural Musical Crying Sounds deep within the Sacred Cave, and I could now see why it was said that if a person had fear in their heart, they'd race out of the cave into the night and get lost. But if you were at peace within your heart, then the Holy Voice of the Mother Earth passed through you with ease, refreshing your Very Soul.

The celebration lasted for three days. This was when we heard that another tremor had happened at the capital. Pierre began to understand the Holy Forces that stirred deep within the bowels of our Mother Earth. She was Alive and Holy, and we were her children, and she had very strong feelings for us.

I asked Jan to please explain to Pierre that it was not what the shamans did that caused earthquakes. It was what people carried inside themselves that caused phenomena. Jan explained this to Pierre, and our special guest said that he, too, could now hear the Holy Voices of the cave and feel them pass through him with ease.

After this, the Spirit World must have become visible to Pierre, because he suddenly gave a shout of joy and stripped off his clothes, dancing with the Indians and howling to the moon. The coyote was obviously his Spirit Guide, a very powerful and tricky totem, so I guess this was why Pierre had the great ability to survive in the world at the capital.

On the last day of the celebration we were serenaded by natural Holy Music of the Violin, which echoed with the wind throughout the cave. Angels had come down from Heaven and joined us here on Mother Earth, and they were singing, too.

CHAPTER 37

Jan

That winter Mireya and I went down to Chihuahua City and were officially married, with Rochín acting as our best man. Jorge Ramos and Silveria attended our wedding and rented a beautiful suite for us in the most luxurious hotel in town. Before Mireya and I left the city, we met with Jorge and his wife, who told us that some close friends of theirs wanted to help us build an environmentally friendly culture park in Creel for the Tarahumara.

"So you finally spoke up to them," I said to Jorge, laughing.

"Yes," he said, also laughing, "and what I thought was going to become a confrontation became a miracle of generosity and understanding."

We just looked at each other for a long time, then started laughing with *carcajadas*. "So how does it feel to start stepping into the World of Miracles?" I asked.

"Well, what did it," he said, still laughing, "wasn't so much their faith in miracles, but your little joke when you came back from the United States."

"What joke?"

"When you said to our mutual coffee-drinking friends that yes, you were responsible for our governor's sudden resignation, but not for the earthquake, at least not this time. When our friends heard this, they decided maybe it was best for them to buy a little insurance. They don't want earthquakes coming to Chihuahua the way they came to Mexico City when a couple of the cabinet members refused to resign. Jan, your fame has grown even more! My hat is off to you! What I told you could not be done has now been done, and very nicely, too! It's astonishing that de la Madrid was able to accomplish what he did!"

He turned to Mireya. "I hope you understand who this man is you married."

"I do!" said Mireya. "I was just a child when my distant cousin came back from the lowlands with the sickness of the evil eye and stole my grandparents' ranch from them, by staking my wonderful uncle Oscar and his brother on an anthill. I began to believe only people with the evil eye could get ahead in this modern world of fast cars and paved roads, but then I began to hear about a *gringo* with a red beard who Father Rochín had brought up to live in a tent by our largest lake. His eyes were as pure as the eagle, they said. He played his guitar and serenaded the night, making the spirit of the trees and the rocks and the water herself happy. I was in love with him before I ever saw him. He was kind, they also said. He was handsome and strong, but most important of all, he had a noble heart, just like a mother bird or deer who's willing to give her life for her family."

Tears came to her eyes. "And even as a young girl I knew how hard it was to find such a man. My grandmother and mother both explained a lot of things to me about life, way before I began to pass the blood of being a woman. I love my *gringo!* He's *mi esposo de la vida!*" she added with that huge, contagious smile of hers. "And I'd die for him, I love and trust him so much, because, you see, he has shown us all that the evil eye of greed doesn't really work, even in our modern world. And it feels beautiful to know this in *mi corazón!*"

Smiling, Jorge and Silveria took each other's hands. They, too, were now in love with Mireya. How could they not be? There wasn't a bone of confusion or fear in her body. She was totally at home within her Heart and Soul and Mind, no matter where she was, because she was always in the Sacred Flow of God's *Amor.*

It snowed that winter, and Mireya and I spent a lot of time alone in our new cabin. It was wonderful, and so peaceful and quiet that we could hear the snowflakes landing on our roof. Often people become antsy and start getting irritated with each other when they spend so much time together, but I can honestly say that this never happened to Mireya and me. We were at peace with each other even after being together day and night for months. The world could not break us, as Mireya's mother had suggested to her could be the case. The world had, in fact, made our love stronger, and this I do believe is the case when two people include God in their Love and also in their lovemaking.

Then in the spring, just a few weeks before the kids' camp was to begin, three of the *mayoris* of the 13 different *ejidos* came to see Mireya and me. They said that a special celebration had been prepared for us. We got in our red truck, with them in the back, and drove away from the lake over hills and across *mesas* for about ten miles, and then we were told to park in the shade of some large pines.

The *mayoris* asked us to take off our sandals and told us that we needed to walk barefoot to the location for the Sacred Ceremony so we could feel Mother Earth with the soles of our feet. I had never been to this part of their land. We walked on deer paths— there were no roads—for about six miles. Then when we came to a beautiful small valley, one of the *mayoris* went up on a ridge to keep watch as we continued up the valley. There were wildflowers everywhere and an abundance of bees and butterflies.

About half a mile up the valley, a canyon forked off to the right. Here we stopped and the *mayori* who'd gone up on the ridge now came back down with four other respected elders. They told us we had not been followed.

We went up the canyon for about another half mile, and then to my surprise, we backtracked, walking backward for about 200 feet over our own tracks; then we turned to the right and walked from stone to stone, leaving no tracks, and slipped behind a large boulder, then passed through a crack between two rock walls . . . and here was the entrance of a beautifully sculptured hidden cave that you would have passed by if you didn't know about it.

Inside the hidden cave were gathered all the rest of the 13 *mayoris* and their *curanderos* and wives. All the *ejidos* of the Tarahumara were represented. They'd been having a ceremony of silence as we'd come in, but now they greeted us with great joy. The women started cooking, laughing as they cooked. There were long stalactites hanging from the 30-foot-tall cave that were black with soot of many fires.

The Three Wisemen, who now mostly lived in the Spirit World, came to Mireya and me and explained that only the *curanderos* and *mayori* knew of this Sacred Cave. The Tarahumara people knew nothing of this Holy Womb, because it was only used for rare, special occasions. The Wisemen explained that this was where the Spirit of the *peyote* herb first came to the Dream-Consciousness of the Tarahumara and to their cousins, who'd gone north a few thousand years ago.

I was sworn to secrecy, so I cannot tell you anything about our ceremony, which lasted four days and three nights, except that I was officially made a *mayori* and given the name of *apolochi*, Sacred Grandfather Keeper of Wisdom. Mireya was taken in by the women and given her own name and title, which had never been given to one so young in Tarahumara history. The women told Mireya that she was given this honor because they'd all seen what a great warrior she had been in helping to get their Sacred Lands returned to them.

For three nights I thanked the stars, and I began to understand with every bone of my being that this ceremony had brought me full circle . . . to the fulfillment of the experience I'd had as a kid when I'd seen the golden eyes of the mountain lion.

All we human beings have a job to do here on Mother Earth.

All we human beings have our totem to find, so we can activate our Kingdom of God.

All we human beings are Sacred and Holy and Wonderful beyond belief!

I was now no longer alone. I was complete and as round and smooth as river rock!

The ceremony ended with the *mayoris* of the 13 different *ejidos* giving Mireya and me nearly 5,000 acres, as a gesture for the *rancho* that Mireya's grandparents had lost. We promised the *mayoris* that we would build a University for Harmony and Peace and a community of Visions and Love on these 5,000 acres so that people could come from all over the world and experience the Sacred Ways of the Tarahumara, thereby regaining respect for their own families' indigenous story.

Mireya and I were now welcome to walk hand in hand into the World of Miracles.

Three weeks later we opened up the children's camp, and I couldn't believe HOW OUR NEW LIFE TRULY BURST INTO MIRACLES! Who brought their kids up to our camp? Not just Emma, but Catalina, too! And I was finally able to spend time with all of my children—Nathan; Aaron; Jan, Jr.; and Jamie. MY HEART SOARED THROUGH THE HEAVENS!

Jorge and Silveria kept their word, too, and came up by train with a group of wealthy people, who gave us the money so we could start the cultural park for the Tarahumara and the two other tribes of the area. It was beautiful! Just like Mireya had kept telling me all winter she could feel in her bones, the Holy Tide of Creation had changed in our favor, and good things would now be coming to us for a very, very long time.

This is when we and the Indian leaders of the different *ejidos* were invited to the great national Indian Market in Denver, Colorado, the largest assembly of native-made wares in the entire United States. Twenty-six of us went, including the original three women and their daughters who'd come to Mireya complaining about Van Housen—who, by the way, had aged terribly in the last few months and now even had trouble getting around on his own. And who helped care for Van Housen? It was the very people he'd abused.

We took sacks full of goods, and the people who ran the Denver Indian Market gave us a booth. Our Indian leaders quickly made friends with many of the elders of other tribes, and some of these elders said they'd heard through the grapevine about the millions of acres that had been returned to the Tarahumara. Also, it was well known by the elders that Our Three Great Indian *Curanderos* Wisemen had been the ones who'd caused the earthquake in Mexico City, when the government had almost decided not to give back the Sacred Lands.

After the Denver Indian Market, we were invited to Taos, New Mexico, to the Sacred Pueblo where no white people were ever allowed to enter. Mireya, of course, was accepted, but they had to talk it over with our Indian leaders before I, too, could be invited in. What happened there for three days I was sworn to never tell, except to say that once more I was ushered deeper and deeper into the Holy World of the Miraculous. At the end, 26 different tribes smoked the peace pipe as we took turns sitting on the Sacred White Buffalo Rug.

It was after this that we were invited to Mesa Verde, Colorado; and when we got there, our Indian leaders instantly told Mireya and me that these were their long-lost cousins who'd gone north after they'd had their *peyote* visions thousands of years ago. Then our elders began explaining the cliff dwellings to us and to the superintendent of Mesa Verde National Park, Robert Heyder. They told us that this room was used for this, and this other room had been used for this other purpose. Heyder was astonished. He said he and his staff of so-called experts had it all mixed up.

Then our Indian leaders asked Mireya and me to tell the curator what it was we'd done at the *tesgüinada* in the cave the year before. I was halfway through my explanation when I could suddenly hear the Holy Sacred Voices here, too. I cocked my head this way and then that way, and I was being told through Holy Song and Sacred Music that these Ancient Ones of Mesa Verde were the Living Tarahumara of today. Robert Heyder started cocking his head and also heard the Voices, and told us that he now understood why he'd devoted his life to these ancient ruins. They were Truly Alive with the Holy Voice of God!

We returned to Creel with a new understanding of the culture park we were building. Our Vision now included the whole southwest of the United States and northwest of Mexico, a land that had once been free of boundaries to all these interrelated tribal people. With the help of Robert Heyder, a network was set up so the indigenous people we'd met in the U.S. could come down to visit us in Creel.

IT WAS BEAUTIFUL!

IT WAS FANTASTIC!

THE WORLD OF MIRACLES HAD BURST OPEN WITH HOPE AND ABUNDANCE BEYOND ALL MAN-MADE BORDERS! And it was so easy! So very, very easy once we did as Confucius said to do: "Row, row, row your boat, gently down the stream! Merrily, merrily, merrily, life is but a dream!"

And, of course, most authorities believe that this children's nursery rhyme came from the English during the 16th century, but it didn't. It's way older, and it originated in China and definitely shows us that life is a Dream once we get into the Holy Flow of Creation with God. This was what Jesus came down to Mother Earth to tell us, to trust our Kingdom of God that's within us; and row, row, row our boat gently down the stream—not *up* the stream.

Then merrily, merrily, merrily, life is but an EASY, EASY DREAM!

BOOK SEVEN

DESIGNS
BEYOND COMPREHENSION

CHAPTER 38

Mireya

LIFE WAS BEAUTIFUL! I, Mireya, a person without education, had found out that you really didn't need the evil eye to get ahead in this modern world of fast cars and paved roads and big cities. No, a Noble Heart still counted for something. But then one night back in Mexico, two years after we'd been at Mesa Verde, armed men dressed in black with painted black faces came in at night and tied Jan and me up very quietly, then took him away.

There was something different about these large men. They weren't cruel and abusive. No, they'd come in on us as silently as cats, and they did everything so quickly and quietly that I knew these were not soldiers or police. These were men of a much higher and more refined training. I lay still—what else could I do? They'd known what they were doing when they'd tied me up, and it wasn't until midmorning when my mother came looking for me and found me tied up in bed that I was freed.

"We thought we heard something," she said. "But then we figured it was just you and Jan, like you two sometimes get a little loud in your lovemaking."

"They took him, *Mamá!* And these aren't the local judicial police or army."

"No, they aren't," said my mother. "They didn't leave a trace."

We didn't know what to do, and it was Coco who got the idea that we should not report it to any of the local authorities, and instead we should contact Rochín in Chihuahua.

CHAPTER 39

Jan

The moment they came upon us, I knew they were different. They didn't hit me. They simply taped my mouth shut and tied my hands behind my back, and gently, too. Not rough at all. In fact, so quickly and gently that at first I thought it was a joke or something. But then when they put me on a blanket, rolled me up, and carried me swiftly out of our cabin and ran down the road with me for quite a distance and put me in the backseat of a car, I then knew this was no joke. These men were strong and in excellent shape and knew exactly what they were doing. These were not local police or soldiers. These were highly trained individuals who'd probably been trained in the United States by the CIA or the FBI.

The car drove down the road for several miles before they unwrapped the blanket off of me. I'd had trouble breathing, so it was hard for me to catch my breath at first. I was in the backseat between two large men dressed in black workout clothes, with their faces painted black, too. The two men in front were smaller, especially the driver.

"Excuse me," the man in the front passenger seat said to me, "would you like some water before we blindfold you?"

I nodded. I couldn't say anything with my mouth taped up.

"Okay, we will take the tape off your mouth, but not one sound, not one word, not one question, or we will instantly cover your mouth and nose with chloroform and knock you out."

I nodded again. I believed this man. All these men were so different from all the law-enforcement people of Mexico I'd met before. They were so calm and detached and professional.

"It's going to hurt a little bit," the large man to my left told me, "so just close your eyes, and I'll be gentle."

I closed my eyes, and I felt his fingertips gently grip the tape on my left cheek and pull slowly, carefully, then give a quick yank, and it was off. I opened my eyes. He was smiling.

"See, not so bad," he said to me, then turned to the man in the front seat. "Should I untie him?"

"No, not yet. Let's see how he behaves."

The man on the other side of me now put a bottle of water with a straw to my lips. It was purified water. Nothing but the best. I drank and drank, and all this time I could see that the driver kept glancing at me in the rearview mirror. He wore a beautiful Panama hat, and yet I could see his large, dark eyes.

"Okay now," said the man in the front passenger seat, "now put a hat on his head and blindfold him, but I don't think that we'll have to retape his mouth. Am I right?" he asked me directly. "Remember, not a word. Just nod, if you agree."

I nodded, and they put a blindfold on me—the type you could get at an airport—then placed a hat on my head. I guess to the outside world I looked like a man wearing dark shades under his Panama. We traveled for hours, and then more hours. I've always had a good sense of direction, so I figured we drove east toward Chihuahua City and then headed north. I don't know why, but I began to figure they were taking me to the border at El Paso. But if

I were being deported once again, why hadn't they just given me papers to sign like last time?

Then we stopped, turned right, and took a bumpy dirt road. I suddenly knew what was going on. I was going to disappear this time for sure. De la Madrid had just stepped down from office, so most probably this . . . this was the first official business of the new presidential regime . . . to get rid of the troublesome, no-good *gringo*. The car stopped, and they took off my hat and blindfold. It was nighttime, and we were out in the middle of nowhere. The doors opened, and they pulled me out of the car. I could see city lights in the distance.

"Untie him," said the man who did all the talking. "He probably needs to piss as bad as all the rest of us, and if he tries to escape, just shoot him."

He was right. I had to pee so badly, I was dying. I couldn't have tried to make a run for it if I'd wanted to.

"Can I talk now?" I asked.

"Sure, go ahead," said the talker man as he began to piss. "But not too much, and no questions."

"You're right. I need to pee. So if you untie me, I promise not to try to escape."

"Good. My students and I like to keep things easy and under control."

Students? This man had called these other men his students. They untied me, and I moved a couple of feet away and began to pee. I could now see that the city lights in the distance stretched out for miles.

"*Ciudad Juárez* and El Paso," the talker said to me, "and this is where you will get your final freedom, my friend, and you should have no fear. For you're a man who's done so much good in the world that you are sure to go directly to Heaven."

I finished peeing. I didn't know what to think. These were an entirely different type of people from the others who'd been sent to do me in. They had no anger toward me, and no fear or remorse about what they were doing. It was obvious that their leader was well educated. I had a thousand questions to ask him. What university had he attended? Had he been a philosophy major? Had he also gone to college in the United States, because he spoke perfect English as well as Spanish?

"Yes," he said, as if reading my mind, "I also studied in the United States. Harvard, to be exact. And in Europe, too.

"The shovel," he said, turning to his two large students who'd ridden in back with me. Each had a shovel in hand that they'd gotten out of the trunk of the car. "Would you like to dig," he asked me, "or would you prefer that my students dig your grave for you?"

I looked at him.

"I assure you, this really isn't as far-fetched a question as you might think. Most men, for some reason, like to dig their own graves. I assume some think that with a shovel in hand, then somehow they will figure out a way to defend themselves and escape. Others, I believe, accept their fate and just want to keep busy before they die. So what would you prefer?"

"I'll dig," I said.

"Good. Give him one of the shovels."

One of the two large men handed me a shovel, and I began to dig. At first the digging was tough, because the crust of the land was as hard as granite, but then once I got down a little ways, the ground was sandy and quite easy for digging.

"You'd better hurry," the talker said to me, "or let one of my students help you, because we want to get this whole thing done before sunrise, and there's a little light in the eastern sky. You know, you've had a good life, Jan. Do you mind if I call you Jan, Mr. Milburn?"

"No, not at all, but what is your name, so we can be properly introduced?"

He laughed. "No questions, remember?"

"Oh yes, I forgot. Excuse me," I said as I continued digging alongside his large student.

"I've read about you many times in the past, Jan. Your life and mine have not been that different. You have been very successful in recruiting young people to the Light, and I have been successful in recruitment to the darkness. Your life and your reputation have been quite extraordinary, as has my life and reputation. In many ways it saddens me that you are now going to your final freedom, but of course, your disappearance will actually enhance your legend, and will also give comfort to those who just don't know what you might try to do next. Give the whole state of Chihuahua back to the Indians? You are a very powerful man, Jan Milburn. You brought a group of incredibly powerful individuals to their knees, as if they were spoiled children.

"Jan, you are respected and feared and also admired, just as I am also respected and feared and admired, but you see, the difference is that I am available for hire and you aren't. So our earthly powers think it is best for you, like all great heroes who only listen to the voices of Heaven, to be on the other side of living so they don't have to worry about what you will do next.

"Okay, the hole looks just about ready. Step aside," he said to his student who was down in the hole digging with me. And this was when the driver, the smallest person among them, stepped forward with a pistol in hand and aimed it at me. I closed my eyes and began to pray . . . and I heard the first, second, third explosion, and then an entire series of rapid fire, but I didn't feel any pain.

I opened my eyes. The small driver was standing directly in front of me. All three other men were on the ground, and their eyes had been shot out of their heads.

"Hurry, get in the car!" the driver said to me. It sounded like a woman's voice. "I'll take you to the border, but you have to promise not to come back. I can't keep protecting you!"

I got in the car. Was this *la Mano Negra?* And was this most infamous of all assassins a beautiful, delicately made young woman?

She pulled up at the foot of the bridge going from *Ciudad Juárez* to El Paso, Texas, to drop me off.

"Please, may I ask you just one question?"

She breathed and breathed again. The lights of the bridge danced on her beautiful, delicately made face. She had to be in her 30s. "One question," she said.

"Were you across the street from me the night I spoke to you?"

She nodded. "Yes, I was."

"Thank you," I said, "thank you! You are the most powerful living soul in the entire world! You are one of the greatest of God's great angels! You are—"

"GET OUT! GET OUT! Wasn't it enough that I just killed my own father for you?"

"My God," I said. "May . . . may I hug you?"

"HUG ME?! What do you think we've been doing since that night, if not hugging every night! NOW OUT!"

I got out and quickly went across the bridge, and once I was on the U.S. side, I called some people I knew in Texas and asked them to come and get me. I was at the park with all the homeless people and drunks. I couldn't get that young woman out of my mind. What had ever possessed her to kill her own father? What would she do after this?

Then it hit me like a lightning bolt, and I now knew why it had been a female lion who'd led me home when I'd been 11 years old. It was the Female Part of God, the Holy Creator, who was now coming forward and leading us to the Light. My heart was pounding! The female, nurturing side of our Creator was coming into power, and she, *la Mano Negra,* was part of this, too. God and the Devil were both becoming a Female Energy and were Globally becoming more Compassionate and Loving.

My friends came and got me, and after showering and getting some clean clothes, I called Rochín. He contacted Mireya, who now had a passport, and they came to see me in El Paso. I told them what had happened, and I couldn't believe it: the first thing Rochín wanted to know was if *la Mano Negra* was a man or a woman.

"A woman," said Mireya without hesitation. "And she's beautiful and . . . and she's in love with my *gringo,* isn't she?" she said to me, with tears streaming down her face.

"Yes," I said, "she's a woman."

"Of this woman, I am jealous," said Mireya, "because her love for you must be so great and pure that this is why she has been doing all these things for you. So tell me, did you two kiss?"

I started laughing. "Mireya, this wasn't a date I was on. These people had been hired to kill me."

"After she killed everyone, her teacher and fellow students, did you two kiss? Answer me! This I must know!"

"No, Mireya, we never kissed or held hands or anything else."

"But you were willing to kiss her, weren't you?"

"Mireya, please. We'll talk later. You see, one of the men she killed, their teacher, was her father."

"Her own father?"

"Yes."

"I think I'd best leave you two alone," said Rochín. "My God, oh my God, all through history we have examples of students disagreeing with their teacher and starting a new school, but this is definitely a much larger change. Her own father. My God, but I guess there was no other way to do it, especially considering the line of work they're in."

Rochín left, and Mireya looked me in the eyes. "Do you want to be with her? Obviously, she wants to be with you. And I don't want to be living the rest of my life wondering what night she will come to get you to be hers with all of her great skills."

"Mireya, I want to be with you. Only you."

"Did you tell her that?"

I burst out laughing. "Mireya, this wasn't a date! Can't you get that?"

"No, I can't get that, because, Jan, this was a date. A date of Soul to Soul of the highest order to cause her to kill her own father. CAN'T YOU GET THAT?!"

I went pale. She was right.

"Mireya, I suggest we pray. My God, I hadn't seen that. Once more you are right."

So we knelt down to pray, and pray we did, asking Our Lord God for guidance.

The couple I knew in El Paso drove Mireya and me to Mesa Verde to stay with Robert Heyder, a man we'd become very good friends with. I figured that Mireya and I should lay low for some time. Then we got word from Pierre, through Rochín, that he'd known about my kidnapping, and the drug lords were not the only people who knew how to hire the greatest assassins of all of Mexico.

Mireya and I were dumbfounded. Then did this mean that Pierre knew *la Mano Negra* was a woman and she was going to kill her father-teacher and her fellow students? Oh, this was just too much to fathom! But then that night my Three *Curanderos* came to me while we were at Mesa Verde, and I realized that all was well. There was a much Larger Design going on beyond all, all, all human comprehension, larger than we could ever imagine!

Definitely we were All United in the Flow of this Great Design, as sure as the rain came down from the Heavens and drip-dropped off the trees and leaves, gathering into little waterways on the rocks to become the streams that had carved even the great canyon of *las Barrancas del Cobre* and went out to sea!

LOVE-*AMOR* WAS THE POWER OF CREATION!

LOVE-*AMOR* WAS THE HOLY VOICE OF GOD, and it was Love-*Amor* that had caused that beautiful young woman, *la Mano Negra,* to give her teacher-father his final resting place, so that a whole new brave world could come to be!

BOOK EIGHT

SOUL-TALK SUMMATION

CHAPTER 40

Joaquin

I just don't get it.

I ask my mom a question, and she gives me one answer; then I ask my dad the same question, and he gives me a different answer. Like, I have asked them both where I was conceived, and my father always tells me I was conceived in Denver, Colorado, in the great big beautiful bed at the house of some friends of the superintendent of Mesa Verde. My dad and mom were on their way to New York to identify some material that had been collected by a guy named Carl Lumholtz who had gone into the *Barrancas* in 1890 and didn't come out until 1903. The dude had been a real Indiana Jones—not an actor, but the real thing. He started out with 32 men and 77 mules and horses, and after 13 years he came out of the canyon with just one Indian and two horses. Man, what a story! What a movie! But my dad says they must've been mules that he came out with, because horses couldn't have even gotten down in the canyon back then, with only little goat trails twisting down those sheer cliffs. Those old trails were sometimes only six inches wide.

Then I've asked my mother the same question, and she tells me I was conceived at Mesa Verde, because she was visited by a Sacred Bear in her dreams, so this is why she knew that, different from my dad, the Bear would be my Guide in life, not the Lion. In fact, when I was finally born in Creel, the local Spirit Healers came to us and gave my mom a shaft with bear claws and eagle feathers. This is who I am, they say—the Sacred Spirit of the Eagle and the Bear. But I don't know. This is all so confusing to me. My mom says she didn't even realize she was pregnant with me until they were in New York and my dad was going every day to the Offices of International Affairs for the National Park Service.

My dad tells me that the building was strictly out of *Star Wars,* but I say it sounds more like something out of the last *Harry Potter* movie. The building was—and still is, I guess—about six stories tall inside and as big as three Walmarts or four Costcos, and they have all these boxes suspended about halfway down on thick cables. Each box is about the size of a large bedroom or bigger, and they have skinny little rinky-dink metal staircases going up to each box. The box they called my dad in to see and identify things was number 118, and 118 had a key that was one foot long and hadn't been opened since 1904 when Lumholtz got back to New York with all the stuff he brought back. I think he died shortly after he returned, because for all those 13 years, he'd been writing passionate love letters to his fiancée, but then when he got back, he found out she'd married someone else years ago and the last five years of his letters had never even been opened. Man, what a kick. I mean, that's not how it works for Harrison Ford in his *Indiana Jones* movies.

Anyway, it took about two weeks for my dad to go through all the stuff this real Indiana Jones had brought back from the *Barrancas*. And my dad says that everything was in mint condition after all these years. Even the corn tortillas he'd brought back looked like they'd only been made that morning. The people who'd built this place and stored everything in suspended rooms really knew what they were doing. My dad said that it was easy for him to identify everything, because the Tarahumara had basically not changed their way of living in the last 15,000 years.

All kinds of people wanted to meet my dad and mom in New York because his reputation had spread, and mostly because of Robert Heyder, who, I guess, had been the superintendent out at Mesa Verde for a real long time. But my mother wasn't feeling very well, so she didn't attend all of the great big get-togethers that were arranged in their honor. Finally, she went to the doctor and found out she was pregnant with me.

My mother says that it was definitely the happiest day of her life, because for nearly ten years they'd been trying so hard to get pregnant, and now that they were, she was so happy she could scream . . . so, of course, that's what my mother did—SCREAM HER HEAD OFF—RIGHT THERE IN THE MIDDLE OF A BIG NEW YORK PARTY!

My dad says that after New York, they went down to Washington, D.C., and met with some people from *National Geographic* and signed a contract for some future articles, then met with the director of International Affairs for the National Park Service, and it was agreed that Mesa Verde and the village of San Ignacio of *las Barrancas del Cobre* would become Sister Parks. By this time, my mother says she was tired of all the people and the big cities, and she wanted to go home. But what happened next blows me out of the water.

On their way home, they stopped by to visit an old motorcycle-riding friend of my dad's from his days in Haight-Ashbury. This guy had started up a business called Pancho Villa Motorcycle Tours in Mexico and had heard all about my dad's great success in getting the Indians' lands back to them. He offered my dad a deal he couldn't refuse.

The man said he'd pay my dad a small fortune to be the leader and guide for the three motorcycle tours he already had lined up. My mom, who I figured would say no because she was pregnant with me, loved the idea. She says she'd always wanted to ride on the back of a big old Harley.

For the next four months, I "traveled" with my dad and mom on a motorcycle and in the big truck that carried the parts and supplies for the tour group. There were about 50 people, my dad says, and when everyone would come roaring into a town, even the cops and *burros* scattered. It was the perfect cover-up for my dad and mom to get back into Mexico. Nobody expected my dad and mom to be with a bunch of bikers, and these weren't ordinary bikers, I'm told. These were mostly professionals who liked to play the role of bikers on road trips. They were lawyers and doctors and dentists and teachers and businessmen, but they all pumped iron and really looked the part.

My mother says I loved it, that she could feel how happy I was inside of her, especially when we pulled into *las Barrancas del Cobre* on a big old Harley and sat around the campfire at night, singing old songs. This is how my mom perfected her English, she tells me—by singing songs out of the '60s that my dad played on his guitar.

Those three road trips were so successful that my dad's friend wanted to hire him for the following season, but my dad told him he couldn't commit, that he and my mom had a child on the way, which was their priority.

My dad says that he and my mom bought an old yellow Chevy pickup with the money they made on the motorcycle tours. My mom, of course, immediately named the truck *Quira Va,* which in Tarahumara means "Hi, how are you?" And they still had the yellow Chevy when I was growing up. My dad says that my mom would sing to the old Chevy and bless it, and this is why it was good for 685,000 miles without ever having one bit of trouble, except when they had to replace the transmission at 500,000 miles.

Those were the years when my parents began driving back and forth between Durango, Colorado, and Creel, then followed the Indian Powwows from California to Arizona and from Colorado to New Mexico, then a couple of times up to Oregon and Washington State, too. My mother's connections, through her store at the train station in Creel, were pouring out with enough goods for them to sell at all the Powwows throughout the western

United States. They were wholesalers, too, getting their wares into places like Sundance and other top outlets.

But all this came to a temporary halt in the ninth month of my mother's pregnancy. They knew I was so big that it was going to be a difficult birth, so my mom wanted to be home with her mother and aunts and sisters. My dad was at my birthing, too, and he says he'd never seen anything like it, and he'd helped in many birthings. It went on for 12 hours, and they had my mother stand up and pull on a rope from the ceiling in the old Indian way, but it didn't help. My head was showing, but I just didn't want to come out.

Then my grandmother took a knitting needle and poked the water bag, but still that didn't do it. She then warmed up some cooking oil and poured it around my head and down my mother's vagina and—pop—I came right out.

My mother and everyone else were exhausted, but still my dad took the cord and the afterbirth, and he climbed the cliffs behind Creel, walking for miles until he came to a place that spoke to him. He says this is when his Three Holy Healers came to him, and together they buried what I'd brought with me from the stars. That place is now Sacred, my dad tells me, and in fact, is the place for which the Tarahumara and my dad are now raising money so they can build an eco-friendly community for people who wish to come to live near Our Sacred Canyon.

All these things I was told about my life before I was born; and now I'm 16 years old and the year is 2008, and we're on our way to the airport in Albuquerque, New Mexico, so we can fly to San Francisco to see where this whole Spiritual Journey of my dad's got started when he saw those big lion eyes in the snowstorm at the age of 11.

As for me, I'm real excited, and yet kind of scared, too. What if it doesn't turn out like I think it should? What if I don't get it, and feel left out? I don't know; part of me almost feels like not going, because so much could go wrong. But on the other hand, my dad and mom both agree on one thing, which is that a person just has to stop thinking and jump in and start living. Maybe they're right. Maybe I should just relax and go for it.

Anyway, the three of us are now at the Albuquerque airport with that big old Indian statue with the huge eagle in his grip. My dad always teases me, saying that they used his gorgeous body as the model for the statue. But I know he's only kidding. I mean, my dad now looks real old and fat and out of shape. It's hard for me to believe that he was able to really do all the things he did. My mom, on the other hand, still looks lean and strong and quick. I wouldn't want to mess with her. I'm sure she could knock me on my ass, even though I'm on the football team and pretty fast and strong myself.

Oh well, here we go. It's boarding time.

CHAPTER 41

Mireya

Jan likes to tell people that we conceived Joaquin in Denver at the house of a good friend of Robert Heyder's, but he and I both know that's not true. We conceived our son at Mesa Verde, surrounded by the Spirit World of the Ancient Ones, who came to me in my sleep and presented me with the Holy Shaft of Bear Claws and Eagle Feathers.

I was told very clearly that Joaquin is a very Old Soul, and he is of the next generation of Ancient Warriors who will do great things in helping heal and protect our Mother Earth. In fact, I was told that he and his generation will do far more than his father's generation did, because Soul People with Noble Hearts have been gathering across the Heavens in larger and larger numbers. It is now Our Holy Human Time to Unite in Sacred Song—as young people did in the '60s, and just as we did that night outside of the prison at Cuauhtémoc—and bring down the old walls of fear and hate and anger and confusion all over our Mother Earth!

But of course, I do not tell any of this to our son anymore, because when he was little and his mind was still full of Holy Dreams and wide-open imagination, we could tell him this, planting seeds in the back of his head, but now that he has begun to question, Jan and I have both stopped telling him, so he can go out into the world and learn about his own seeds that he brought from the Heavens.

It is well known that if parents keep telling their children about their Sacred Spirit and Destiny, especially when they start to question, then their offspring will get very confused and become rebellious for years. This is why the first seven years of a child's life are so important in the old Indian way of thinking, and why boys are raised as girls for these first seven years, so then their hearts will remain open, even as they later learn the ways of men.

Now we are at the airport in Albuquerque, New Mexico, and are about to board the plane to San Francisco. I remember well when I boarded my first plane in Denver to go to New York City. I'd never even been near a plane before, and I was so nervous. Jan started laughing, telling me I had no fear of rattlesnakes or leaping off the rim of our great canyon and taking flight like an eagle, but here I was afraid to board an airplane. I hadn't laughed. I didn't think it was funny. I was surrounded by so many people and all this glass and iron and such long hallways. Nothing seemed natural to me, especially not the airplane.

"But Jan," I told my husband, "back home at our canyon, I go into my Dream World, and it is within this Dream World that I have no fear to leap from our canyon's rim and take flight."

"So then go into your Dream World right now, too," he said.

"But how? Even the smells are so unnatural here."

"Close your eyes," he instructed, "and remember the smell of the flowers and great ferns where we got married down in the canyon by the three waterfalls."

I closed my eyes.

"Can you smell those flowers?" he asked.

I nodded.

"Good, now leap into your Dream World."

I leaped, and it was true. When I reopened my eyes, everything all about me was different. I had no more fear. My eyes could now see everything, so calm and smooth and beautiful. Even the people looked like Angels. I laughed. This was really good. So I took my husband's hand, and we'd started down the ramp to board our plane to New York City . . . and here we are today, 17 years later, preparing to board our plane in Albuquerque on the way to San Francisco. But this time I am holding two large manly hands. The one hand of *mi esposo* and the other of our son, Joaquin, the joy of my life, the fruit *de nuestro amor!* OH, I AM THE HAPPIEST WOMAN IN ALL THE WORLD as I walk down the ramp to board our plane.

CHAPTER 42

Jan

I didn't want Mireya and Joaquin to know what was really going on inside me as we held hands and walked down the long, twisting ramp to board our plane to San Francisco, because I was so nervous that I was actually having trouble breathing. This was why I'd booked us to fly in to San Francisco instead of San Jose. I wanted us to have some fun and happiness before we went up Freeway 17 to go to my family's estate at Los Gatos in the redwoods.

My brother and sisters had not contacted me when our mother had died. But I'd known that she'd passed, because I awoke in the middle of the night and told Mireya.

"My mother just died," I said to her.

"I know," said Mireya. "I, too, can feel that her Spirit has come to us. She's lost and not happy, Jan."

"No, she's frightened and she needs us to help her," I said.

So Mireya and I both got out of bed, put on our robes, and lit three candles for my mother and began to pray, helping her leave her earthly body and go into her Soul and Final Rest. All that day and for the rest of the week, I waited for my brother and sisters to contact me. Instead, three months later, what did I get? An official letter asking me to sign some papers. I felt sorry for my brother and sisters. Was this all they were worried about, the inheritance and making sure I didn't get anything?

This was what I was thinking about as we walked down the ramp to board our plane. My brother had been willed the estate in the redwoods, and my sisters had gotten the beach house in Santa Cruz and the monies from the insurance.

This, I could take. This, I could accept from my brother and sisters, having wanted to get everything for themselves, because I'd basically left all that behind when I had become a minister at 17, but . . . what I could not and would not take was if they were rude or nasty to my Mexican wife and my half-Mexican son. This I would not tolerate for a moment, and I didn't care how much my brother and sisters would try to hide behind the fact that they were devout Christians.

I was beginning to see how nowadays so many Christians had lost the True Spirit of Christlike living, and they conveniently used Christianity so they could justify their narrow-mindedness and judgmental attitudes. Also, I could feel that I, personally, wasn't at my best as we boarded the plane. I had to calm down. I had to have more faith in God and not be so upset about something that, well, might not even happen. Maybe my brother and sisters would accept my Mexican family and me with open arms. I kept breathing and trying to relax, and I guess that Mireya thought I was nervous because of our flight.

"Jan, it's okay," she said to me. "Just close your eyes and go to that place deep in the canyon where we got married, and smell the flowers. This, too, is all a Holy Dream. You have nothing to fear, *querido.*"

I laughed. This was wonderful! Mireya and I had now been together over 25 years, and I was still as much in love with her as the day she'd come to my cabin in the snow and knocked on my door, telling me she was 18 years old.

I TRULY WAS THE LUCKIEST MAN IN ALL THE WORLD!

334

CHAPTER 43

Joaquin

I got a window seat, and my mom sat down next to me and my dad sat down on the other side of her. All the way from Albuquerque to San Francisco I looked out my window. It was very interesting. I'd never realized there was so much open land and desert and mountains between us and California. My mom and dad held hands the whole way. It felt really good to see two old people still in love. My mom was in her 40s, and my dad was in his 60s. They were over 20 years apart, and in the last few years, I'd become good friends with my half brother Aaron, who was from my father's first marriage to Catalina, a minister's daughter.

Aaron was going on 30, and he was a real fine person. He'd come to live with us in Durango for a while, and my mother liked him a lot, too. He was the one who had introduced us to a book called *Rain of Gold* that's about *las Barrancas del Cobre*, and Aaron told our dad we should contact the writer and get him to write his life story. My dad read the *Rain of Gold* book and fully agreed with Aaron, who is now currently trying to get this to happen.

It felt really great to have an older brother, but I'd never met any of my dad's family in California, so I wondered how they would treat my mother and me, since we were obviously not white, like them. Aaron, he was dark like me and way smart. He learned English so quickly and got into college and did real well. I hoped my mother and I would be accepted by my dad's family. It would be real embarrassing if we weren't.

These were the kinds of thoughts I was thinking as we flew west and I looked out the window of our plane. The human mind can really jump around all over the place when it's nervous. Oh, I really hoped my dad's family accepted us. I mean, my mother's family totally accepted my dad, a white guy, so what could be the trouble? I just didn't get it. After all, we're all God's children, like my dad always says.

CHAPTER 44

Aaron

I, Aaron, first met my dad when my mother, Catalina, took us up to the kids' camp on a lake up in the mountains of Chihuahua. I instantly took a liking to him. He was funny and happy and immediately gave me big hugs and kisses, telling me how much he loved me. And his new wife, Mireya, was real good to me, so when I finished high school, I went up to the United States to live with my dad, Jan, and my stepmother so I could learn English before I started my studies at the University of Chihuahua. This is when I met my little half brother Joaquin, and I immediately liked him, too. He was as happy and playful as a little wild bear, and he even looked like a bear cub.

A bunch of my Mexican friends and I had just read the book *Rain of Gold* by a Chicano author from Oceanside, California, before I crossed the border to spend the summer with my dad and his new family in Durango, Colorado. While reading the book, I found that the author's mother had been born and raised in the Rain of Gold canyon, just a tiny finger of the great, immense

Copper Canyon of northwest Mexico. I couldn't believe it: a whole book had been written about the same little canyon where my mother's mother had been born and raised.

I spoke to my old grandmother before I left for Durango and told her about the book and how the story was about the youngest daughter of the Gomez *familia,* and her name was Lupe. My grandmother's old wrinkled face lit up with joy!

"Lupe Gomez!" she shouted. "I grew up with her and her sister Carlota and her brother Victoriano! They lived right next to us in *la Lluvia de Oro.*"

The book I had was in Spanish, so I read most of it aloud to my grandmother. And she'd say yes, of course, that was true and this was true, and then she'd add her own stories that hadn't been written about in the book. My grandmother and I lived for weeks together inside of that book, experiencing those years of the Mexican Revolution, which had happened about 100 years ago.

On my bus ride going north from Chihuahua City to El Paso, Texas, and then across the state of New Mexico to the southwest tip of Colorado, where Durango is located, I couldn't get the *Rain of Gold* book out of my mind. In the past, so many of my grandmother's stories of how she'd grown up in a mystical canyon, literally called the Rain of Gold, hadn't been believable to me. Her stories had just seemed too far-fetched and supernatural and full of daily miracles. But after reading the book to my ancient grandmother and seeing how her face lit up with so much joy as she told me that the stories were true in the *Rain of Gold* book, that she'd seen many of those things happen with her own two eyes, adding even more information, little by little I began to understand that the written word was Holy. It gave a credibility to a story far beyond the time when it was orally told.

By the time I arrived in Durango, I knew why so many friends of mine had also taken the book home for their parents and grandparents to read. We were all hungry for validation, not from Europe, with the Bible and all of Europe's other great writings, but for a Voice of Truth that came from our own soil *de México.*

This was when it entered my mind as I traveled north to Durango that I should encourage my dad to contact the author of *Rain of Gold* so he could write a book about him, my father, a white guy, whose story was also unbelievable—how he'd risked his life over and over again, and then with the help of God was able to get all the Sacred Lands back to the Tarahumara Indians.

But when I got to Durango to spend the summer with my dad and his wife, Mireya, and my half brother Joaquin, I found that they knew nothing about the *Rain of Gold* book or its author, so they had no idea what I was talking about, much less how important it had been for my grandmother, an old Indian woman, to have the life she'd lived—not just validated, but given breath and respect and honor and dignity and believability.

My father and Joaquin and I went down to the local bookstore in Durango and purchased *Rain of Gold* and the two other books of the author's trilogy, *Wild Steps of Heaven* and *Thirteen Senses.* My father and stepmother couldn't stop reading the three books once they'd gotten started, and they were both amazed how much this author knew about the Spirit World.

Why, the book *Rain of Gold* started out with the sentence: "High in the mountains in northwest Mexico, an Indian named *Espirito* followed a doe and her fawn in search of water." So this, then, meant the author knew that this Indian was over 78 years old and an Elder of the Spirit World, and this was why he'd been able to see the gold raining down the mountainside—because to see was to manifest.

Together we read the entire trilogy, and the author's family became our *familia,* and we prayed for the Holy Forces of Creation to bring us together with the writer. Then the following week, just like a Miracle, we read in the local paper that Victor Villaseñor was coming to Durango to give a series of talks to the local schools and community.

We were so happy!

It truly was like my dad, Jan, always said: Pray and you will receive. The rest, you already know. I went to one of the author's talks and told him that he should meet my dad and write the story of his life at the Copper Canyon, 100 years later. I did. It worked.

And now we have been working with the author for over two years. Twice he's come down to Chihuahua City, and I've personally driven him and his staff out to Creel. I've met his son Joseph—a big, tall guy—and his brother-in-law Eddie Kramer, and they filmed our Indian Holy Week celebrations.

The author says that everything is going very well, and soon he will have a first draft for us to look at. He tells us that he's really not a writer, but a rewriter, and with each draft the Spirit World speaks to him more and more. We can hardly wait to read what he has written, and we're all sure that it will be wonderful. But he has warned us that we won't like the book at first—that we'll disagree with much of what he's put on paper. He explained that at first his own father hated *Rain of Gold* and tried to stop him from getting it published.

But then he lied to his father, saying, "*Papa,* I've rewritten it. Please read it again." His father reread it and said it was getting better. Twice more he lied, not changing a thing but telling his dad that he'd rewritten it again.

Finally his dad said, "*Mijito,* if you'd become a businessman and made a hundred billion dollars, I would not be as proud as of you as I am for having written this fine book. You portray my mother, God bless her soul, in such a way that the whole world can see what it is to be a woman connected to God! Her power! Her cunning! Her vision! You got it all! I'm so proud of you, *mijito!*"

Well, I don't think we will hate what he writes about us, as his father hated *Rain of Gold* at first. But who knows? He's the writer and has the experience. We don't. So maybe he's right, and at first we'll hate what he has written.

CHAPTER 45

Mireya

IT WAS ALL SO EXCITING!

We rented a car at the airport in San Francisco and drove into the world-famous city! I wanted Jan to immediately take us to see the Golden Gate Bridge and then go to Haight-Ashbury, but he wasn't feeling that well and suggested we first go to our hotel room. The hotel was beautiful! It was right at Union Square and had a balcony overlooking the famous square, which was full of tourists with large cameras hanging around their necks.

I told Jan to give our son, Joaquin, some money and a list of things to go buy for us to snack on, but Joaquin well knew what I was really saying! And as soon as he was gone, I leaped on Jan, wrapping my legs about him. I loved my old *gringo!* He was as exciting to me as he was when I was 18 and I'd walked through the snow to be with him. But Jan, for the first time in 27 years, wasn't in the mood to make love with me.

"I'm just not feeling well," he said.

"Jan," I said to my husband, "what is it? All trip long you have not been the happy man I've known all of my life. Is it *la Mano Negra?* Are you now in love with her and not me anymore?"

He laughed.

"Jan, do not laugh. I am serious. What is it?"

"I'm sorry I laughed," he said. "No, it is not *la Mano Negra* or any other woman. What I'm worried about, Mireya," he said, taking a deep breath, "is my American family. I can accept that they didn't contact us when my mother died, but if they don't accept us as family with open arms, then this *I* will not accept. They claim to be Christians and read the Bible every day, and yet—"

"No more, *mi esposo,* not another word. Let us just pray and send our *amor* to them and ask God to help us. After all, we all have the same Sun, the same Right Eye of God, greet us each morning and the same Left Eye, the Moon."

"You're right," he said to me. "Getting run over by cars, being tortured almost to death, having Chato and so many of my other boys tortured and killed, I have been able to live with, yet this fear of my American family not accepting my Mexican family is hurting me so deeply, Mireya, that I feel powerless. My mother never came to see her own grandchildren; and then she died a frightened, lonely death. And it was us, her Mexican *familia,* who were able to go to her on the Other Side and calm her down and help her forgive herself and go to the Light. Why is it, Mireya, that my American family only sees money and inheritance and not the Love and Soul of us, their Mexican family?"

I shrugged my shoulders and said, "No more talking, Jan," and I took him in my arms and began kissing him slowly, gently; and then I caressed his ears, and oh, did he come ALIVE! We then made *el amor* and everything got better.

Afterward, we bathed together, and once again we felt wonderful and totally in love. Over and over my grandmother told me that a woman had to take good care of herself and her man with *amor* on a regular basis or the Delicious Warmth and Love of Marriage would fade away.

That evening I walked the streets of San Francisco with my two big men, looking at all the beautiful stores and strangely dressed people. Then we didn't use the car we rented, but instead we took a taxi out to Haight-Ashbury, which is way across town toward the southwest. It was beautiful, just as Jan had described it. And we saw the huge fern tree at the park where Jerry Garcia and so many others used to play their free music on the grass.

Jan explained to us that the place had been fixed up, that it had looked real run-down in the old days. We searched and searched but couldn't find the basement that he'd turned into a coffeehouse. Finally, one man told us where he'd heard that years ago there'd been a coffeehouse basement run by a motorcycle-driving young minister.

I screeched and told the man that the young minister was my old *gringo!* The man took us to the place, but we couldn't go in. The basement was locked up.

We got hungry, so we found a place to eat. Joaquin and I were so excited and proud of Jan. After dinner, we got ice-cream cones and walked up and down Haight and Ashbury, window-shopping. It was still very hard for me to imagine all those lost kids coming from even good homes all across the country to this place. Why hadn't their parents come with them? They could have all had a very good time together.

We didn't get back to our hotel until close to midnight. We'd had so much fun and seen so many things, and the people didn't look strange to me anymore. I loved it. The next day we took our car out of the garage, and we drove across the Golden Gate Bridge, parking on the other side. The bridge was magnificent, and Jan pointed out the famous island of Alcatraz, where the prison had been, and also Nob Hill back in San Francisco.

We had lunch at a beautiful marina across the bay from San Francisco. I'd never had so much fun in all my life. I was with my two men!

For three more days we stayed in San Francisco. We went down that steep, twisting, narrow red-brick road; and we also went in a trolley car to Fisherman's Wharf. Then the day we were to leave,

Jan told Joaquin and me that we had to talk before we drove down to San Jose and Los Gatos. I wasn't surprised. I knew well that my *gringo* was still very worried about how his American family would treat Joaquin and me.

Myself, I wasn't worried. How could they not fall instantly in love with our son and me? We each had such a big, beautiful smile, full of gorgeous, large teeth, just like a horse screeching with joy! And our eyes danced with happiness and trust and *AMOR!*

CHAPTER 46

Jan

Mireya and I had already talked, but I didn't quite know how to, well, I guess, open up my conversation with our son, Joaquin, because I didn't want him to take on my baggage. I mean, maybe my American family had come a long ways in the last few years, and they would treat Mireya and Joaquin very well. But on the other hand, if they didn't, then I wanted to prepare my son, as I'd prepared Mireya, so they wouldn't take it personally. After all, what we'd really come to see were the gigantic redwood trees and the place where I'd seen the lion eyes as a boy.

"Joaquin," I began, "your mother and I have already talked, but I think that it's also important for you to know this before we go down to Los Gatos, so you don't get your feelings hurt if—"

"If your family doesn't like my mother and me, because we're Mexican looking and not white?" said Joaquin. "Dad," he continued, "I've already thought about this. I live with it every day of my life in Durango. I'm an American, and yet I'm . . . I'm not really accepted. You don't have to tell me anything. However they treat us will be fine, because I know that you love my mother and me, and this is all that really matters to me, Dad—your love."

Tears came to my eyes.

"Is this still bothering you, Jan?" asked Mireya. "Don't be silly. Joaquin and I are strong. We'll be nice to them, even if they aren't nice to us. I promise you, Jan, you don't have anything to worry about. I'm not going to kick the ass of any of your American family members," she added, laughing. "Well, at least not this time."

Joaquin burst out laughing, too. "Mama's right. We won't kick any ass, Dad, so you can relax."

I joined in their laughter. This was exactly why I'd originally been drawn to work in the fields when I'd still been going to high school. I'd see field-workers laughing and being so happy as they stood on the street corners waiting to be picked up to go to work. It would be cold or hot or even raining, and still they'd be joking and happy and laughing as they waited to be picked up. And here my Los Gatos family and I'd had so much, and we'd hardly ever laughed. We'd read the Bible and feel smug and superior to everyone who wasn't a Christian, and we were even critical of other Christians, especially the Catholics, because, in our opinion, they didn't follow the letter of the law of the Bible.

I now laughed, loving my happy, fun-loving Mexican *familia* who found humor and goodwill in everyone and in the whole world, no matter what!

CHAPTER 47

Joaquin

My dad took us on the mountain route of Interstate 280 between San Francisco and San Jose. It was one of the most beautiful drives I've ever seen: rolling green hills with oaks and huge, beautiful houses with the most expensive-looking horse barns I'd ever seen. Coming into the San Jose basin, the town stretched clear across the whole valley to another mountain range of rolling green hills on the eastern side.

My dad told my mother and me that this whole basin of San Jose used to be nothing but agriculture when he was growing up and still had had a lot of farming when he'd come here with Emma in 1985 when he'd been deported from Mexico. I didn't know Emma, my dad's second wife, but I did know her kids. From what I could figure, she and her kids were mad as hell at my dad and blamed him for pretty near everything that had gone wrong in their lives.

"We can go directly out to Los Gatos," said my dad, who was driving even though he usually let me do most of the driving since

I'd turned 16. "Or we can go through downtown San Jose and over to Willow Glen, where I established our first coffeehouse."

My mother and I both wanted to go to Willow Glen first. I guess that even though we didn't admit it, we were both also a little wary about meeting my dad's family. I mean, they'd never once come down to meet us, even when my dad kept inviting them.

San Jose had a lot of high-rises that my dad said were all new. We drove past my dad's favorite restaurant, called Original Joe's, and then went past San Jose State college and headed south. Willow Glen was just a little ways from downtown San Jose, but was a city of its own, and tiny—I mean, only about three blocks long—with real pretty shops and old English-looking houses. We parked across the street from an old-fashioned movie theater.

"Right next door to the movie house," he said, "is where we rented the basement and Father O'Neil and I set up our first coffeehouse. He was a heroic man. His church, like my church, was totally against what we proposed to do—to create a safe place where the hippies and lost skid-row people could come off the street and learn about Jesus through actions instead of words. Those were crazy days. The whole world was split down the middle."

"And you'd ride your Honda 300 from here to San Francisco?" I asked.

"Yep. Sometimes two, three times a night."

"Was this place also run-down?" asked my mother.

"Oh yeah. Haight-Ashbury and this place were skid rows back then."

"Weren't you scared, Dad?"

"Sure, I was scared, yet I knew I was—"

"Yeah, you were doing God's work," I said.

"Yes," he said. "What is it, Joaquin?"

I shrugged. "I don't know, it's just that, well, I'm 16, and you were only a year older than I am and already a minister and doing all that stuff."

Tears came to my eyes. We were parked, and I was in the backseat and didn't want my parents to see me crying. But he'd seen me in the rearview mirror, and my mom had turned around.

"Look," said my mother, "I, too, used to think I'd done nothing compared to this great, brave man who fought the drug lords in the lowlands. I thought I was uneducated and had nothing to offer, but then my *gringo* taught me how to see my own life so differently. He showed me I was brave—that I knew how to handle a rattlesnake and walk through the wild country full of jaguars and mountain lions and coyotes. And that I knew about the changing seasons of the year and how the birds and animals and plants are affected.

"Pretty soon, I began to see myself as a very knowledgeable, brave person who was also very capable and smart. I could never have gone up against Van Housen and opened up my store if I hadn't learned to see myself differently.

"You, Joaquin, are by far the most levelheaded person among all your friends. You, Joaquin, are honest and trustworthy; you don't smoke or drink or take drugs; and, most important, you have a Noble Heart, just like your father. And any girl who can't see this, then she isn't the type of girl for you to get involved with, because this means she doesn't have the eyes to see who you are and what are the really important things in life. And I say all this to you, not because you are my son, but because what I say is true, and I have the intelligence and wisdom to see these truths. Your father and I are very proud of you. You are a fine, wonderful son."

Now I was really crying. I'd never heard my mother talk so much in all my life. My dad was always the talker, not my mom.

"Okay," said my father, "do you think we're now all ready to take that drive out on Freeway 17 past Los Gatos?"

My mom and I both nodded yes.

"Good," he said, "because I agree with everything your mother just said; plus, Joaquin, I also think you're pretty cute in a weird kind of way."

We all burst out laughing. I loved my parents. They were good people, and no matter what, we always seemed to be having such a good time together. This was why all my friends liked to come over to our house and hang out. They wanted to get away from their own parents, who were always coming down on them and showing them what they did wrong. My parents didn't do that. No, they made everyone feel happy and at home and that it was okay to screw up. No big deal. Just learn and be responsible and keep going and going!

CHAPTER 48

Mireya

I know I'd promised I wouldn't kick any of Jan's American *familia*'s asses if they mistreated us, but down deep inside, I didn't know if I could keep my word. I mean, our son, Joaquin, was having enough trouble adjusting to life on both sides of the border, and it would really help him if Jan's family accepted us.

I put some music on the radio as Jan drove us back across the valley to catch Freeway 17. I could feel that both of my big strong men were very apprehensive, so I knew I had to calm down and be happy. I'd always been told by my grandmother that a woman was the Heart-Center of *la familia;* and it was her Holy duty to sing when she cooked, to whistle and be happy as a bird in a tree when she gardened and milked the goats, because it was very difficult for the rest of *la familia* not to be happy when they felt the Heart-Center laughing and singing. So this was my Sacred Job as a mother and as a woman and as a wife, to keep my woman's Heart-Center full of healthy good happiness, because the woman's

Heart-Center was the Holy Sacred Voice of God Living within *la familia*.

Oh, to make *tortillas* by hand, slapping them from palm to palm, was so relaxing and Holy. To soak the beans in water overnight, then use that water for the plants was wonderful, because the fresh water that you put in the pot to cook the beans took the *pedos*—the farts—out of the beans, and the old water gave nourishment to the plants. Working with two hands in the kitchen, in the garden, and with the goats and chickens was relaxing and Holy and Sacred. Poor rich people who had others to do this soulfulfilling work for them. Small wonder Jan's family was lost and bitter and so unhappy. Working with your God-gifted hands to put Love-*Amor* into the food you ate was a blessing of the highest order!

CHAPTER 49

Jan

The three of us drove southwest on Freeway 17. I'd forgotten how far Los Gatos was out of San Jose. Then just past the city of Los Gatos began the tall, green, wooded mountains. My heart started beating loudly. How many times had I run all the way home from here because my mother had left me? Dozens of times? No, closer to hundreds. And yet I guess those five-mile runs up the side of the old highway and then the two miles up the steep mountainside were what had built my legs into track-star quality.

So looking back, I guess, my mother had done me a favor. Her wimpy choir-boy son had become a real handsome stud in high school. But a virgin stud who wanted to save himself for marriage, and had preached to all the hippies not to take drugs and save their lovemaking for marriage. At least half a dozen beautiful young hippie girls had taken a vow to de-virginize me, but I hadn't succumbed, even when a couple of times a girl or two had crawled naked into bed with me.

"Is this our turnoff?" asked Joaquin.

"Yes," I said, "this is it."

I had to brake hard to make the turnoff. I guess I'd been daydreaming so much that I'd forgotten where we were. The climb was steep.

"Right up ahead is where I saw the mountain lion," I told my wife and son, pulling over to the side of the road. "Let's get out and walk."

"Sure," said Joaquin.

The three of us got out of our rental car and walked up the road. It was truly steep. I'd forgotten how steep.

"I'd run uphill all the way from school alongside the highway," I explained. "By the time I got to our turnoff, I was pouring with sweat, and usually I didn't have any 'go' left in me, but this day it was snowing, and I was cold and still had some energy left and came sprinting up this steep grade in the snow. But then I suddenly realized that I had no idea where I was—or if I'd even taken the right turnoff. Everything was white with snow, and also, you see, back then 17 wasn't really a freeway. It was more like just a good wide road, and the turnoffs just had little wooden signs."

"Was 17 paved?" asked Mireya.

"Yes, it was paved, but the turnoffs were dirt, and they all looked the same—real steep. So suddenly I lost confidence, didn't know where I was, and all the sweat on my body began to turn to ice. I got scared. I was freezing. I thought I was going to die. I began to hate my mother for having left me once again. I was feeling so bad and sorry for myself that I didn't care if I died. Nobody loved me, and this was when I felt something off to my right and I turned and here, no more than five or six feet away from me, up on that short embankment, stood the largest mountain lion I'd ever seen. She looked the size of a horse. Remember, I was only 11, not very tall yet, and she was up on that higher ground."

"Where exactly?" asked Joaquin.

"Right about here," I said, climbing a few feet up the embankment of the road. "They widened the road a little when they paved it, but not much."

Joaquin came up beside me and reached out with open hands, palms toward the earth. "Right here, Dad?" he said. "Your lion totem was right here that day, and she was facing this direction?"

I nodded. "Yes, exactly."

"And fear came into you with so much power, Dad," said Joaquin, "that you forgot all about feeling sorry for yourself or hating your mother or anything else, right?"

I nodded again. "Yes, exactly. I was petrified, so I closed my eyes, said a little prayer, and when I reopened my eyes, everything was different."

"The mountain lion wasn't so huge anymore," said Joaquin, "and her eyes, they looked so calm and detached, almost indifferent to you."

"Exactly, and I wasn't afraid anymore, and even the snowflakes that had been coming down real hard and hitting me in the face weren't freezing cold and hurting me anymore. It was like the whole world had become gentle as I now watched the snowflakes come floating past my eyes down to the ground."

Joaquin smiled. "And Dad," he said, "isn't this how we will get approval from your American family, by us looking at them with our hearts open and our eyes as calm and sure and full of love as the lion eyes you saw that day?"

My son was right! Absolutely right! Or, as it is said in so many native cultures, my son had just become his father's father. Tears came to my eyes. In one lightning-fast move, my son had moved out of his head, through his heart, AND ENTERED HIS ETERNAL SOUL!

"Thank you," I said to our son, Joaquin. "You've just become my father."

"I know," said Joaquin, wiping the tears that had come to his eyes. "I can feel your lion with me here, right now, Dad. I really can, and I don't feel scared either."

"I guess that's because you're a bear," I said. "And even larger than a mountain lion."

"I can feel the lion here with us, too," said Mireya.

"This is so wonderful," I said. "I don't have to explain anything to you two."

"Of course not," said Mireya. "We all have our Spirit Guides. How could we live without their help?"

I breathed. "Yes, exactly. I remember that day so clearly when I looked at the lion and she looked at me, and we held eye-to-eye for the longest time. Then she turned and walked off through the snow and those great, huge redwoods right there, which were gigantic even back then. I don't know why, but I felt invited, I guess, Soul-to-Soul, so I followed her, losing sight of her now and then, but I'd see her deep paw prints in the fresh snow, and then here I was, safely home."

"I know what you mean, Dad," said Joaquin. "I feel like I'm being invited, right now, too."

I reached out and put my hand on my son's shoulder. He was taller than I was. Joaquin had gotten his height from Mireya's side of the family. Both of her uncles were much taller than I was. "I can now see that if this encounter with the lion had not happened," I said, "then I don't think I would have ever had enough guts inside of me to venture out and grow. Because it was only after this, when I was finally able to push all those bad feelings out of me—of feeling sorry for myself and unloved by my mother— that I was able to let go and go completely to God. Am I making sense? My whole life changed, right here. At this exact place."

"Of course," said Mireya, "because this is what it means when a human being finally greets their totem, taking its Holy Spirit into their Heart and Soul."

"So, then, Mama, it is okay for us men to be scared?" Joaquin asked his mother.

"Of course," she said. "Fear is natural."

"Your mother is right," I said. "Fear, I can now see, is what helped me clear out a lot of my garbage, and we need to clean out our baggage before we can be open enough to let in the Light of God."

"Then, Dad, are you telling me that all these years when you've done all these great things, you were afraid?"

"Yes, of course I was afraid . . . yet I also knew I wasn't alone, and I had faith, if not in me, then in my lion."

"Oh wow!" said Joaquin. "Then this is why so many of my friends are all screwed up and taking drugs. They think they're all alone."

"Poor lost boys," said Mireya, making the sign of the cross over herself. "How can a person ever find peace if they think they are alone?"

"They can't," I said. "That's why we're all lost souls until we find our totem, who automatically leads us to the Holy Spirit of Jesus. Because I can now see that it was the terror of seeing the lion up so close that got me past all my petty feelings of hating my mother and feeling sorry for myself, and . . . and I don't think I could've reached that depth of prayer if I hadn't been so petrified."

Joaquin broke down, crying and crying. And Mireya went to hug him, but he pulled away.

"No," he said to his mother, "please, I, too, need to get down into all my fears, like Dad and you have done, Mom. And I need to do this alone. So could you two please go back to the car or walk up the road a ways and leave me alone at this place where my dad saw the lion eyes and a whole new life began for him?"

The tears were pouring down his face. I took Mireya by her shoulders and turned her around so our son could be alone, and we walked up the road. Our son, Joaquin, was right on schedule. It was now his turn to stop listening to us and instead, listen to his own Spirit Guide, the bear. He wasn't a bear cub any longer. He was 220 pounds of strong young bear-man.

And mother bears feed and take care of their offspring for about three years, and then one day the cub waits for them by a tree or rock, and they never come back. For the first two or three days, the big cub cries and calls for his mother, then gets angry and begins to search for her. But then his hunger overcomes his anger, and he begins to look for food. This is when his own life begins, when he begins to feed himself. Humans are the only species to keep our offspring for more than a few years. Even the great whales only keep their young for five to seven years.

We could hear Joaquin crying behind us as we walked away. A whole lot had been locked up inside of our son that he was now finally unlocking, just as I'd had to do that day when I'd been 11 years old. Our son, Joaquin, would be okay. We'd raised him good and strong, and he was now taking the bull of life by the horns and stepping into his Own Spiritual Powers.

Coming into a grove of redwoods, I caressed my wife's hand, kissing her fingertips. She turned and took me in her arms; and with that huge, contagious smile of hers, she began kissing me. We were all right now. We'd turned everything over to God, and this always felt so good!

CHAPTER 50

Joaquin

I began to feel better and stronger the farther my parents walked away from me. It was like I, too, could now feel and almost see this mountain lion my dad had seen. I mean, I was 16 years old, and I hadn't seen my own bear eyes yet, but it was okay. I wasn't so old that maybe sometime in the not-too-distant future, I'd come face-to-face with my own Spirit Guide, as my dad had done when he'd seen his totem's eyes at 11 years old—especially since we had so many bears around Durango. But those I've always seen at a distance. Never up close and eye-to-eye.

Suddenly I felt very happy. It was like somehow I'd let go inside myself, and I wasn't trying to measure up to my dad anymore, so the whole world all around me had changed into a friendly, happy place and I could now actually feel like Mother Earth was purring to me.

I began climbing up the steep hillside into a brushy area between two groves of gigantic redwoods. I mean, these trees were way bigger than any of the trees we had back home, and we still

359

had quite a few big trees left outside of Creel. It was really steep climbing up through the thick brush, and I had my head down, looking where I stepped . . . and then I suddenly had this strange feeling that I wasn't alone.

I turned and looked up and saw nothing. My heart was pounding! What did this mean—that I was just imagining things? Or that a bear was really here only a few feet in front of me, A HUGE BLACK BEAR, but I just couldn't see him?

I breathed and breathed, trying to understand, because I'd truly felt something, as if I wasn't alone. I breathed again, and wiped the tears from my eyes. Then I closed my eyes, like my dad had said he'd done, said a quick little prayer, reopened my eyes, and still there was no bear in front of me, yet I also didn't feel alone. No, I felt that now . . . now that I'd prayed, I was somehow connected.

I smiled. This was it. Life was so easy once we knew we were connected and not alone. Yes, I could now see and feel that we were always connected, whether we came face-to-face with our totems or not. In fact, it was already done! Finished! Written in the stars, from where we all came and to where we all returned! The stars! Our True Home!

CHAPTER 51

Aaron

I wasn't at all surprised when my dad and Mireya and Joaquin came back from California and my little brother, who is actually taller and heavier than I am, told me he'd almost met his Bear Totem in the Santa Cruz Mountains of California, at the exact same place where our dad had met his Lion Guide when he was a young boy. I told Joaquin how the Red-tailed Hawk was my Spirit Guide, just as it was for Victor Villaseñor, who was now busy writing the book about our dad's life.

"You see," I told my little-big brother, "one of the main reasons why we have so many problems in the world is because young people aren't initiated into the Ancient Ways of Our Ancestors anymore. You read the newspapers today, and you see there is unrest everywhere. In Mexico there's a war going on between the drug lords and the government. It is currently estimated that the trafficking of weapons from the United States into Mexico is as large as the trafficking of drugs from Mexico into the United States. We need to return to the balance and harmony of Our Ancestors, a time when everything was rooted in Spirit."

"Yes, I totally agree with you," said Joaquin, unzipping his backpack. "I brought you a little present from California," he added, bringing out a piece of cardboard with large hand-printed letters.

I took it and it read:

WITH KNOWLEDGE AND DESIRE TO LEARN
EVERYTHING IS WITHIN OUR REACH
A LIMITLESS WORLD—
THE FARTHEST STAR—
THE HIGHEST DREAM!
Los Gatos Elementary 1923

"Wow!" I said to Joaquin. "This is incredible! So here was the secret to life written above the entrance of our dad's elementary school for him and his fellow students to see every day of their growing-up years."

Grinning, Joaquin nodded.

"So tell me," I said, "how did our dad's family treat you guys?"

Joaquin started laughing so hard that he could hardly speak. "They looked so scared of us that my mother and I felt sorry for them. I guess they felt guilty they'd stolen our dad's inheritance and thought for sure he'd come to reprimand them or threaten to sue them."

Joaquin couldn't stop laughing. "And the more our dad told them not to worry about any of that—we'd come only to see them because we're *familia*—the more and more nervous and scared they got," he added, laughing with *carcajadas*.

"So, they weren't rude to you and your mother?"

"Oh, no!" he said, wiping the tears from his eyes from laughing so much. "The poor people just couldn't do enough for us, but I could also see they wished our visit would be over as soon as possible."

"I'll be," I said, laughing, too. "Then maybe this is how all of the U.S. feels about us Mexicans. They're scared that we might want to take the lands back they stole from our Indian brothers and sisters, plus what they took from Mexico."

"And they were all real old and sick looking," added Joaquin. "Their windows were closed, and they smelled of rot and death. They aren't happy people like our dad. Before we left, Dad wanted them to pray with us, but even this was difficult for them. I guess they just had trouble accepting our love," said Joaquin, laughing again.

I, too, was now laughing with *carcajadas*. "I guess Americans, in general, feel this way—guilty because they're less than 5 percent of the world's population, yet they consume more than 27 percent of our earth's natural resources. So then, the more our dad told them not to worry about his inheritance, the more uptight and guilty they got," I said, laughing.

Joaquin nodded. "Yeah, I think that's it," he said.

We continued laughing together until we both had tears running down our faces. Oh, it was so beautiful! It was like we were— not just half brothers, but soul mates and totally connected with the JOYFUL *CARCAJADAS DE DIOS!*

Oh, I felt so happy I'd made the decision to get to know my dad and his new family instead of being bitter and get into blaming, like my mother and older brother did, for all the aches and pains we'd had to endure.

Life was so much happier when people had faith and turned their lives completely over to the Holy Creator!

I couldn't stop laughing, because even inside my head, I was beginning to sound a whole lot like my dad—full of joy and miracles!

AUTHOR'S NOTES

Off and on for three years I interviewed Mireya, Jan, Joaquin, and Aaron. Then they came to our little *rancho* in Oceanside, California, a week before Thanksgiving to stay with us and help do our Snow Goose Global Thanksgiving Celebration for world harmony and peace. But Jan's legs and back were in so much pain that he could barely get around, so I took him to see my two sisters Linda Villaseñor and Sita Paloma Villaseñor, who are both healers and live in the old part of Carlsbad, just two miles south of the *rancho*.

My sister Linda specializes in animals and works on human couples who want to get pregnant. She has about a 98 percent success rate. My sister Sita Paloma, the dancer of our family, is a licensed Rolfing practitioner and also does psychic healings. Sita told me that when she closed her eyes, said a little prayer, then lowered her hands, palms open and facing down, to begin to work on Jan's body, SHE LEAPED BACK AND BURST INTO TEARS!

"Nothing like this has ever happened to me, brother," she later said to me. "I mean, I always read a person's body energies before I work on them, and his body energies told me this man's BONES AND LIGAMENTS AND MUSCLES HAVE BEEN TORN APART so horribly that it's a miracle he can sit or stand, much less walk!

"This poor man's body has been crushed and broken beyond all human-being comprehension, yet he still functions! He, Jan, is a walking, talking Miracle—that's all I can say! God is truly with him, and this is what has got to come through for the world to know when you write his book!

"All of us humans are now moving into an Age of the Miraculous, and Jan is here to prove this to us. I couldn't stop crying. In all my years of working on bodies that have been in car wrecks or have come home from the wars overseas, I have never seen a human body like this. Truly, it must be the Spirit of the Lion he saw that day as a boy that is keeping him together. The man shouldn't even be able to sit up straight, much less stand up and walk like normal. I had to do a lot of deep breathing to calm myself down enough before I could do my Healing Work on him.

"The man is a saint, I tell you, but not a goodie-goodie saint. I see how he looks at his wife, Mireya, and sometimes at other women, too. He's a man, just a man—no better and no worse."

So my little sister Paloma worked on Jan's broken-up body, and I'd like you to know that the Spirit World is, indeed, with Jan, just as the Spirit World is with all of us. He walks. He talks. And he continues being proof of a Living Miracle, just like all the rest of us who live in Service.

I feel privileged to have written this book, and if you have any questions and/or simply wish to further understand the Indigenous World of the Tarahumara and other Native Americans, read my trilogy *Wild Steps of Heaven, Rain of Gold,* and *Thirteen Senses,* which are currently in production for a miniseries. Truly, back at one time we were ALL INDIGENOUS PEOPLE THE WHOLE WORLD OVER, and we lived with Total Trust in a Spirit World WHERE ALL WAS POSSIBLE!

Also, I'd like you to know that once the 2 million acres were deeded back to the Tarahumara, the Elders of the 13 different *ejidos* gave Jan and Mireya 5,000 acres just outside of Creel in a gesture of giving Mireya's family back their old *rancho.* Now Jan and Mireya have brought in one of the world's leading eco-friendly building consultants, and they are presently working with the

Tarahumara to build a University Community that teaches World Harmony and Peace through Our Natural 13 Senses, which then automatically activate Our Heart and Soul and Open Our Doorway into Our Cellular Memory of yesteryear.

So come and help us take our U.S. celebration of Thanksgiving, where Native Americans and the European pilgrims ate in peace and harmony, and go global with it! Thanksgiving, where two very different cultures got together and gave thanks to God and Mother Earth, is by far OUR GREATEST U.S. CELEBRATION! Since 1992, every Sunday before Thanksgiving, thousands of us have been getting together at our *ranchito* in Oceanside at 1 P.M., and we share joy and food and music. IT'S FREE! IT'S A POTLUCK! Bring your family and friends and a dish for 12 made with loving hands. Come in walking shoes, bring folding chairs and/or a blanket and your own plates and cups, and be prepared to clean up after yourself. We want a garbage-free event.

Our little *rancho* is located in south Oceanside, just one block west of the big Interstate 5 freeway, a block north of California Street at the end of Stewart Street. Drop your party of people off at the gates and then go find parking, and be prepared to walk a few blocks with a smile. Be happy and grateful that you can walk. Thank your feet and legs for helping you all these years. No valet parking. Everyone is equally special.

There will be plenty of food and laughter and music and love, and then at sundown, we will light candles and face east. To the west we came with heads full of conquest and taking and taking, and now to the east we go with hearts full of Love and Harmony and Giving and Giving with Abundance for All . . . and then Peace on Earth is our by-product!

All of our other 6 Sister Planets have already reached Global Love and Harmony with Abundance for All, and they're rooting for us! Where do you think all these advancements came from that we've developed in the last 100 years? Einstein knew. Ask him. He'll tell you. Where do you think he got his theory?

SO BACK TO THE FUTURE WE GO, WHEN WE WERE ALL INDIGENOUS PEOPLE! AND WORLD HARMONY AND PEACE ARE IN THE BAG!

This is what 2012 of the Mayan calendar is all about! We are moving out of 26,000 years of male-based energy and into 26,000 years of female-based energy! Indigenous People have known this for 100s of 1,000s of years, and modern society is just beginning to learn about this, because they are now able to prove it to themselves with their computers.

COME JOIN US! We need 1,000 locations of giving thanks by 2012, and 100,000 by 2026, and 1,000,000 and/or more by 2052, so our Sacred Mother Earth can then feel our Critical Mass of HEART-LOVE-DREAM-CONSCIOUSNESS-ENERGY CHANGE. Then she, Our Sacred Mother Earth, will then INSTANTLY heal herself, because like any good mother, she will rejoice once she realizes how we, her children, finally do TRULY LOVE HER AND RESPECT HER, AND THIS WILL GIVE HER HEART!

Wars will no longer exist!

Armies will be used as loving "arms" for helping and rebuilding areas of natural disaster.

Truly, we aren't even the species we think we are! Hate and war aren't part of basic human nature. Greed and selfishness aren't part of basic human nature. Happy, loving, sharing, playing human beings are who we all used to be and are returning to be, AS WE ONCE MORE AWAKEN TO THE WHOLE HUGE SPIRIT WORLD ALL AROUND US! Jan did it! An ordinary white dude! And we can do it, too! Ask any surfer! Ask any skateboarder! Ask any old person and/or child who's running, leaping, playing, and having fun on their feet or in their wheelchair!

Check out my website: **www.victorvillasenor.com**.

Thank you!
¡Gracias!
Victor E. Villaseñor

EPILOGUE

by Jan A. Milburn

I truly believe that the Spiritual Consciousness of the Indigenous Ancestry that flows in the veins of Victor Villaseñor is the reason he was chosen by our guides to capture the true essence of the last 50 years of my life. For without his Mexican-Indian background, he could not have understood my feelings for the wonderful people and their culture that have been my life journey. Not only that, but Victor has been very open to the gifts that Spiritual Understanding brings. Through these gifts, he is able to bring to his readers the power we all have within us, but don't realize it.

In 1989, after the last kidnapping and coming back over the border into the United States, we were invited to live in Mesa Verde National Park as VIPs for a year. The then-superintendent Robert (Bob) Heyder and his wife, Katherine, along with their daughter Gretchen, had been to visit us in Arareco, Chihuahua, and been with us during that year's Easter ceremonies. Bob had become extremely interested in the theory of mine about the relationship of the Raramuri (Tarahumara) culture and the Anasazi group of the Four Corners region of the U.S.

We spent the year there researching the Anasazi-Tarahumara Connection and had the opportunity to expand our own understanding of the different cultural groups that form the indigenous base of the Southwest and Mesoamerican interchanges that have taken place for the last several thousand years. The Spirituality of Mesa Verde alone is wonderful and can be felt deeply, as my mentors Tonio Rivas and Benito Juárez said when they first saw Cliff Palace in 1985. They were both quite moved. As we walked over to the overlook of the ruins, they stopped and looked down, and in a hushed silence stated, "We are here; our Spirits have come home."

From that moment on, I knew that the most profound Spirituality has no limit as to time, distance, or ethnic group. As it is, I believe that the Raramuri are Mogollon-Anasazi and must be listened to and honored as the last cave and cliff dwellers of the Americas. And it will be groups like these that will survive whatever the future holds for us who put our human consciousness before our Spiritual Consciousness. For them, 2012 is hope for the new beginning that will give *all* hope for renewal.

While living in Mesa Verde, I realized that our lion was still with us. One day while I was busy in the museum, Mireya decided to take a hike. She wandered off into a remote area and lost track of time. As dusk approached, she headed back to where she thought the museum area was. She quickly realized she was lost. Uneasiness set in, as she had no way of communicating with me and had not seen a soul for hours. She felt she was being followed but saw no one.

As darkness hit, she ran into a gate. Not understanding English, she had no idea what the sign on the gate said but decided to follow an arrow that was painted on it. Problem: the gate was high and locked. She, however, was able to climb up and over it and made it home to our small house that the park had provided for us. She was upset with herself for having lost her sense of direction, but felt she had been protected.

A few days later, the park rangers discovered lion tracks on the same path that Mireya had been lost on. And following them, they found where the lion had killed a deer. The lion dragged the deer for a long distance and had hidden it across the street in front of our house. The lion was never found.

As the summer came closer, the park needed our house for the permanent rangers who would be coming on for the season. We were moved to the section that was reserved for the Native American workers at the park. We were given a tent platform dwelling that felt like home to us. These tents are built around a common area where bathrooms and showers are located.

One night late, Mireya needed to use the bathroom, but as it was dark and a bit far to walk alone at that hour, she decided to heed nature's call outside the tent in the trees. As she was squatting there, she heard a thundering noise coming at her. Before she could even stand up, a group of deer came flying by, almost hitting her. She quickly jumped up and ran for the tent. As she reached the step, a large mountain lion ran by her, brushing her leg, in hot pursuit of the deer.

Today we laugh at the situation and recall the holding of each other the rest of the night—laughing, crying, and full of emotions that are mixed at a time like that. But what I wonder is: has my lion continued protecting us through all these trials, and has she become a part of Mireya's protectors, giving her the same care she has always given me? I truly believe so. Mireya and I have become one. Probably always have been and always will be.

A short time after that, we left the park, as our time was up, and relocated to Durango, Colorado, not far from Mesa Verde. We were invited to several powwows and followed the circuit. Mireya was honored by many friends and was brought into the Native American healing circle and given the name of Morning-Eagle by a Cherokee Elder. Later, that same elder, along with a Mescalero Apache Healer, came to Durango and blessed our newborn son,

Joaquin, and gave him his eagle feathers and Bear-Eagle as his new name.

We made new friends quickly, and they became interested in the stories I spoke about during lectures and presentations we were giving about the Tarahumara and the theory of their relationship to the area. We had also opened our first gallery in the U.S., in downtown Durango. This gallery was dedicated to Mireya's people and was a true cottage-industry gift shop. Good friends of ours, Tom Caver, Jr., and Wardine Lee, thought it would be good to set up a foundation for helping these indigenous groups.

As always, money was a problem from the beginning. My mother had passed on a couple of years earlier, and my family had finally sent me a $1,000 check as my part of a very large inheritance. So, with that money we were able to form and register THE MILBURN FOUNDATION, INC.—a nonprofit, tax-exempt corporation for "International Environmental, Cultural, and Indigenous Relations and Preservation." Little did my mother, who had very little confidence in anything I ever did, know that this would turn into *un milagro de Dios*. From there, medical clinics have been established, schools have been built and additions put on, legal help for the indigenous has been provided, and programs for women and children have flourished and continue to grow year after year.

The Foundation has become an international group that lately has been able to save thousands upon thousands of acres of forest land, where two major projects are in the works: one is an Environmental Sustainable Eco-Touristic Green Development; and the other is a World Institute for Cultural Understanding Through Peace and Harmony. All this has been made possible through Friends of the Foundation tax-deductible gifts.

During the last 20 years of travels and lecturing on the themes that are so dear to my heart, people are constantly asking me how one mixes Christianity with primitive cultures. Good question, with a relatively simple answer: FAITH and RELIGION are two separate things. Yes, they interact with each other; however, each does take its own path and at times becomes confusing.

It's easy to work within "primitive" cultures as a Christian, especially if you respect people for who they are. Both faith and most organized religions have very basic foundations that are essentially the same: the relationship of one to the earth; to one's brothers and fellow man; and to the cosmos, better known as the Heavens. Once you understand and respect this, and leave out the inner politics that are true to all organized religions, then you are there. Respect and responsibility become one of your major goals.

When I first went into the Sierra Madre, I quickly learned that my "preaching" as a minister had no place there. The Raramuri had survived over 350 years of religious impact and had nothing but heartache and disillusionment. They had survived because they did not believe in the *chavochi* (white man). They saw his destruction not only of the earth by way of lumbering and mining, but also of his fellow man by destroying the basis of their faith that was their right, by imposing another religion on them, often by force. All respect for the white man was lost, and he became the *chavochi-chauwami*—the bearded white man, better known as "the Devil's first cousin."

I, being a bearded white man, was up against a concept that preceded me. The only thing to do was to respect and honor the Raramuri for who they were and shut up. This took many years, and it wasn't until our imprisonment and the terrible beatings that they saw someone different in this Christian *chavochi-chauwami*. One of the most moving parts in my life was that night as I lay on the cement floor of that prison, bleeding and hurting. I knew that I had become part of them. We had but one blanket between all eleven of us. The principal chief or governor, Fransisco Sabastian, took the blanket and covered me with it. He then lay close to me on one side to give me warmth, and Jose Ayala, a leader, lay on the other side. Fransisco then announced in a quiet voice, "You are now our *APOLOCHI* [grandfather]." I now knew that it is what you do that proves who you are, not always just what you say.

I have seen on occasion the leaders of Raramuri ceremonies actually run a priest out of the church with whips when, while leading the religious part of the ceremony, he would begin to preach. When I asked about that, I was told that not even the governor could talk in the church because "the way of men would get in the way of God." This is an example of faith versus religion. The true expression of the Raramuri was in the celebration through ceremony, not in a certain man's opinion.

Indigenous groups that I have had the honor of knowing believe in simplicity and not making things complicated. The churches I have known and become involved in seem to have forgotten this very aspect. Things have become complicated with many rules, and according to all of the groups I know, that is where the problem begins. And because of that, our destinies are in danger of not being fulfilled. I would like to explain how that has been a major part of how a Christian minister can be so comfortable living with, and being part of, primitive indigenous groups.

I believe in destiny and how that may affect transformations. First, let me say that when you make a commitment to a higher being, such as I have with the Holy Trinity (Father, Son, and Holy Spirit), you must have total Faith that what happens to you while carrying out your work on this being's behalf is predestined. Whether you know what's coming or not, in the greater plan, you become only an INSTRUMENT that is part of that plan. Your path will constantly be crisscrossed with elements that are needed to fulfill that plan. These can be people (that is, *curanderos*) or totems. In my case, my ANGELS and the LION fulfill those roles, in part, along with circumstances and happenings.

Much of the time you are chosen to pass hardships and endure unpleasant situations that may cause even death—as in the case of martyrs. This is why I have been able to do so many things and still come out on top. It's not my game; it's the Lord's! Things can go wrong that are part of destiny. This happens when you allow your HUMAN CONSCIOUSNESS to get in the way of your

SPIRITUAL CONSCIOUSNESS—in the pursuit of money and power, for example.

If you remain true to yourself and your promise, nothing can stop that. When you are in this powerful state of being, it is easy to become part of the unexplainable. Transformations are a good example: *curanderos* flying or changing form. Seeing, feeling, and hearing nature, which is very alive, can and will be part of your journey's work. Rocks, water, rain, and the canyons themselves are examples.

The reason why many cannot see this is simply that they are not true to their commitments and only live things halfway, not ready to give all that is needed to give. For example, the priests wish to control through their own power and not that of their CREATOR.

In summing up this thought on destiny, the HEART and SOUL, along with FAITH, is the indigenous way and supports all that *Lion Eyes* is about. One should always remember: be careful what you pray for; you might just get it. I prayed for the opportunity to serve my Lord—and I really got it!

Gracias, Victor!

Be Blessed,
Jan Milburn
March 2011

These Bible scriptures have been important to me for the last 50 years:

Romans 8

[28] And we know that all that happens to us is working for our good if we love God and are fitting into his plans.

[31] If God is on our side, who can ever be against us?

[35] Who then can ever keep Christ's love from us? When we have trouble or calamity, when we are hunted down and

destroyed, is it because He doesn't love us anymore? And if we are hungry and penniless, or in danger, or threatened with death, has God deserted us?

[38–39] For I am convinced that nothing can ever separate us from His love. Death can't, and life can't. The angels won't, and all the powers of hell itself cannot keep God's love away. Our fears for today, our worries about tomorrow, or where we are—high above the sky, or in the deepest ocean—nothing will ever be able to separate us from the love of God demonstrated by our Lord Jesus Christ when He died for us.

Blessings,
Jan

AFTERWORD

Okay, you have just finished reading *Lion Eyes,* and it was a good, fast read and you enjoyed it, but now part of you is wondering if certain parts of this story are true, or if it's all fiction and/or mostly an exaggerated lie by me—the author—and Jan Milburn.

Well, if you have any of these thoughts and doubts, let me tell you, you are not alone. I myself, Victor E. Villaseñor, received 265 rejections before I sold my first book, *A La Brava*—the title of which my New York publisher Bantam changed to *Macho!*—and it was compared to the best of John Steinbeck by the *L.A. Times.* And in the case of my first bestseller, *Rain of Gold*—the true story of my dad and mom and my two Indian grandmothers—I had to buy the rights to that book back from the New York publisher Putnam, because Phyllis Grann, the chairman of the board and president of Putnam, wanted to call it fiction. All this is well documented in my book *Beyond Rain of Gold.*

In fact, all your doubts and questions are addressed in *Beyond Rain of Gold.* You see, simply, what I have been writing about for more than 50 years is completely outside the box of Western civilization, which is based on 5 senses. So for you to doubt and not accept what I write about as being true is expected, because for you to understand this incredible Spiritual Journey that Jan Milburn, "a white guy" (as his son Joaquin calls him), went through, you'd have to be outside of your "civilized thinking head" and return to those days when we were all "indigenous" people the whole world over and we were WILD OF HEART AND ALIVE OF SOUL AND WE UTILIZED ALL OF OUR NATURAL 13 SENSES!

And the extent of this gap of credibility is larger than the Grand Canyon, yet I really didn't fully comprehend the size of the gap until I'd interviewed Jan and his *familia* for well over three years and I'd traveled to Durango, Colorado; and Chihuahua and Creel, Mexico, several times. Then . . . finally, I began to realize that in my attempt to make sure Jan and Mireya's story was believable to a modern-day reader, I saw that I'd gathered way too much information, so my job as a writer would now be to thin things out and assemble a more focused story that would be reader friendly.

You see, the same thing happened to me when I'd been working on the original *Rain of Gold,* which took me more than 16 years to write and get published. Why? Because bluntly, I, too, at times had difficulty believing that my parents' stories were true, so in trying to make sure their story was believable, I also just kept gathering information on top of information until I finally had a 1,500-page book with more than 300 characters.

This was when my dad one day told me in frustration that I'd never be able to understand the life he and my mother had lived, because I'd become too *gringo*-ized. *"Mijito,"* he'd said to me, "understand this, your grandmothers didn't believe in God. Get it! They *lived* with the Almighty with their every breath! But you've become so *tapado* in your head that you can't see this, because your very eyes are covered over with *caca!"*

What could I say? I'd almost felt like quitting, because what my dad was telling me was that I'd never be able to understand what he and my mother had been through with my two Indian grandmothers, because I was so "constipated" in the brain that my very eyes were covered with shit. My dad had never been one to be subtle. Then he'd also added that my heart had been tamed, and in order for a soul to live, the heart had to be WILD!

But I didn't give up. In fact, what my dad told me motivated me to get into an even higher gear, and I rewrote the entire 1,500-page book five more times and then finally broke it down into the trilogy of *Wild Steps of Heaven, Rain of Gold,* and *Thirteen Senses.* And this time I didn't question and try to understand what it was that my dad and mom told me. No, I just wrote it down as they gave it to me.

So please, dear reader, don't be too hard on yourself and/or on *Lion Eyes,* which you've just finished reading, because you wouldn't even be reading these pages if you weren't a person who's ready to let go of what you know to be reality and LEAP BACK INTO THE FUTURE where we were once all indigenous people!

A civilized plant, like a rose, you need to water and spray and feed or it will die; but to an indigenous plant, like a weed, you give it nothing and it lives. You poison it and it comes back a year later. You pour cement over it and it will break the concrete reaching for the sunlight of God, and this is where we are all going collectively: back to a time when we were ALL WILD OF HEART AND ALIVE OF SOUL AND AS INDESTRUCTIBLE AS WEEDS!

Read *Beyond Rain of Gold* and the original *Rain of Gold;* then return to *Lion Eyes* once again, and you will then see how Western civilization has basically taken over the whole world with 5 senses and the languaging of English, so, of course, it is now nearly impossible for us to step outside of our "civilized, English-speaking, Western-thinking, boxed-in reality" long enough to "see" anything that's different and/or outside of that box!

So realizing this, I could now "see" that I had a far more serious problem with Jan's story than I'd ever had with my dad and mom's story, because with theirs, I'd had their indigenous mothers explaining things to them, and in Jan's story I had no such people.

Jan, a white dude, had managed to leap out of his cultural box and into this world of yesteryear with nothing but his own personal guts and faith and the feeling that there had to be something more to living life other than what his upbringing offered him. And there are a few stories of white men doing this back in the days of the western movement across the Americas, stories of frontiersmen and even priests who became Indian-ized.

But different from those stories, Jan, a Christian minister, didn't reject his faith and/or culture. No, Jan kept his faith intact. And so how did he do this miraculous feat? This was the challenging dilemma I had before me if I was to do his story justice. But also, I didn't want to spend 16 years on his story, as I'd done with my parents' book.

So, at first, I tried writing *Lion Eyes* in the third person, figuring that this way I could interject all of the knowledge I'd accumulated about indigenous people over the last 40-some years of interviewing my immediate family and relatives in the U.S. and Mexico. But it didn't work. My own voice, my own point of view, kept interfering with the wonderful voices of Jan and Mireya and Joaquin and Aaron, which were so beautiful and authentic on their own.

I finally stopped that and started to write only through Jan's point of view. I began the story in Los Gatos, California, and then in Haight-Ashbury in San Francisco, but by the time I got to Chihuahua, Mexico, I was exhausted, confused, and had lost the heart of the story I was trying to write. Or, as my sister Sita Paloma said so well when she'd done her healing work on Jan's broken-up body, I had to be sure to do justice to this incredible man's story.

Back to the drawing board I went a dozen more times, and then one morning at about two, something magical happened. I went outside to look up at the stars, and I suddenly saw so clearly how I needed to write Jan Milburn's story. I had to write it not as if he were special, but as if we were *all* special and he was the norm of how special and miraculous we all were.

Because over and over my Yaqui grandmother had told me that we were all Walking Stars. Every human being was a 5-pointed walking star, and we'd all come across the heavens gathering stardust from the different stars to plant on Mother Earth for the Holy Creator's ongoing garden. And that each and every generation brought their own stardust, and each and every individual brought his/her own unique dust, and God depended on us because the Holy Creator couldn't do it without us. God needed us as much as we needed God. We were a team, Us and God, and Together it was our nature to do GREATNESS!

This was how I would write Jan's story, showing that he was the norm—the direction in which we were all headed, collectively, as Human Beings doing Service on Earth. That the time had come for us to ask ourselves not what Mother Earth can give us, but what we can give her. This is what *Beyond Rain of Gold* was all about.

I BEGAN TO DANCE, SHOUTING WITH JOY, LOOKING UP AT THE STARS! Because I now understood that I wasn't writing Jan's story. No, I was writing the story of every "civilized person" who'd been raised within the structurally limited reality of Western civilization, and I could now feel deep inside of me, as I gazed up at the infinite vastness of stars and moonlight, that all of us, collectively, had reached a point in our Human-Being Development where we all wanted to LEAP OUT OF OUR UPTIGHT CIVILIZED BOX!

YES, OH YES, we didn't want to play it safe and reasonable anymore! We all yearned to break loose from our collars, shake off our shackles, and go back to YESTERYEAR WHEN WE HUMAN BEINGS WERE ALL FREE AND WILD OF HEART AND ALIVE OF SOUL AND LIVED LIVES OF INCREDIBLE ADVENTURE AND PURPOSE, JUST LIKE JAN!

This was what the Spirit of those frontiersmen who'd gone Indian had been all about! And this was what the Spirit of skateboarding and surfing was all about! This was what the Spirit of skydiving and rock climbing was all about! This was what crazy-*loco* drinking and doing drugs was all about! EVERYONE AND HIS/HER BROTHER AND SISTER wanted to get out of our stranglehold of "Western civilization" and be free AT LAST and WILD OF HEART and ALIVE OF SOUL and HAVE EXCITING LIVES FULL OF FOCUS AND PURPOSE AND MEANING!

In other words, we all wanted to roll back history to a time when we humans lived lives of heroic proportions with Total Love and Devotion to Spirit/God and the natural exciting adventure of daily living! A time of young boys scaling cliffs with their father-teachers to learn how to capture a baby eagle so it could grow up to become their hunting partner! Of boys seeing their fathers and uncles and older brothers going after bears and lions with nothing but a spear! Of men riding the high seas in canoes and going after whale and seal, and some getting killed. Yes, of course, some meeting their glorious fate with open eyes and loving hearts, and the other men coming home to share their great adventurous stories around the campfire with their wives and aunts and sweethearts and daughters and the widows of the great ones who risked it all!

No hate!

No egos!

No enemies!

All just part of Living Life to the Hilt, and the women and girls being happy and excited to receive their warriors, who were, of course, gone a lot of the time, so that then they, the women, the timekeepers of knowledge, could run things.

Why? Because back then all men knew deep inside themselves that women were directly connected to the Mother Moon with their monthly passing of blood, so it was within their very nature and wisdom to keep the tribe in Harmony with the Forces of the Universe. Read *Wild Steps of Heaven* and see how my dad explained to me that even in the middle of the monstrous Mexican Revolution, he'd watched his short little Indian mother keep their lives full of faith and love and daily miracles!

This was why my father always listened to my mother and was the first man in the *barrio* of Carlsbad, California, to get his wife her own car and put her in charge of going to the bank by herself and doing the banking. My dad and mom were a team! No confusion between the sexes! This is what the book *Thirteen Senses* is all about: a man and a woman with their FOOT TO THE PEDAL AND FIRE IN THEIR BELLY!

Suddenly I was riding on a beam of light, just like Albert Einstein, and I realized that my dad had told me the truth. I truly had been so constipated in my head that my eyes had been covered over with shit.

The whole world is in our hands and full of Magic and Wonder and Adventure once we let go and live a life of TOTAL LOVE AND TRUST AND FAITH IN THE ETERNAL GOODNESS OF GOD AND NATURAL CREATION! And this was what Jan's story was all about, a very different story from his Christian, God-fearing, judgmental brother, who'd stayed safely home and did so well at IBM.

So it's all up to you, dear reader: doubt and question and criticize, and/or LEAP INTO A WORLD OF MAGIC AND WONDER AND ADVENTUROUS SPIRIT!

Myself, I long ago let go and LEAPED!

I totally, completely, let go and LEAPED!

In other words, I was/am no longer concerned and/or worried about what you, my modern-day reader, might think, because I was/am looking up at the stars as I write, and I can now "see" that I am writing about all of us! Not just Jan! And now everything falls into place and makes so much sense to me!

And yeah, sure, of course, this was also the case with the story of my dad and mom, and how I'd finally had to let go, so I could write their story, too.

Then when I'd finished my parents' book, thinking I'd written a masterpiece, life threw me a curveball I hadn't seen coming, and I'd had to ask my poor old mother to mortgage her home, the only thing she had left, so I could buy the rights of their book back from Putnam. Because Phyllis Grann, the highest-paid woman in all of publishing at that time, decided to call my parents' life story fiction. But my brave, stout-hearted mother backed me up, because the poor, lost, rich, most powerful woman in the publishing world had been so full of doubt and fear that the only way she could feel safe publishing the original *Rain of Gold,* which was full of miracles and incredible heart-moving stories, was to "believe" it wasn't true, even though she knew about all the years of research and interviewing I'd done, and . . . and she'd originally bought it as nonfiction, calling *Rain of Gold* one of the greatest books she'd ever read.

All this I also documented in *Beyond Rain of Gold,* of meeting Phyllis at her fancy restaurant in New York City (Alex Haley had told me how to pull this off after she wouldn't return my calls), and you can "see" for yourself how, obviously, this once-wild-hearted, brilliant woman had gotten her heart so "tamed" by the things she'd had to do to get to the top of the publishing world that her soul had dried up, and hence, she no longer had the guts to believe . . . because believe-you-me, it takes guts to believe in heart-moving stories and miracles, when we "see" so much crap and greed and awful things happening all around us in the world!

For me, Marianne Williamson says it best: It's not the darkness we fear, but the incredible bright light beings that we are. Yes, a thousand times yes, we humans are fantastic, Great Beings of Miraculous Light and Wonder once we get out of the confines of our "Western thinking head" that's dictated by 5 senses and we begin living Life, *la Vida,* with all of our Full Natural 13 senses!

Then Jan and Mireya's story becomes OUR NORM!

My dad and mom's story becomes OUR NORM!

Jesus Christ and Buddha and Gandhi and Mother Teresa and Martin Luther King and César Chávez and Nelson Mandela ALL BECOME OUR NORM!

And the story of all these people are full of Love and Purpose and Meaning and Miracles and Infinite Beauty and Hope and Indestructible Faith, because once we humans move into Our Full Natural 13 Senses, then we can do no other, but live and breathe in Greatness because we are never, ever alone again and instead are FOREVER SURROUNDED BY THE LIVING, BREATHING FLOW OF GOD'S ONGOING CREATION CREATING!

So, what are these 13 senses? Okay, I'll now tell you, but I need you to know that I, too, didn't know anything about all these other senses until the night of my dad's passing.

It was March 14, 1988. I was 48 years old, and my dad was 86 years old. He'd announced his death on New Year's Eve, three months before. It was evening, and I was with him at our smaller new house across the grass from the big old main house at our *rancho* in Oceanside, California. All week my mother had been staying with my dad, so I'd suggested that she take the night off and I'd stay with him. You see, my dad had been getting weaker and weaker every day since he'd announced his death, because he'd basically stopped eating in preparation for his Passing. All this is documented in *Beyond Rain of Gold.*

My mother agreed and went across the grass to the big house where everyone was staying, and I was left alone with my dad.

"I'll be staying with you tonight," I told him.

"Good," he said, taking my hand in both of his huge hands and soothing it with such warm, gentle love. "You know, *mijito,* I've been doing a lot of thinking lately about life, and I can now see that . . . that the main reason we have so many *problemas* in the world is because people don't use all of their senses."

"Oh," I said, "that's very interesting, *Papa.* So which of the five senses are you talking about that we don't use?"

"What five senses are you talking about?" he asked me.

"All of our five," I said. "That's what we have, *Papa,* is five senses."

"Who told you such a big stupid damn lie?!" he said.

"Everyone, *Papa.* At school and in the books and—"

"Even the Church says this?" he asked.

"Yes, of course, *Papa,* even the Church," I said, knowing he was referring to the Catholic Church.

"Well, I'll be," he said in astonishment. "No wonder the whole world is such an upside-down mess. *Mijito,* we got 12 or 13 senses. I don't remember which, but it's a hell of a lot more than 5. Look, once I'm on the Other Side, I'll ask my *mamá* to explain it to me, and then with the help of the Grandmasters, I'll come back and tell you everything. But—and this is a big 'but'—you got to be paying attention when you sleep. Remember, *mijito,* that all real learning happens in our sleep, when we finally stop thinking and start listening."

All my life he'd told me this, that we humans never really learned anything when we were awake, because we were then always "thinking" and not really listening.

"Okay, *Papa*," I said, not actually taking too seriously what he was telling me. I guess, because I was awake and thinking. And yet all his life, my dad had also spoken about going over to the Other Side every night when he'd slept as if this was the most natural thing for us to do in all the world—to interact with our loved ones on the Other Side in our sleep.

But we didn't get to talk about this anymore, because that very night my dad passed over, and he passed with such peace. In fact, when I'd asked him if he was afraid, he'd said, "Of what? Death? Absolutely not! Passing over is part of life, and I've had a good life, so I'm not going to insult it now!"

It was totally amazing. When my dad announced his death on New Year's Eve, he'd taken us all by surprise because he'd been in perfect health, but he'd said that his life on Earth was done, and it was now time for him to go over to the Other Side to be with his mother, my brother, and all of the rest of our *familia* so he could continue to do his Holy Work—that he didn't want to hang around until he got so weak he couldn't wipe his own ass, because that was stupid—that any person of sound mind and heart passed over while they were still strong and healthy. All this is also well documented in *Beyond Rain of Gold,* which starts with my dad's great, wonderful funeral.

Anyway, a few months after my dad's passing, I was in New York City, and I was feeling so lost and desperate that I didn't know what to do. Phyllis Grann, the president and chairman of Putnam, had destroyed my parents' book. The advance bound galleys that she'd shipped across the country for reviewing had the word FICTION in large letters on the cover. And when I called and protested, she'd told me to relax, that *Rain of Gold* was her lead book, and she was going to make me rich.

That night in my New York hotel room I was a total mess. I truly thought that I'd let my parents down after all these years of dedicated work, because the world would now never know how great and true my parents' story was, and we Latinos NEEDED OUR REAL-LIFE HEROES, TOO!

Oh, I just felt awful, but I guess I was finally able to fall asleep, because the next thing I knew, I smelled my dad's cigar, and in my delirium, I'd forgotten that he'd died, so in my sleep I began to talk to him. And suddenly, just like magic, here was my dad in my hotel room with me. All this is also well documented in *Beyond Rain of Gold,* and it was after this that the whole Spiritual World came BURSTING INTO MY LIFE, and my dad began coming to me on a regular basis in my sleep and giving me advice.

Soon, my dad became my Spirit Guide from the Other Side, just as his mother had been his Spirit Guide from the Other Side when he'd been here on Earth, and I began living in a Dream Consciousness of Infinite Possibilities, interacting with my dad and his mother and all of our *familia* on the Other Side, plus the Grandmasters. This was when the Spirit World began moving my life out of our limiting 5 senses and into Our Full Natural 13 Senses so that I could then comprehend what was going on within the LARGER-DESIGN PLAN OF CREATION CREATING and not go crazy-*loco* insane!

And/or as Jesus so well said, "The Kingdom of God is within each of us," and I could now "see" that . . . my Kingdom of God within me had truly been ACTIVATED!

NO JOKE! I WAS NOW FLYING LIKE AN EAGLE ACROSS THE HEAVENS! My totem, the Red-tailed Hawk, was me! Totally! Completely! And I was so happy! BIG BIG HAPPY!

Okay, here you have it! And we can now finally go directly into Our Natural 13 Senses, so that then, even as a modern-day reader, you will be able to understand and maybe accept the world of my parents and their indigenous mothers, and also the Spiritual Journey of Jan Milburn.

And/or I ask you, could any of us now go back just 100 years and explain to people then how we live with TVs, cell phones, computers, freeways, jets, and airports, and that we've traveled to the moon? You would probably be called crazy*loco* and locked up. Well, this is how far we are now going to go, and you will then "see" that we aren't even the species we "think" we are, once we get out of the "prison" of our 5 senses and enter into the Miraculous

World of Our Natural 13 Senses. It will be like a 13th-century European suddenly being told and shown that the earth isn't flat, but round, and that there's human life and whole continents just across the seas.

First of all, my dad explained to me that we have three centers for processing information, not one center (the brain), as Western civilization has led us to believe.

- Center 1 is the Brain, located at the head, and it has 4 senses.

- Center 2 is the Heart, the chest area, and it has 3 senses.

- Center 3 is the Soul, located in the gut, and it has 6 senses.

The 4 senses that work with the brain are specific and give specific and separate information, and these are all located at the head. They are eyes for seeing, ears for hearing, mouths for tasting, and noses for smelling. And please note that these are the only senses that we've been educated to utilize for the last few thousand years.

The 5th sense, feeling, which is our broader sense of touching, has been discounted, because if men go into their sense of feeling, they are considered wimps; and if women go into their sense of feeling, they are considered too emotional.

So long ago society decided that in order to protect itself and keep things reasonable, people would be educated to only respect and acknowledge the 4 senses that are located at the head, and to separate feeling from touching, so that then this 5th sense of feel-touching could be kept under control.

But my dad explained to me that his mother and the Grandmasters told him that in Oaxaca, where my dad's mother was originally from, these cousins of the Maya knew that we humans needed to incorporate our whole body so we could utilize all of Our Natural 13 Senses, and that the 3 senses that go to the heart—feelings, balance, and intuition—are not specifically located in the human body, nor do they give specific and separate information, like the 4 senses that work with the brain. We don't just feel-touch with our hands and fingers. We feel-touch with our whole body, and beyond our body 26 arms' lengths in all directions all around us, AND IN HIGH INTENSITY!

Have you ever walked into a room and instantly felt that something wasn't right? Of course you have. We all have. Have you ever walked into a room and just felt that everything was fine? Of course, and how did you know this? Not with "thinking," which is way too slow and works only with the Head Center. No, you knew this with a feeling, with an instinct, with your intuition, which is 10,000 times faster than thinking because it doesn't operate with words, and instead operates with "feeling" from the Heart Center, which instantly, in a flash, generates a KNOWINGNESS BEYOND ALL THINKING!

Why? Because feeling comes to us from the whole body, our whole Total Being, while thoughts come to us only from the head, with specific information from specific locations—eyes, ears, nose, and mouth—and hence keep us divided, cautious, incomplete, and in a state of infinite self-separation.

And so, of course when we stay in our "thinking heads," my dad explained to me, we are then forever full of doubt and worry and can't believe in anything we can't see, hear, smell, and/or taste; and that's why we've actually been taught to say, "If I can't see it, it doesn't exist." But in pre-Columbian Oaxaca, these cousins of the Maya weren't afraid to go into their feelings, because the 6th sense was balance, and balance was and is the key to health and happiness and all the rest of our senses.

And balance is also done with the whole body, just as feeling is done—not just with the touching of our hands and fingers, but with the whole body, too. And balance, the 6th sense, unites us, integrates us all together within ourselves and with our surroundings, and this is why my dad was taught by his mother, even while he was on This Side of Living, that balance is the most important of all of our 13 senses!

We can live without sight.

We can live without hearing.

We can live without taste and smell, but we cannot live without a sense of balance, and yet have we been educated by Western civilization to acknowledge and understand that balance, which comes from our feelings, is our most important sense for survival and health and happiness? No, we haven't been. And why?

Because once we accept and acknowledge our feelings as paramount so that we can then balance ourselves with our surroundings and automatically go into our intuition, our instincts, who's more intuitive, men or women? Women, by far! Because, as my dad explained to me, men can't control women who are connected to their feelings and know how to balance them so that they can then trust their inner voice, their intuition, which comes from their hearts, their Kingdom of God.

I was astonished!

This all made so much sense!

Now I could see why on his deathbed my dad had said no wonder the whole world was such an upside-down mess, because with 5 senses, then we didn't have the tools with which to go inside ourselves and activate the Kingdom of God that Jesus Christ had so clearly spoken about that we all have inside of ourselves, and then harmonize ourselves with our surroundings.

With 5 senses, the best we could do was "believe" in what Jesus and other enlightened human beings told us, but with just these extra two senses, balance and intuition, we can then move into A WHOLE NEW relationship of knowingness with Jesus and other enlightened human beings, and then, COLLECTIVELY, BURST INTO A WHOLE BRAVE NEW GLOBAL CONSCIOUSNESS—not just with faith, but with SOLID, CONCRETE UNDERSTANDING THAT OUR SURROUNDING WORLD IS ALIVE AND CONSTANTLY TALKING TO US.

And now I could fully understand why the Greeks, a very male-based society, had solidified the concept that we only have 5 senses; and all the rest of Europe followed, never questioning, and our 5 senses became the very foundation of all Western civilization! Because then, with only 5 senses, women would forever be kept off balance and their Intuitive Powers could be held in check and men could conquer and rape and destroy our environment without any worry and/or compassion!

All this and much, much more I began to understand as my dad educated me from the Other Side. And he explained to me that he, too, had never really understood all this until now that he'd joined his mother on the Other Side, where the Grandmasters were also helping inform him as he informed me.

I began looking forward anxiously to each night so I could go to sleep and continue being educated from the Other Side of Living. Soon I understood that thinking was to the brain, as intuition was to the heart, and thinking, which used words for processing information, was slow and cautious, while intuition, which used feelings, WAS LIGHTNING FAST!

I now began to understand why I'd been the chess champion of our entire school, beating all the students and faculty, and at the same time I hadn't been able to learn how to read, so I'd been kept in mentally slow classes. In playing chess I'd used all my 13 senses, and in the classroom I'd only used 5 senses.

I now also began to understand why in my first year of being on the wrestling team and not knowing much about wrestling, I had still been able to tie and go into overtime with the guy, a senior, who took state!

In both cases, in chess and in wrestling, I'd been completely out of my head and totally into my heart and soul—the zone, the flow of Creation Creating—and using all of our 13 Senses, so I'd been far, FAR, FAR more capable than I really am!

And so my dad continued educating me from the Other Side, and this was when magic began happening to me, and all the traffic lights would turn green for me as I drove up to them, and I lived in a continuous state of grace.

No joke!

No kidding!

This was also when I began to understand that there truly were no accidents in life, and the right book and/or person would come into my life just when I needed it and/or him/her. And I'd turn on the radio and the perfect song for me to hear, at that exact moment in my life, would begin to play, like "IMAGINE" by John Lennon.

Also miracle of miracles, this was when Fernando Flores—one of the smartest, wisest, most gifted human beings I've ever met on our planet and who helped reinvent Erhard's Forum—came into my life. An old friend of mine invited me to take a weekend course with Fernando, and by noon of the first day, a couple of doctors and lawyers had walked out of his course, but we, who'd stayed, found out that we naturally learned everything we needed to know about another human being within 15 seconds, but then we spent the rest of our time—minutes, hours, weeks, months, years—arguing within our "thinking heads" with that which we'd instantly known in Our Hearts and Souls to be True!

I was astonished, to say the least!

That which I was being taught by my dad from the Other Side, I was now also being taught on This Side by certain books and songs and individuals! It was as if I was being shown that there really was NO SEPARATION FROM THIS SIDE AND THE OTHER SIDE, and that Heaven and Hell were already here on Mother Earth living with us, side by side, as we breathed and lived. It was all up to us what we made of our Living Life, *la Vida,* here on Earth—Heaven and/or Hell!

I began to get speaking engagements of my own, and I was pleasantly surprised that when I spoke to law-enforcement groups, they instantly knew what I was talking about when I mentioned how we had to balance our feelings so we could then step into our 7th sense, which was our intuition.

The old cops would quickly explain that when they came upon a potentially dangerous situation, they always first got a "feel" for the situation, and then they instantly "knew" in their gut if they needed reinforcements or not. And different from young cops, they didn't ignore these feelings inside themselves. In fact, over the years the old cops said they'd come to depend more and more on these "feelings"—their instincts, their inner voices—after balancing them, and this was what had saved their lives over and over again.

And this was also when my dad began to explain to me the Big Picture and I came to understand that women by their very nature were far more intuitive than men, because they were directly connected to the moon with their periods, just like the tides of the oceans were connected to the Mother Moon, and hence, women were the natural leaders of our planet.

And this was why he, my dad, had been raised by his old Indian mother like a woman for the first seven years of his life—he'd helped in the process of childbirth—so he'd grow up to be a man who was in awe of women's natural powers, and he'd then fully realize that the most important decision any man could make in his life was to know how to choose the right woman to marry and have his children with, because women had the HOLY POWERS of the universe within them, AND A MOTHER, *UNA MAMÁ*, WAS THE "FIRST TEACHER" OF EVERY CHILD!

And so for weeks, for months, I was educated every night from the Other Side, then shown living examples during the day of what it was like to live Life, *la Vida*, once we moved out of the 4 senses of the head and into the 3 senses of the heart.

Then one night it exploded for me outside of Phoenix, Arizona!

I awoke in the middle of the night hearing beautiful music. I quickly got out of bed and went outside. I was staying in a motel, but I couldn't find anybody playing music on their car radio in the parking lot.

THEN I SAW IT! I FELT IT! I HEARD IT!

THE WHOLE WORLD ALL ABOUT ME WAS ALIVE WITH MUSIC!

Check out the gorgeous cover of *Beyond Rain of Gold* and you will see me facing the desert with my back to you, and I have a wild bird perched on my left hand and a baton in my right hand, and I'm orchestrating THE ONGOING SYMPHONY OF A BLOSSOMING DESERT OF SINGING LANDSCAPE AND FLOATING WILDFLOWERS!

A Native American of the state of Arizona, Steven Yazzie, painted this picture of himself, and when I saw it in the lobby of the hotel where I was staying, I instantly knew that Heart to Heart and Soul to Soul this was me that Steven had painted on that magical night when I heard and saw and felt the SYMPHONY OF CREATION CREATING in a motel outside of Phoenix.

And I suddenly realized that I was being told, being shown, that our 8th sense was music; and it was our sense of music that activated Our Soul Center, which moved us from Our Wild Heart Center into Our Living Soul Center, and SUDDENLY I UNDER-STOOD EVERYTHING!

Sure, of course, when God created the Universe, He/She created One-United-Verse, One-United-Song, so everything in Creation was Vibrating, Dancing, Singing! The stars above were Singing, Dancing, Waltzing! The trees and rocks and cacti all about me were Singing, Dancing, Waltzing! All of Creation was one huge IN-FINITE, LIVING, ONGOING, CONSCIOUSLY CONSCIOUS SYMPHONY. And you and I are one little, tiny, happy, joyful note within FABU-LOUS CREATION CREATING!

I screamed!

I danced!

I began to cry, I was so happy! BIG, BIG HAPPY!

Then I hadn't been left out of the superbowl of Creation Creat-ing, because it was still going on! Right Now! Right Here! FOREVER!

And I suddenly understood all of Our Senses! 6 of Our Senses belonged to Our Soul Center, like 3 belonged to Our Heart Center and 4 belonged to Our Head Center. And Our 6 Senses that work with Our Soul Center are (8) Music, (9) Time, (10) Space, (11) Our Interconnected Collective Consciousness, (12) Psychic Awareness, and (13) Being. And Psychic Awareness is to Our Soul Computer as Intuition is to Our Heart Computer, and Thinking is to Our Head Computer.

And just like Feeling, which activates Our Heart Center and reaches out 26 arms' lengths all around us in all directions, Music, which activates Our Soul Center, doesn't work within the confines of Time and Space as the thinking brain "thinks" it does; and, instead, Music, Our 8th Sense passes *through* Time and Space, ac-cessing ETERNITY, REACHING OUT TO INFINITY!

And hence a Human Being now starts Goding, meaning that a person is *now* part of the ongoing Music of Creation Creating; a note with God's Symphony, and he/she is now equally Alive in Our Collective Past and/or Future, because now within Our 13th Sense of Being, we don't believe in God; no, we *do* God. God is a verb. God is what we do. And that's why we'd originally used the words *Supreme Being* and *Human Being* to describe our relationship to Our Holy Creator, because then, in this state of Beingness, we are both Verbs, Verbing, Musicing in an ETERNAL STATE of "BEING," of CREATING TOGETHER, GOD AND US, and this is when all of Our Ancestry, Past and Future, comes BURSTING into Us and We now have a zillion times more cellular memory than all the computers of the whole world put together!

Wow! Oh wow!

And once we became Consciously Conscious of this, We are then living with God-Goding in an Eternal Present with our every breath, just like my two Mexican Indian grandmothers!

We are a team, GOD AND US!

And this is what my dad had been trying to tell me on the night he'd Passed Over!

Oh wow!

My dad had been ABSOLUTELY RIGHT!

My dad had truly spoken "truth" when he'd said I'd become so *gringo*-ized that I was constipated and couldn't "see" because my eyes were covered with shit!

And crap was what we ate from the Tree of Knowledge!

And shit was/is what has kept us locked up inside our "thinking heads" all these years and was/is what has been keeping us from using all of our senses, and . . . and not using all of our senses was/is why we have so many *problemas* here on Earth!

My dad was a genius! A GENIUS GENIUSING!

In fact, We are all GENIUSES GENIUSING once we get out of our 5 senses!

I sang!

I danced!

I thanked God-Goding!

And so now, knowing all this, having received all this information from the Other Side, was what later enabled me to do Jan Milburn's story, because by then I'd been able to totally switch out of 5 senses and go into Our Natural 13 Senses, so I had no *problema* understanding how Jan, an ordinary human being, had seen those lion eyes as a child, then befriended so many lost souls in San Francisco, then even had the guts to send love-*amor* to *la Mano Negra,* and how that great assassin had finally come over to Jan's side of Our HOLY LIGHT!

Because . . .

Because with 5 senses we can only live in our head, and so then we fear to even "believe" in the Light!

And with 13 Senses, We have no such fear!

Because, then, with Our 13 Senses, We Live in the Light!

And you tell me, how can FEAR exist if we are LIVING IN THE LIGHT WITH OUR EVERY BREATH? It can't, because we are *now* never alone AND always forever Living, Breathing within the GREATNESS AND WONDER OF GOD'S ONGOING CREATION CREATING!

And God has no fear! Get it? We can do this! We really can! We can do just like Jan, a white dude, AND LEAP INTO OUR NATURAL 13 SENSES AND LOVE-*AMOR* ALL OUR *PROBLEMAS* OF OUR WHOLE WORLD INTO NONEXISTENCE!

In fact, this is what has ALREADY HAPPENED ON OUR OTHER SIX SISTER PLANETS!

And this was also why I had no *problema* in understanding why that old double-barreled shotgun hadn't fired when they'd put it to Jan's head, yet fired when they'd pointed it at a small pine tree. You can't shoot Light. Also, I'd had no *problema* understanding that when the police had opened fire on the natives of *las Barrancas del Cobre,* none of their bullets had touched them, as they'd run in all directions, and the old healers had LEAPED OFF THE GREAT CANYON'S EDGE, TURNING INTO EAGLES, AND TAKEN FLIGHT!

My mother told me that she'd done this same thing, a story recounted in *Rain of Gold,* when she'd been 12 years old and renegade soldiers had chased after her to rape her. She told me that she'd run down the face of a cliff, leaped across the creek, and squatted down in the great ferns, breathing and staring at them, as she'd been taught to do as a child. And when she saw that the ferns were breathing in harmony with her breathing, she knew she'd become "fern," because she and the ferns had joined in together with the Holy Breath of Our Creator's Sacred Light Breathing. And so the soldiers had never found her, even though they'd passed so close to her that she could smell them and feel their movement among her and her fellow ferns.

My father told me he'd done the same thing when he escaped from prison in Arizona with two Yaqui Indians. He'd been 13 years old, and he'd been put in prison because he'd stolen $6 worth of copper from the Copper Queen Mining Company of Douglas, Arizona, to feed his starving family. The two Yaqui had been put in prison for feeding an Army mule to their starving *familias* after the American Army had confiscated all of their livestock.

My father and those two Indians had gotten sick from the prison food, and they'd been put in the hospital, from where they'd escaped, running in the desert all day and into the night. And when the mounted prison guards and their hound dogs finally caught up with them, the two Yaqui had quickly squatted down among some boulders and begun to chant. And my dad told me that he'd known what they were doing, because his mother had also taught him how to call in the Light Spirit of the Rocks for form-shifting, and so he'd also squatted down and begun to chant, too. The howling dogs and the guards on horseback finally caught up with them, but they were never able to find my dad and the two Yaqui, except for the one hound that sniffed at my-dad-being-stone and found his scent so attractive that he'd lifted his leg and pissed on my dad.

My dad told me that after the guards and their horses and dogs were gone and the two Indians had shifted back into human form, the Yaqui had laughed so hard they'd almost choked, saying they'd never seen or heard of a human becoming such a sweet stone that a dog would piss on him. My dad told me after that, the two Yaqui Indians called him Sweetrock.

These and dozens of other true stories Phyllis Grann and her sidekick editor, Tracy, had me remove from the original *Rain of Gold,* and then even after the removal of all these true stories, which I'd agreed were pretty hard to believe and accept within the limited reality of our 5 senses, those two New York women still insisted on calling *Rain of Gold* fiction! All this is also well documented in *Beyond Rain of Gold.*

By the way, in case you haven't noticed, dear reader, both *Beyond Rain of Gold* and *Lion Eyes* are published by Hay House, a local publisher in Carlsbad, California—my hometown—and not in New York City. And this is no accident. Both of these books I do believe could have never, ever been published in the eastern part of the United States, which still looks for guidance to Europe and that whole world of "thinking" and 5 senses and "If you can't see it, it doesn't exist" mentality.

As a whole, it's only the western part of the U.S., along with Hawaii, that doesn't look toward Europe for guidance anymore, and instead is now looking "within" and finding out that we really do have a Kingdom of God in each of us, just as Jesus Christ so well said.

Truly, Jan and Mireya's love story is the norm, and my dad and mother's love story is the norm, because within Our Natural 13 Senses, Great Love Stories are the Norm! And the stories of Jesus, Gandhi, Martin Luther King, Mother Teresa, César Chávez, and Mandela are love stories above all else!

LOVE STORIES OF LETTING GO, OF "FORGIVENESS" AND INCLUSION!

And now let's add to that list of Enlightened Human Beings a list of women who are currently—I've been informed from the Other Side—also moving us out of Darkness and into Our Collective Light.

Note that before the list had mostly been made up of men, except for Mother Teresa. But now take a look and see that it's mostly made up by women, and this is no accident, because . . . because we are now moving out of 26,000 years of Male-Based Frequency and into 26,000 years of Female-Based Frequency. And this doesn't mean women who think and act like men. No, this means women who are Heart and Soul Centered and are Loving and Compassionate and Motherly.

And this list of Enlightened Human Beings are Amma, the hugging guru; Louise Hay, the you-can-heal-yourself advocate; J. K. Rowling, who's rekindled the Spirit of kids back into a world of magic adventure; Melinda, the "seeing" Heart of the Gates Foundation; and Oprah, who has the gift to "know" how to popularize even esoteric Dream Makers into mainstream consciousness, like the great Eckhart Tolle.

I mean, most people who popularize the esoteric have hidden agendas. Like Darwin—who only mentioned "survival of the fittest" twice, and wrote about love and attraction and cooperation between animals and nature 93 times—was popularized by "men" who wanted to back up what they wanted: a society of "survival of the fittest," meaning everyone for themselves and Top Dog gets it all and is justified to be getting it all.

Not Oprah. Whether she knows it and/or not, when she popularizes a person and/or idea, she is all Heart and Soul Centered, so she automatically makes use of her Full Natural 13 Senses. I've studied her. She's basically beyond ego and personal gain—even though she's rich. And/or as my dad would have said, money doesn't own Oprah. She owns her money. Her vision and purpose are bigger than her money. And most rich people, my dad would always say, are little, lost, lonely poor people with dried-up Hearts and Souls because their money is bigger than they are, and so their money owns them. And where did my dad get his knowledge and wisdom (he never went one single day to school)? From his beloved mother, a little bag of skinny Indian bones from Oaxaca, Mexico. And so to my two indigenous grandmothers, Doña Margarita and Doña Guadalupe, and to Oprah and these other women, plus Marianne Williamson; Clarissa Pinkola Estés, who wrote *Women Who Run with the Wolves;* and Felicitas Goodman from New Mexico, whose all-women spiritual retreat she allowed me to attend for ten days—MY HAT IS OFF TO YOU, GREAT LADIES!

And why is my hat off to you? Because, simply, the Time has come in our Human-Being Development for All of Us to LEAP, COLLECTIVELY, without safety nets, into the ETERNAL INFINITE LIGHT-FLOW OF GOD'S ONGOING LOVE-*AMOR* OF CREATION CREATING!

And above all, you women encourage this! You don't put yourselves on a pedestal and want people to idolize you. No, you have each shown how you, too, were abused and have been down and had to learn how to overcome, no matter what! And you invite everyone to do the same! THIS IS BEAUTIFUL! THIS IS BACK TO THE FUTURE IN A HEALTHY, RESPONSIBLE WAY! AND US HUMAN BEINGS ONCE MORE BECOMING WEEDS, REACHING FOR THE SUNLIGHT OF GOD-GODING CREATION!

And so in this New Female Way of Living, then WEEE, WEEE, WEEE, SNOW GEESE ANGELS OF OURSELVES, GOT THE WHOLE WORLD IN OUR HANDS!

And we have no *problemas* on Earth!

What we have are simply situations that need to be "de-solved," not solved.

And how do we do this? By understanding that with Our Natural 13 Senses, WE can then "see." Because, simply, with Our 13 Senses, our cautious, worried, thinking, self-separating brain is then no longer in charge, in control; and our vision is then no longer covered over with crap. And now, above all else, WE ARE THEN MIRACLE MAKERS OF LOVE-*AMOR*!

ALL OF US!

AND UNITED TOGETHER, WE CAN MAKE A HEAVEN ON EARTH RIGHT NOW! RIGHT HERE!

And this "making" begins not over there with us making judgment calls about other people's backyards, but in our *own* backyard, where we live! You and me!

And when we look at our own yard, we need to remember to pass all information through Our 3 Centers, Our 3 Computers, so that then we have not just one way of viewing a situation, and instead have a flexibility and capability of seeing reality IN MULTIPLE LEVELS AND DIMENSIONS!

For instance, when my big, handsome blue-eyed grandfather Juan Jesus Villaseñor returned in 1913 to *Los Altos de Jalisco, México*, after having been gone for almost a year working on a horse ranch in Malibu, California, he was only able to see that his ranch had been destroyed. That's all he saw, because being a Basque-Spaniard, he saw life through 5 senses, so the world was flat and reality was one-dimensional.

He didn't have the tools with which to balance his feelings and see the larger picture of a multilayered reality. All he saw was that all of his cattle and horses had been stolen, and all his blue-eyed sons had been killed or lost. He couldn't see that my dad, his dark-skinned youngest son, was alive and loved him, and so were two of his daughters still alive and full of love for him. And he also couldn't see that his wife, Doña Margarita, adored him and had done all she could to save what she'd been able to save. He wasn't even able to see how much they'd all suffered while he'd been away, yet no one was blaming him for having been gone for almost a year up in the safety of the United States.

None of this could he see, and since he couldn't see it, then, of course, it didn't exist, so he began to shout to the heavens that it was the end of the world—that God had abandoned them—and he started drinking and died.

And yet my dad told me that his mother, Doña Margarita—nothing but a little bag of skinny Indian bones—saw the very same reality and said, *"Mañana es otro milagro de Dios,"* tomorrow is another miracle of God, and *"con el favor de Dios,"* with the blessing of God, "we will survive," and she took the 3 kids she had left out of the 14 who'd lived out of an original 19, and she went down the mountain with them from *Los Altos de Jalisco* to the valley of *Guanajuato,* and they'd migrated to the Texas border, well over a thousand miles to the north. And in those two years of migration, my dad told me that his little skinny Indian mother never once panicked and/or lost hope.

The Mexican Revolution was pre–World War I and II, so the Germans showed up with machine guns and barbwire and dug trenches to see if they could stop a cavalry charge, and they did, killing tens of thousands of riders and horses on a single charge. And the Americans showed up and joined the other side and tried out the same equipment in preparation for World War I, plus airplanes with crude bombs, and in a period of just a few years, more than one million Mexicans were killed in combat and another half million starved to death—more than in all the American wars put together—and through this nightmare of death and destruction passed my dad and his two older sisters and his skinny old mother.

And sometimes when they'd go to a creek to drink water, after having walked all day and night in the desert without food or water, they'd find it running red with blood and pieces of human and horse flesh. But still my dad told me, with tears pouring down his face, that his tough little Indian mother WOULD NEVER GIVE UP! And if they couldn't find a snake or lizard to eat—which was most of the time—she'd give them little round, smooth river rocks to suck on so they'd make saliva, and they wouldn't choke on their dry tongues. Then at night she'd have them look up at the stars, and she'd tell them a story of the little she-fox who lived on the moon, and how the mother fox was able to once more trick the crafty big old coyote so he wouldn't eat her little baby foxes.

"And we'd laugh and laugh and go to sleep, feeling loved and happy," my dad told me as he wiped the tears from his face, "because always, and especially in the middle of disaster, my wrinkled-up old Indian mother knew that she had to get my sisters and me laughing with *carcajadas,* big belly laughs that shook the whole body, so we'd have life in our hearts and hope in our souls to go on and on, no matter how desperate and hungry we were."

And so this was how I, Victor Edmundo Villaseñor, who was born and raised in the U.S., was taught to look at the world through my dad's and mother's eyes, and why I saw and still see our life here on Earth as a place full of hope and joy AND LOVE no matter what, but—and this is a big but—I still hadn't really understood why my grandfather and grandmother saw life so differently until my dad passed over, and from the Other Side, he gifted me Our Natural 13 Senses.

Only then, after receiving this education from the Other Side, could I begin to clearly "see" that my grandfather Juan Jesus Villaseñor wasn't a bad or weak person. No, it was simply that the poor, lost, delusional man hadn't been playing with a full deck of cards. No, he'd been living life with only 5 senses, so there'd been no possible way for him to see and/or do anything other than what he'd done. Where, on the other hand, my little skinny bag-of-Indian-bones grandmother, as my dad always referred to her, had been playing with a full deck, so she'd been able to "see" and "know" that God hadn't abandoned them; and it wasn't the end of the world, either, but was, in fact, just another challenge, just another Spiritual Request from God Almighty, asking them to come closer and closer to Him/Her through OUR OWN TOTAL AWAKENING HERE ON PLANET MOTHER EARTH, even while we were still in Human Form!

OH WOW!

And/or here is another way of explaining this in modern terms: The other day my sister Teresita received a letter from a friend of hers who lives in Japan. Her friend said that she was sorry she hadn't gotten back to my sister sooner, but the tsunami had destroyed her home and all means of communication . . . yet she was fine. In fact, people were being so good to one another that it was inspiring. People were helping each other dig through the debris, still looking for the bodies of missing friends and family. And when they were in line for water, no one pushed or became impatient. She went on to say that the Japanese people had never treated her better, that old Japanese men with green hats were leaving her water and a piece of fruit by her place now and then. And at night the stars could be seen in abundance for the first time in years, and people sat and visited with one another. That truly, having been reduced to nothing but life itself, people were sharing a side of themselves rarely seen when they'd had so many nonessential possessions.

This is exactly what *Wild Steps of Heaven,* the first book of the *Rain of Gold* trilogy, is all about! My dad explained to me that once their region of *Los Altos de Jalisco* had been totally destroyed by the Mexican Revolution, the women had stepped forward with their children, and they'd begun to help each other in a miraculous way they'd never been able to do before. My dad told me that his old Indian mother had done miracles while Don Juan had been in the U.S. working on that horse ranch in Malibu, California, but he just hadn't been able to "see" it.

My dad explained to me that his mother, Doña Margarita, had even been able to persuade the enemy of their *familia* to help her get my dad's older brother, Jose the Great, released from prison. And even this heroic story my poor, lost grandfather and his 5 senses hadn't been able to hear and/or see, much less comprehend.

Truly, once we get past all the bad news of our daily papers, and all the facts and statistics we are given by the media in order to back up all the bad news of our 5 senses, and we go into Our Natural 13 Senses and the Human Heart and Soul of the matter, then it is possible to catch a glimpse, a tiny fast-fleeing glimpse, of the fantastic love and compassion and understanding that comes through from every bad-news situation; and this is called *balance,* OUR KEY TO ALL OF OUR OTHER 13 SENSES!

WE'VE GOT THE WHOLE WORLD IN OUR HANDS! TRULY, WE DO!

AND WORLD HARMONY AND PEACE ARE IN THE BAG! And we all "know" this deep within Our Collective Cellular Memory because it has to do with water.

We humans are 70 percent water, and so is our planet, and both "waters" are alive and interconnected and receptive to our love and/or anger. Check out Dr. Emoto's books on water. His breakthrough is as big as Darwin and Freud put together.

WE'RE ALL EQUALLY ALIVE!

AND WE'RE ALL, ALL, ALL INTERCONNECTED!

AND UNITED, we can THEN make a GREAT, WONDERFUL, MIRACULOUS difference!

So come join us at PLYMOUTH ROCK, MASSACHUSETTS, where the original Thanksgiving took place between Native Americans and Europeans, and they ate together in Peace and Harmony.

No joke!

No kidding.

Come join us the Sunday before Thanksgiving, November 2011, and we will eat and celebrate together; and then just before sundown, we will light candles, face east, and sing songs of Peace and Harmony, sending Our Collective Love-*Amor* around Our Whole Grandmother Earth, giving her thanks and asking her for forgiveness for all the abuse that we've put Our Grandmother Earth through in the last 500 years.

Truly, come join us this year of 2011 and every year thereafter until 2052 and help us take our Greatest American Holiday—meaning Holy Day, a day of giving thanks to God and Planet. Then the following year of 2012, come fly with us to "see" the Queen of Spain the weekend before our U.S. celebration of Thanksgiving, so that she can endorse us and sponsor us, as Queen Isabella did with Columbus back in 1492.

COME JOIN US IN REDOING "HISTORY" AND GOING GLOBAL WITH OUR GREATEST AMERICAN CELEBRATION, so by 2052 we will be known as the Nation that took the two periods out of U.S. and we became the Dream/Nation of US, OUR THE PEOPLE FOR THE PEOPLE!

YES! COME JOIN US, SO WE CAN COLLECTIVELY MOVE OUR PLANET into "her-story."

COME JOIN US AS WEE, WEEE, WEEE, BECOME SNOW GEESE ANGELS OF OURSELVES and show the WHOLE WORLD how we, America, can still truly be the "good guys" just like Jan, a White dude, and embrace our Indigenous Brothers and Sisters with all OUR HEARTS AND SOULS!

COME JOIN US IN A GLOBAL MOVEMENT OF men "following" in front, as we fly across the HEAVENS IN V FORMATIONS and women and children leading with their happy songs and calls of joy as we fly Eastward, instead of Westward, picking up more and more locations EVERY YEAR IN LOVE and PEACE AND HARMONY AND ABUNDANCE for all!

YES! COME JOIN US going Eastward around the world again and again, so with help of the Internet by 2026 the whole globe will have joined us, and we will have gotten into the Habit and Rhythm of Giving Thanks and Love-*Amor*—not just once a year on Thanksgiving, but every day of our lives; in the morning, at midday, and in the evening, 3, 4, 5 times a day for a full few minutes of quiet, relaxed time by ourselves and/or with our friends and family, Feeling and Giving Genuine Gratitude and Thankfulness for our beautiful GRANDMOTHER EARTH and GRANDFATHER SKY!

After all, look at the Big Picture and "see" that we, we, we are 5-pointed Walking Stars with 13 senses; and our aging process goes in stages of 13, too: 13, 26, 39, 52, 64, 78 . . . and 78 is our most perfect age as Light Beings, and this is why "here" is very little aging from 78 to the age of 104—to the degree that we accept our Spirituality, and slip-slide into 91 and Goding at 104, where we are then in Total Unity with Creation Creating!

Read *Beyond Rain of Gold*. Truly, it's a must-read, and "see" how one miracle builds on top of another from the beginning of the book to the end, and, hence, can open up even a modern-day reader's mind so that then he/she is able to flow with ease into the incredible Spiritual Journey that's all around us, just like Jan Milburn did in *Lion Eyes*.

Truly, by 2052 our Collective Consciousness will be of such Miraculous Energies that wars will be out-of-date, and when soldiers and/or police forces open fire on unarmed groups of loving, peaceful protestors, their bullets will not strike anyone. Why? Because, simply, you can't shoot Light Beings.

AND JAN PROVED THIS!

NO JOKE!

NO KIDDING!

And when disasters happen, like they did in Japan and in Phuket, Thailand, a few years earlier, we will AUTOMATICALLY UNITE GLOBALLY with our Hearts and Souls and send Holy Healing

FOCUSED LIGHT Prayers to those people and help heal them and also restore calmness to our GRANDMOTHER EARTH, who is greatly suffering from all the human abuse we've heaped upon her and each other in the last few thousand years!

WAIT!

HOLD ON! I've just received an e-mail from my friend Gary, who oversees Snow Goose Global Thanksgiving (by, of course, "following" in front), and he tells me that he remembers seeing a segment aired by CBS on the tsunami victims of Thailand, and what really fascinated him was that where the tsunami hit hardest, there were no casualties, because a tribe of sea gypsies who call themselves the Moken knew the tsunami was coming before it came. They are a people who live on the sea. They're born on the sea, they die on the sea, and their kids learn to swim before they walk.

Gary says that *60 Minutes* did an article on a Moken village on an island that had become something of an exotic tourist Mecca before the tsunami. A Bangkok movie star and her photographer were there, taking pictures of the Moken village, when someone noticed the sea receding. The pictures show the Moken on the beach crying, then show the Moken running for higher ground. The Moken who were on their boats saw that the dolphins were swimming for deeper water, so they followed them way out to sea.

Gary found the *60 Minute* segment for me—it's only a couple of minutes long—and I watched it six times, and my God, it's wonderful! The first thing the Moken on the shore noticed was that the cicadas, beetle-like bugs that are usually very loud, suddenly went quiet. Then the segment shows a skinny, wrinkled-up old man who took note of the silence of the cicadas, and he ran around warning everyone that the tsunami was coming, but no one believed him. Even his own daughter told him he was a liar and a drunk. He told her that he hadn't drunk a drop. Finally he was able to convince his daughter and the other skeptics to climb to higher ground, and they were all saved, but nothing was left of the village.

Check it out for yourself on the web and see how the old man, Kalathalay, who took note of the cicadas and the sea receding, said that the tsunami happened because of the angry spirit of the sea, which hadn't eaten people in a long time and wanted to taste them again.

Then see how Dr. Narumon Hinshiranan, an anthropologist who speaks the Moken language, explained how the Moken knew that the tsunami was coming because they have a legend that has been passed down for generations about seven waves when the water recedes quickly.

She says that the Moken call a tsunami "the wave that eats people," and it's brought on by the angry spirits of their ancestors. The legend says that before it comes, the sea recedes, then the waters flood the earth, destroy it, and make it clean again.

Please note that this doctoral anthropologist called the Moken's oral history a "legend," and this is what the "civilized world" has been doing for thousands of years, discounting "Indigenous Knowledge" by labeling it superstition and/or legend.

In fact, looking back I can now "see" that this is what Phyllis Grann wanted to do with my entire book of *Rain of Gold* by calling it fiction. And this doesn't necessarily mean that this anthropologist and/or Phyllis are bad people. No, it's just that they don't know any better. How can they? They only use 5 senses and are therefore trapped in their heads.

Truly, I'd like to some day meet Phyllis face-to-face and make amends with her. After all, she's the only one who bid on *Rain of Gold* in the first place. She's my hero. She just didn't have the guts and vision with which to keep what she saw and knew in the first 15 seconds of meeting my book and me. I swear that Fernando Flores's weekend course should be taken by every corporate executive, so they can LEAP OUT OF THEIR HEAD AND INTO THEIR FULL NATURAL 13 SENSES AND START GENIUSING!

But some people do use all of their 13 Senses without consciously knowing it, and these people can "see." For instance, I noticed that the French anthropologist Jacques Ivanoff didn't use the word "legend," and he said that the Moken don't know how old they are, because for them "time is not the same concept as we have. You can't say, for instance, 'When,' because that word doesn't exist in the Moken language."

And Ivanoff also said "when" isn't the only word missing from the Moken language. "Want" is another. "Yet we use it often," said Ivanoff. In fact, he suggested that we take "want" out of our language, and we will then see how often we use it: "I want this, I want that." Also, he explained that there is no word for "take," because the Moken want very little, and so they don't "take" or accumulate anything, because baggage isn't good for a nomadic people. It ties them down. So the Moken also have no concept and/or desire for wealth.

There are other words also missing from the Moken language. "No 'goodbye,' no 'hello,'" said Ivanoff. "That's quite difficult. Imagine after one year, you live with them, and then you go. You go. That's it."

He also explained that there are no greetings, and since there is no notion of time, it doesn't matter if the last visit was a week ago or five years ago; and now that the tsunami has passed, the Moken are happy rebuilding their boats and their lives, because "worry" is also one of those words that don't exist in their language.

Also, when the Moken were asked why the Burmese fishermen didn't get to safety in time, they said it was because the Burmese didn't know how to "see" anymore.

WOW!

FANTASTIC!

I read and reread the different printouts again and again, and I came to clearly "see" that it doesn't take long for us to get so brainwashed that we get constipated in the head and we can no longer see. I mean, Kalathalay's own daughter didn't believe him and told him he was drunk; and those Burmese fishermen weren't *that* removed from their Ancestral Knowledge, and yet they also hadn't been able to see the signs of the sea. Truly, understand that

Collectively we need to quickly move back into Our Natural 13 Senses and/or we are all going to end up like those lost fishermen.

Breathe, breathe, breathe, and understand that Living Life is a Constant Ongoing Prayer. Truly, breathe, breathe, breathe, and allow yourself to realize that Life, *La Vida,* is an Ongoing Continuous Prayer, and with Prayer is how each of us balances ourselves within Our Holy Kingdom of Goding, and also by Praying is how we harmonize ourselves with Our Blessed Surroundings—the Holy Sea, the Grandmother Earth, the Grandfather Sky—so that then we, too, can "see," and read signs in Mother Nature, just like those Moken were able to do once they'd balanced themselves within and harmonized with their surroundings.

And the Moken did this by using all of their Full Natural 13 Senses, and this is why they are Home Free and able to Live a Life with no worries and no *problemas.* Just like we all used to do when we were Indigenous People all over the earth. And to pull off this Miracle of Miracles, all we have to do now in modern times is get out of our "thinking heads," out of our confining 5 senses and the language that we've inherited, and then we, too, are HOME FREE AT LAST AND ABLE TO LIVE A LIFE OF NO WORRIES AND/OR NO *PROBLEMAS!*

AND WE THEN GOT THE WHOLE WORLD BACK IN OUR ADORING HANDS!

AND THE WHOLE WORLD THEN HAS US BACK IN HER LOVING HANDS, TOO!

AND THE TIME HAS COME FOR US TO REALIZE THAT THERE'S ONLY ONE RACE, THE HUMAN RACE, ALL OVER THE GLOBE, AND ONE LOVING GOD, and bring Harmony and Peace to our planet, as our other Six Sister Planets have already done, with women and children leading and men "following" in front!

THIS IS WHAT 2012 IS ALL ABOUT!

THIS IS WHAT JAN MILBURN'S STORY IS ALL ABOUT!

A Brave New World Consciousness that happens every 26,000 years, with Male-Based Energy moving into 26,000 years of Female-Based Energy, and then back again!

WE'RE ON OUR WAY, and world harmony and peace are in the bag!

And it has very little to do with countries and politics and laws, and has everything to do with water and with the movement of the HEAVENS, from where we all came!

God Bless You!

God Bless Me!

God Bless All of Us!

We're All Walking Stars!

WE'RE ALL, ALL, ALL LIGHT BEINGS OF INCREDIBLE POWER ONCE WE ACCESS OUR KINGDOM OF GODING THAT'S WITHIN ALL OF US WITH OUR NATURAL 13 SENSES!

¡GRACIAS, AMIGOS! And remember, it's not the life you live that counts! It's the Courage and Heart and Soul and Miracles that you *bring* to Your Life with Your Natural 13 Senses!

Look at Jan and Mireya's life! THEY'RE MY HEROES! AND YOU, DEAR READER, WHO'VE STAYED WITH ME THROUGH ALL THIS, YOU ARE MY HERO, TOO!

I just drove down to San Diego to see the movie *Cave of Forgotten Dreams* by the German docu-filmmaker Werner Herzog, about a cave recently found in southern France with extraordinary art that dates back about 40,000 years—20,000 years further back than any other man-made artifacts ever found before. At that time our planet was covered with ice, and the seas were 300 feet lower and a person could walk from Paris to London on foot.

It's a "must-see" film! Take your friends and family and kids, and truly understand that this is just the beginning of what we will shortly start finding out everywhere, particularly on islands that are presently under the sea! And in my next book, a continuation of *Lion Eyes* and *Beyond Rain of Gold*, we will journey back 76,000 years, and we will "see" that island people used to sail all over the globe and interacted with our Outer-Space Sailing cousins from our other Six Sister Planets, who consider Our Mother Earth so beautiful that we were/are THEIR VACATION PLANET!

No joke!

No kidding!

And this ain't science fiction, but, instead, nonfiction, once we "see" reality through Our Natural 13 Senses.

Look around, and truly see how beautiful we are!

And with Our Collective Natural 13 Senses, then we automatically SEE THIS! LIVE THIS! KNOW THIS WITH EVERY CELL OF OUR BEING!

In fact, you already know this.

I am not telling you anything new. It's all part of Our Collective Cellular Memory, once we activate Our Kingdom of Goding that's within each of us!

God bless! God loves us! No doubt about it!

Also, last night we drove up to L.A. and participated in a session with the Hugging Guru Amma, along with about 5,000 other people. Marcos, a friend of ours from Panama, flew in just for this event. The Hugging Guru is all about the Female Energy that we're Collectively Being drawn to for World Harmony and Peace. She's clean! She's radiant! And her followers are such gentle, loving people. I loved it! She, too, is a Walking Star who has found her life purpose and mission.

¡Se están juntando! We are all coming together from all walks of Life, *la Vida;* Being drawn to the Light of God-Goding Female Energy for the next 26,000 years!

WALKING STARS ARE WE!

SINGING!

DANCING!

LAUGHING OUR WAY BACK TO THE FUTURE!

WOW! I was just told that what I'm writing about is absolutely coming true! That they just saw a rerun on the Internet—a picture of the survivors of the earthquake in Haiti, I do believe, dancing wildly in the rain with fire and destruction all about them. And when they were asked why they danced, they said that it was important to keep their Spirits High and Full of Love so they could handle the disaster that had just happened.

So dear reader, SING! DANCE! *¡CANTA! ¡NO LLORES!* And especially in the midst of chaos and disaster! KEEP YOUR HEART WILD

SO THAT THEN YOUR SOUL CAN BE ALIVE! GOD BLESS! And a great big juicy hug from me to You!

¡Con Dios! ¡Gracias!
Victor E. Villaseñor

P.S. By the way, in case you want to know why Gary Gernandt, an Irish American *gringo,* is "overseeing" Snow Goose Global Thanksgiving, which was "gifted" to me by the local Native Indians of Portland, Oregon, the answer is simple.

I didn't know Gary. I'd never seen and/or heard of him, and so when I arrived to give a talk at Borrego Springs High School, made up of mostly Latinos, it turned out that he was the principal, and we immediately hit it off. In fact, he later told me that the instant he saw me, he knew that he'd be quitting his job and coming to work with me.

For over 25 years, Gary has been a practitioner of *A Course in Miracles,* and at that time I'd never heard of the *Course,* but since then I have, and a lot of people I seem to hit it off with have been longtime practitioners of that *Course,* including, I do believe, Louise Hay, who is now my publisher.

Anyway, I, too, felt an immediate Heart-to-Heart and Soul-to-Soul connection with Gary, knowing deep inside myself that he and I were on the same path. And after he heard me speak, he told me that he knew his intuitive evaluation had been correct, so later that same day he told his wife, Debbie, a therapist and active crisis counselor and ex–Nordstrom model, and she believed him and . . . backed him up with an early retirement.

Now Gary and I are both pooling our own monies together—which aren't much—in order to support Snow Goose Global Thanksgiving. And even though Gary has recently lost his home, he and Debbie and their two beautiful grown children are still Totally Committed and Happy and Know deep within their Hearts and Souls that Abundance is just around the corner for ALL OF US! WORLDWIDE!

Gary, just like Jan, long ago made his decision and LEAPED with Total Faith in God and the conviction that no matter what, people are basically good, wonderful people all over our planet, just as I have also jumped time and again with the same conviction and faith!

Presently, Gary's working with Natives out at several Indian Reservations East of us, and we're forming a coalition of Indigenous people with our backs to the Pacific Ocean from Alaska to South America, facing East, so WEE, WEEE, WEEE SNOW GOOSE ANGELS OF OURSELVES CAN UNITE AND TAKE OUR GLOBAL THANKSGIVING VISION OF HARMONY AND PEACE TO THE WHOLE WORLD!

Contact Gary, who knows how to "follow" in front, at: **www .snowgoose.org**. Gary has also informed me—he reads a lot and listens to the news, which I don't do either very much—that women are coming into leadership all over the world, especially in Europe. Intuitively, whether we know it and/or not, we are all waking up and returning to Our Natural 13 Senses and Our Female Energy Frequencies of the next 26,000 years.

ABOUT THE AUTHOR

Victor Villaseñor is the author of the national bestsellers *Rain of Gold, Thirteen Senses, Burro Genius,* and *Crazy Loco Love,* the last two of which were nominated for the Pulitzer Prize; as well as other critically acclaimed books, such as *Beyond Rain of Gold, Wild Steps of Heaven,* and *Macho!,* which was compared to the best of John Steinbeck by the *Los Angeles Times.* He is also the author of five ancestral-themed bilingual children's books, and has written several screenplays, including the award-winning *The Ballad of Gregorio Cortez.*

Villaseñor, a gifted and accomplished speaker, continues to live on the North County San Diego ranch where he grew up. The original *Rain of Gold* trilogy is now being developed into a wonderful movie, worthy of the books that are so loved!

For more information, please visit: **www.victorvillasenor.com.**

NOTES

NOTES

NOTES

NOTES

NOTES

NOTES

NOTES

NOTES

NOTES

NOTES

We hope you enjoyed this Hay House book. If you'd
like to receive our online catalog featuring additional
information on Hay House books and products, or
if you'd like to find out more about the
Hay Foundation, please contact:

Hay House, Inc., P.O. Box 5100, Carlsbad, CA 92018-5100
(760) 431-7695 or (800) 654-5126
(760) 431-6948 (fax) or (800) 650-5115 (fax)
www.hayhouse.com® • **www.hayfoundation.org**

Published and distributed in Australia by: Hay House Australia Pty. Ltd.,
18/36 Ralph St., Alexandria NSW 2015 • *Phone:* 612-9669-4299
Fax: 612-9669-4144 • www.hayhouse.com.au

Published and distributed in the United Kingdom by: Hay House UK, Ltd.,
292B Kensal Rd., London W10 5BE • *Phone:* 44-20-8962-1230
Fax: 44-20-8962-1239 • www.hayhouse.co.uk

Published and distributed in the Republic of South Africa by:
Hay House SA (Pty), Ltd., P.O. Box 990, Witkoppen 2068
Phone/Fax: 27-11-467-8904 • www.hayhouse.co.za

Published in India by: Hay House Publishers India, Muskaan Complex,
Plot No. 3, B-2, Vasant Kunj, New Delhi 110 070 • *Phone:* 91-11-4176-1620
Fax: 91-11-4176-1630 • www.hayhouse.co.in

Distributed in Canada by: Raincoast, 9050 Shaughnessy St.,
Vancouver, B.C. V6P 6E5 • *Phone:* (604) 323-7100 • *Fax:* (604) 323-2600
www.raincoast.com

Take Your Soul on a Vacation

Visit **www.HealYourLife.com®** to regroup, recharge,
and reconnect with your own magnificence. Featuring
blogs, mind-body-spirit news, and life-changing
wisdom from Louise Hay and friends.

Visit **www.HealYourLife.com** today!